Leaning into the Future

Princeton Theological Monograph Series

K. C. Hanson, Charles M. Collier, and D. Christopher Spinks,
Series Editors

Recent volumes in the series:

T. David Beck
The Holy Spirit and the Renewal of All Things

Ryan A. Neal
Theology as Hope

Abraham Kunnuthara
Schleiermacher on Christian Consciousness of God's Work in History

Paul S. Chung
Martin Luther and Buddhism

Philip Ruge-Jones
Cross in Tensions

John A. Vissers
The Neo-Orthodox Theology of W. W. Bryden

Stephen Finlan and Vladimir Kharlamov, editors
Theosis: Deification in Christian Theology

David A. Ackerman
Lo, I Tell You a Mystery

Leaning into the Future

The Kingdom of God in the Theology of Jürgen Moltmann and in the Book of Revelation

POUL F. GUTTESEN

PICKWICK Publications • Eugene, Oregon

LEANING INTO THE FUTURE
The Kingdom of God in the Theology of Jürgen Moltmann and in the Book of Revelation

Princeton Theological Monograph Series 117

Copyright © 2009 Poul F. Guttesen. All rights reserved. Except for brief quotations in critical publications or reviews, no part of this book may be reproduced in any manner without prior written permission from the publisher. Write: Permissions, Wipf and Stock Publishers, 199 W. 8th Ave., Suite 3, Eugene, OR 97401.

Pickwick Publications
A Division of Wipf and Stock Publishers
199 W. 8th Ave., Suite 3
Eugene, OR 97401

www.wipfandstock.com

ISBN 13: 978-1-55635-513-4

Cataloging-in-Publication data:

Guttesen, Poul F.

Leaning into the future : the kingdom of God in the theology of Jürgen Moltmann and in the book of Revelation / Poul F. Guttesen; foreword by Richard Bauckham.

xiv + 264 p. ; 23 cm. Includes bibliographical references.

Princeton Theological Monograph Series 117

ISBN 13: 978-1-55635-513-4

1. Moltmann, Jürgen. 2. Bible. N.T. Revelation. 3. Kingdom of God. 4. Bible—Hermeneutics. I. Bauckham, Richard. II. Title. III. Series.

BS2827 G88 2009

Manufactured in the U.S.A.

Scripture quotations, unless otherwise noted, are from the New Revised Standard Version Bible, copyright 1989, Division of Christian Education of the National Council the Churches of Christ in the United States of America. Used by permission. All rights reserved.

For my parents,
Marita and Leivur Fossdal Guttesen,
and in memory of Louise M. Houston

Contents

Foreword by Richard Bauckham / ix

Preface / xi

Abbreviations / xiii

1. Introduction / 1
2. Witness to the Promised Kingdom: The Bible in Moltmann's Theological Approach / 16
3. The Kingdom of God as Symbol of Hope / 38
4. The Passion of the Kingdom in the World / 68
5. The Crisis of the Kingdom and the Book of Revelation / 110
6. The Future as Regime Change / 123
7. The Presence and Reign of God in History / 175
8. Conclusions and Anticipations / 236

Bibliography / 251

Foreword

IN RECENT YEARS THERE HAS BEEN A MOVEMENT ON THE PART OF SOME biblical scholars and some systematic theologians to bring their disciplines back together after a long period of alienation. This is not a matter of dissolving one into the other, but of finding ways in which serious dialogue can bear fruit. Poul Guttesen's work is an exemplary contribution to this. By engaging Jürgen Moltmann's theology and the biblical book of Revelation in a mutually illuminating dialogue Guttesen is, of course, hosting such an encounter within the creative theological context of his own engagement with both. He enters with sympathy and perception into both of these visions of the kingdom of God, with their very different theological idioms, and explores both the consonances and the tensions he finds between them.

As supervisor of Guttesen's doctoral studies, I followed his work with great interest, because I am myself an enthusiastic student of both Moltmann's theology and the book of Revelation. I have written two books on each, and doubtless each has influenced my reading of the other, but I have never attempted systematically to bring them together. So I have been delighted to see this done so well.

Guttesen importantly recognizes the *situatedness* of Revelation, of Moltmann's theology, and of his own work. As the seven messages to the churches in Revelation show, we cannot live out an orientation to the coming kingdom of God (in Guttesen's phrase, "leaning into the future") without prophetic discernment of the historical moment at which the church finds itself here and now. As Guttesen argues, the focus on *resistance* (in Revelation) or on *engagement* (in Moltmann) is a relative difference that reflects the continuity of the two within the mission of the church on its way to the kingdom.

Where differences between Moltmann and Revelation become apparent, they concern especially the nature of the sovereignty of God that the biblical symbol of God's kingdom entails and the relationship between the church and the kingdom. These are vital issues that the church has all too often got dangerously wrong in the past, as both Moltmann and Guttesen recognize. We need all the help we can find to get them right in the present, and Guttesen's engagement with both Revelation and Moltmann at these points of divergence points some ways forward.

In commending this book, it is a pleasure also to be able to welcome a theological voice from the Faroe Islands to the international theological discussion.

Richard Bauckham
Cambridge

Preface

THIS BOOK BEGINS WITH A LIE. YOU HAVE ALREADY READ IT. IT IS ON the cover. If it takes a village to raise a child, it takes an extended community to write a book. And yet I am listed as the sole author of this work. As an act of penance, allow me to acknowledge a few of those without whom this book would never have seen the light of day. I owe thanks to more people than I can mention, but must name a few: my editors, Charlie Collier and K. C. Hanson, for their interest in my work and patience with the time it took for the final manuscript to arrive; my supervisors at the University of St. Andrews, Prof. Alan Torrance for helping me give the project shape and encouraging me throughout, and Prof. Richard Bauckham for guiding me confidently and graciously through two areas of research few know as well as he; my thesis examiners, Prof. Christopher Rowland and Dr. Stephen Holmes, whose questions helped refine my own convictions; wise guides, Prof. James Houston, who so often has been the gracious hands of God in my life, Dr. Sven Soderlund, whose kind wisdom has sown hope, and Dr. Charles Ringma, who gently lead me through the personal experience that was the seed of this book; my flatmates, Sharon Jebb, Louise Lawrence, and Nathan and Claire MacDonald, who made life enjoyable even in the hardest of times; close friends, who have encouraged and helped me along the journey, Gisela Kreglinger, Keith Hyde, David Rudolph, Wayne Coppins, Stefan and Sherry Lukits, Ivan and Julie Khovacs, David and Chelle Stearns, Matt and Julie Canlis, Tony and Antonia Clark, and Dirk and Marion Jongkind with their six wonderful children. I am also grateful to Tyndale House for the year I was able to spend there. I would like to express my deep felt gratitude to the Faroese Research Council (Granskingarráð Føroya) for a generous research grant that made my PhD research economically possible. My parents, Marita and Leivur Guttesen, deserve a special mention, not only have they supported me throughout my long academic journey, but their unconditional love has been an anchor throughout my life. To Louise M. Houston, who passed away in 2008, I also owe special thanks. When I arrived in St. Andrews she welcomed me with open arms, and through her hospitality she constantly brought me back to what is significant, living in and through the Love of God. She has now moved into the mystery of the divine presence, which arrival those await who lean into the kingdom of God. To my parents and in memory of Louise this book is published.

Soli Deo Gloria

Abbreviations

Works of Moltmann

CoG	*The Coming of God*
CPS	*The Church in the Power of the Spirit*
CrG	*The Crucified God*
EH	*The Experiment Hope*
EiT	*Experiences in Theology*
FC	*The Future of Creation*
GHHC	*Die Gemeinde im Horizont der Herrschaft Christi*
GiC	*God in Creation*
GSS	*God for a Secular Society*
HP	*Hope and Planning*
IGEB	*Im Gespräch mit Ernst Bloch*
HTG	*History and the Triune God*
IEB	*In the End—the Beginning*
JCTW	*Jesus Christ for Today's World*
Man	*Man*
OHD	*On Human Dignity*
RRF	*Religion, Revolution and the Future*
SL	*The Spirit of Life*
SoL	*The Source of Life*
SW	*Science and Wisdom*
TH	*Theology of Hope*
TKG	*The Trinity and the Kingdom of God*
ThT	*Theology Today*
WJC	*The Way of Jesus Christ*

1

Introduction

Prelude

NODAL EXPERIENCES OCCUR IN THE MOST UNEXPECTED OF PLACES. Earning a credit toward a master's degree, I spent an early spring weekend at Westminster Abbey, a Benedictine monastery, resting on a hill over Mission, British Columbia. That retreat constituted a fundamental shift. Time took a 180 degree turn; God's future turned me upside down. The future ceased to be the empty space I sought to populate with my own dreams and became a gift from God, his homeland that beckons us to journey toward it and let our lives be shaped by it. Those early spring days of 1999 are the roots of this book, giving me the basic question I brought to my doctoral research: how does a Christian notion of the future as divine gift beckon people to live? I wanted to explore how eschatology shapes a Christian understanding of the world. If the future is the gift of God to his creatures, what difference does it make? How does the hope for the coming of God shape Christian existence, and how is this God who will come already present among us?

Considering this dual concern, and since I desired to probe the question from both a systematic and a biblical angle, the choice fell quite naturally on Jürgen Moltmann and the Book of Revelation. Moltmann emerged as a significant twentieth-century theological voice with his groundbreaking work in *The Theology of Hope*.[1] Ever since, eschatology

---

1. Works on Moltmann are legion. For an extensive bibliography up to and including 2001, see Wakefield, *Moltmann*. Of the many portraits of Moltmann's thought, pride of place goes to Richard J. Bauckham's two studies (*Messianic Theology* and *Theology of Jürgen Moltmann*); of Bauckham's work Moltmann says: "It is not easy for me to reply to Richard Bauckham . . . he knows too much! He knows my theology, with its

has been a shaping force in his theology.[2] But, while his early work was singularly focused on hope, Moltmann, as his theology has developed, has become increasingly interested in how the God expected is now at work in the world, orienting it toward its future in him. A similar dialectic between the expected future and how it is to shape present existence is also found in Revelation.[3] A contrapuntal tension between heavenly reality and earthly actuality drives the book forward: Although God is the rightful sovereign over his whole creation, the earth is at present occupied by forces antithetical to God. The whole book is oriented toward the resolution of this tension. The finale of the visionary complex is the descension of the heavenly city and its divine ordering center to the earthly realm, the latter finding its Edenic fulfilment in the arrival of the former. This eschatological climax shapes the book's judgments on what is real, true, good, and so on.

It was relatively easy to settle on these two literary contexts as the textual sites for my explorations in how faith in the coming God should shape Christian existence. It proved to be far more difficult to find a conceptual hook that could bind such disparate texts into conversa-

---

strengths and weaknesses better than I do myself. His books . . . are far and away the best accounts of my theology" ("The World in God," 35).

2. Meeks rightly observes that Moltmann constantly attempts "to make the eschatological revelation of God concrete in relationship to the present" (*Origins*, 88).

3. Academic interest in Revelation has grown exponentially in recent years. In addition to a multitude of articles and monographs, two monumental commentaries were published in the late 1990s (David E. Aune's three-volume WBC and G. K. Beale's NIGTC volume); since then, substantial commentaries have also been published by Ian Boxall, Grant R. Osborne, Stephen S. Smalley, and Ben Witherington. In 2004 Judith Kovacs and Christopher Rowland published a commentary focusing on the history of the interpretation of the book (*Revelation*). In addition to the extensive bibliographic information in Aune and Beale, see Witherington, *Revelation*, 51–64, for a helpful overview of critical works on Revelation. Of specific interest to the present study is Michael Gilbertson's *God and History*. Not only is he concerned with the relationship between the Bible and theology but he conducts a very similar dialogue to the one I construct, comparing Moltmann's and Pannenberg's understanding of history with Revelation. I will interact with Gilbertson throughout this study, and have especially benefited from his excellent analysis of Revelation's temporal and spatial categories (81–142). His study is complementary to my own as both are concerned with how eschatology and transcendence shape our understanding of the world. However, while Gilbertson is primarily concerned with how Moltmann and Pannenberg appropriate apocalyptic in their respective views of history and as such is focused on "the debate about the significance of history per se" (1), I am concerned with the concrete function of the kingdom of God in Moltmann and Revelation.

tion. It needed to be a theme or notion that was prominent both in Moltmann and Revelation, and it had to be a conceptual framework into which both texts were easily translatable. Initially I planned to work with broad conceptualities as transcendence and imminence. As the work progressed, however, the abstract character of this approach moved the conversation too far from the concrete ways in which both Moltmann and Revelation deal with God, the future and existence. Probing both "texts" further, a theological motif emerged which both have in common, the Kingdom of God. The kingdom is an operative symbol in Moltmann's thought, which, as we will discuss later, runs throughout his entire corpus. Although βασιλεία τοῦ θεοῦ ("the kingdom of God") is not frequently found in Revelation, the book is rife with political language, and the reign of God is of central concern. God as creator is sovereign over both heaven and earth, and he will come as such to the latter, the realm that now languishes under the occupation of his enemies.

Grounding the Conversation

This conversation between Moltmann and Revelation on the kingdom is a theological construction that lies within the recent surge of interest in the role of the Bible in theology and in theological interpretation of Scripture. However, there is far from a consensus on how these questions should be approached, or whether bridging the modern divide between Biblical Studies and Systematic Theology is a good thing.[4]

---

4. Central to the advent of modern biblical studies was the liberation of the Bible from the heavy yoke of dogmatic tradition. The biblical books should be allowed to speak with their own voice from within their own historical context. If this was the urgency 200 years ago, many find the opposite to be the case today, the need to free the Bible from the objectivist constraints of modern biblical studies (on calls for a theological interpretation of Scripture, see e.g., Fowl, *Engaging Scripture*; and Watson, *Open Text*). The present study is one attempt, and one among many, to let contemporary theological concerns and Scripture exist in enriching dialogue. However, several scholars, while acknowledging the impossibility of a purely objective stance vis-à-vis the biblical text are nevertheless committed to the historical and descriptive task of biblical studies (e.g., Barr, *Concept*; Räisänen, *Beyond New Testament Theology*). In defence against the charge of objectivism or positivism, several scholars claim they seek to counter their own bias through the application of a certain 'neutral' methodology. This does not hold. Positivism is precisely the belief that through method one can achieve the ideal of approaching the first century "without," in Stendahl's words, "borrowing categories from later times" ("Biblical Theology," 425). Barr reflects this sentiment (*Concept*, 205),

Therefore, some words on what I aim to do in this conversation is in order, including what I hope to accomplish and why I believe my particular approach is methodologically justified.

First, what I do not claim. I make no claim of *normativity*. I do not try to exemplify *what* the constructive relationship between biblical studies and theology *should be*, but only seek to develop one way it *can be* constructed. And although I privilege my analysis of Revelation over my discussion of Moltmann, I am not proposing a baton-passing approach to the relationship between biblical studies and theology, in which the biblical scholar *must* first determine what the text meant in its original context before the theologian can articulate what it means for Christians today.[5] While there is some wisdom in the division of labour between the Bible scholar and the theologian in the modern academy, it is detrimental to both, when the one attempts to dictate how the other should work. The reason why I believe the voice of a biblical book should be privileged is not because the NT scholar should determine how a theologian should work, but because I believe that the

---

when he says the biblical scholar must hold his own commitment in suspense if it is to be questioned by the text itself. Precisely because of this, theology is inadmissible in the academic life of the Biblical scholar (222). Such an attitude wrongly assumes both that one can suspend one's faith commitment in favor of a methodological stance that provides objectivity, and that one's commitment cannot be challenged if one brings it to the text. Watson also notes (*Text*, 2) how strategies for reading that are over-determined by a particular methodological stance falsely assume that all texts are alike and therefore can be submitted to a "single-reading-perspective." This is not to deny that certain methods may uncover what otherwise would be missed nor to dismiss they may help us gain a certain critical distance from our own commitments, only that our own subjectivity is not to be dismissed in our reading and that methods are not value neutral.

5. The baton-passing approach of the biblical theology movement is perhaps best encapsulated in Krister Stendahl's influential essay, "Biblical Theology." On the history of biblical theology, see Reventlow, "Theology (Biblical)." For a particularly insightful critique of Stendahl's distinction between the supposedly descriptive task of biblical studies and normative task of theology as well as his distinction between what the text meant and what it means, see Ollenburger, "Krister Stendahl." The critics of biblical theology usually point to one of two alternative roads. There are those who are sympathetic and committed to the descriptive task of biblical theology but restrict it to the historical task of determining the various and even contradictory theologies of the biblical texts (e.g. Barr, *Concept*; Räisänen, *Beyond New Testament Theology*). Others want to abandon it in favor of an intentionally theological interpretation of Scripture (e.g., Fowl, *Engaging Scripture*; see also several of the essays in Watson, *Open Text*, and the essays in *Theological Interpretation*, edited by Fowl).

Bible is normative for all Christian theologians, whatever the academic guild they labour in.[6]

Nor do I claim to be *comprehensive*. This is but a small but hopefully valuable contribution to much larger discussions. This is not an analysis of the significance of the Kingdom of God in contemporary theology, but a close reading of how it functions in one significant modern theologian. Likewise, I am not proposing a comprehensive biblical theology of the kingdom, but present an attentive reading of how Revelation deals with the kind of questions and concerns Moltmann's view of the kingdom raises. I am also keenly aware that my interpretation of Revelation is shaped by the particularity and contingencies of the socio-historical place I occupy. Therefore, my reading must be seen within the long history of the interpretation of the book. However, I am sufficiently confident that my reading lies within the semantic field of the book, and therefore can make a valuable contribution to larger concerns.[7]

Then what do I claim? I believe the present work paints worthwhile portraits of how the Kingdom of God functions in a major contemporary theological voice and in an important, though often overlooked, biblical text. While these portraits must be seen within the limitations outlined above, they show the crucial role the kingdom must have in Christian theological reflection, and can hopefully make some contributions to this task. The aim of the study is also to show the importance of an engaged conversation between the interested parties that have been bifurcated in the modern academy, between the biblical scholar and the theologian, not by proposing another theoretical framework for how this should be done, but by exemplifying one way in which it can be accomplished.

Considering the particular approach of this study, the way in which it allows contemporary theological concerns set the questions an ancient text is to answer, and the way in which Revelation is read, two quite different objections might be raised. The first objection emerges within the guild of biblical studies. Since I allow my appraisal of a particular theological concept in a modern theologian to set the agenda for the questions I set a biblical book, is my project not a step backwards,

---

6. My view on Scripture will be further elaborated in the next chapter.

7. On the history of the interpretation of the book, see Wainwright, *Mysterious Apocalypse*; and Kovacs and Rowland, *Revelation*.

giving back territory which the modern academic study of the Bible fought hard to gain? Is the point of biblical studies not to read texts within their first context? And is a fundamental fallacy not to read later concerns into earlier texts? If this is the case, then is this study not an exercise in futile anachronism?

The other question, which arises from the particular way in which I analyze Revelation, results in the opposite concern. Although I set the agenda through my appraisal of Moltmann's view of the Kingdom (and thus for some, commit fallacious anachronism), I still claim that my interpretation of Revelation on this matter lies within the field of possible meanings that are consonant to what was encoded in the text in the first place. Considering how the objectivist ideals of biblical studies have been decisively undermined within the last few decades, do I not commit the arrogant modern mistake, claiming to unearth the original meaning of the text that has been obfuscated by tradition? I will attempt to answer both of these concerns by appealing to what I believe are two fundamental aspects of texts, their communicability and their referentiality, i.e. texts are constructed to *communicate something*. In doing so, I also hope to further clarify, elucidate, what this study aims to accomplish.

The Communicability of Texts

First, although the critique of the objectivist claims and aims of modern biblical studies is to be applauded,[8] the task to understand what an author desired to communicate through his or her texts remains—texts are produced to *communicate*.[9] Authors write in the hope that the meaning their readers will decode corresponds to what they sought to encode in their texts, what they purposed to communicate through them.[10] Therefore, if texts as communicative acts are to be successful,

---

8. For an insightful discussion on the modern misconception of hermeneutics as going beyond interpretation to apprehend what is as it is, see Smith, *Who's Afraid*, 34–53. Smith, drawing on Derrida, rightly notes that reality is essentially interpreted; says Smith, 39: "when Derrida claims that there is nothing outside the text, he means there is no reality that is not always already interpreted through the mediation lens of language."

9. This discussion on textual communicability is primarily drawn from Vanhoozer, *Meaning*, especially chs. 5–6.

10. My appropriation of terms used within Speech-Act theory, is drawn from Vanhoozer, *Meaning*. In doing so I only aim to describe how I understand communica-

there has to be a sufficient level of correspondence between what an author sought to encode and that which a reader decodes. Despite both often misreading and at times being misread, the astounding success of textual communication is seen in that people continue to read and write in order to understand and be understood.[11]

A consideration of the kind of literature read as well as the purpose for which it is read must be kept in mind when reading an elusive, liminal and complex text as Revelation. Such texts have usually a fairly wide field of meaning; how it is read is highly dependent on the purpose an interpreter brings to it.[12] Some of these readings are likely closer to

---

tion and make no claim regarding how others, such as Wolterstorff, employ the theory in their understanding of divine discourse.

11. This is not to deny that there are other motivations for both reading and writing, but to understand and to be understood remain two primary purposes for textual communication. If this is the case, the attempt to recover the meaning an author sought to encode in a text is not only valid but honorable, it respects the communicative purpose of most texts. However, this claim must be qualified. The attempt to decode what an author sought to encode does not make one's own reading less situated, it only means that one seeks to hear the text as well as one can precisely where one finds oneself. Even the most painstaking attempt to elucidate the "there" where the text was produced is still undertaken in the "here" in which the interpreter stands. He or she can neither enter an author's mind to see his intention nor travel back to a text's first hearers. But although an interpreter cannot move back into the world of the text, the text, with some of its world, has journeyed to him or her. As such, all reading is always anachronistic, always read in another spatial and temporal coordinant than the one in which it was written. It is always an "I" that reads *here* what another wrote *there*. Shall I seek what the author sought to make present? Of course, but this does not mean teleporting from where I am and who I am to another place. It means paying attention to the voice that speaks from elsewhere and is heard where I am.

12. The attempt to hear the text within its broader historical context does not limit its meaning to *one particular interpretation*, only to *a field of meaning* within which any good reading must stand. What constitutes a good reading, and the width of its semantic field, depends naturally on the type of text one reads, and for what purpose one reads it. If a poem is read in the same way as an instruction manual, it most likely will be read badly. And a marketing student and a child will likely read a children's magazine differently because of their purpose in reading it. Although some texts have a strictly limited field of meaning, like a construction manual, others have a wide field, especially texts that venture into the liminal field of the meaning of existence. In *Metaphor and Reality* Philip Wheelwright helpfully distinguishes between the one-to-one correspondence of symbol and referent in stenosymbolism (as in an IKEA instruction sheet) and the shifting patterns of association in pensive symbolism (as in a poem or rich novel). It is this latter type of texts that have the capacity to live beyond their first contexts (see Gilbertson [*God and History*, 68] for a brief overview of Wheelwright's discussion). And it is these kinds of texts that tend to survive, they are not forgotten. Unlike an

the purpose the author had in writing the text, but even readings that lie far from this purpose can nevertheless be consonant with the semantic field the text signifies. While the semantic elasticity is fairly limited in a car manual or a trigonometry textbook, the Book of Revelation, with its expressionist style, visionary content, complex intertextuality and textured religious tradition (both the traditions it builds on and the ones which it has spawned), contains a multitude of interpretive strands. Kovacs and Rowland have provided a helpful taxonomy of the ways in which the book has been interpreted.[13] They plot interpretations of Revelation on two axes. On a chronological axis interpretations can be classified by whether they deal with the past, present or future. The other axis plots whether interpretations try to decode the text's imagery in order to unearth the message encoded in it, or whether they perform a "repeat actualization" of the text, conveying "the spirit of the text" in a new context. The former has tended to discover the one meaning of the text while the latter sees it as multivalent.[14] Within Kovacs' and Rowland's taxonomy, my interpretation primarily focuses on how the text might have been decoded in the late first century.[15] I try to cipher how John was employing his visionary symbolism in order to empower his first-century readers with an alternative imagination, one that could

---

IKEA instruction sheet, they delve into those regions of life that transcend the passing of time. They can move on because what is imbedded in them goes beyond their author and first readers, they delve deep into matters that are not limited to particular peoples and times. Revelation is a good example of such pensive literature; e.g. Rome is not identified as Rome but in the textured symbol Babylon. But precisely in clothing Rome in the textual garments of Babylon, the symbol and its associations live on after Rome has fallen, waiting for news ways it can uncover the evil cities of the world.

13. Kovacs and Rowland, *Revelation*, 7–11.

14. Although Kovacs and Rowland seem to prefer the latter, there seem to be enough direct and indirect matters in the text that call for it to be decoded. However, this does not preclude new actualizations.

15. By this I do not claim to return to the first century, but rather seek to discern how the text can be heard when we consider how it might have been received in the late first century. Nor do I claim that there is a one to one correspondence between the meaning the author sought to encode and the meaning I seek to decode. What I claim is only that important to this project is the *aim* to decode the meaning that is consonant with the *field of meaning* the author likely sought to encode, not an exact representation but a reading that lies within trajectories of interpretation of which the author likely would approve.

withstand the symbolic web with which the Roman empire encoded its populations.¹⁶

In focusing on this aspect, I do not preclude other ways of reading it. However, differing from some recent interpreters, I do not believe legitimate readings of the text can be contradictory; rather, they must complement and be consonant with one another. Therefore, although Revelation can be approached from many angles, in different ways and with various purposes, they all must strain toward occupying a place within the legitimate field of the text's meanings. To the extent they are at odds with one another, we are reminded of the eschatological nature of interpretation, that every reading is partial and faulty, and must await the fulfilment it strives toward.

Critiques of attempts to regain what the author sought to encode in a text are usually levelled against certain ways of approaching ancient texts. However, while the attendant difficulties of this task might be most evident in reading ancient texts, they are not limited to such texts but are equally applicable to contemporary texts. The difference is not in kind but of degree. While readers of this book may be more likely to question how I read Revelation, they ought not do so unless they level the same critique of my analysis of Moltmann. Therefore, when I write "Moltmann claims" or "Revelation shows," I naturally mean that I think that this or that stands within the field of meaning which Moltmann or the author of Revelation would see as adequate readings of their texts, to paint portraits that are sufficiently consonant with what they hoped to lay into the text.

---

16. By this I do not deny the validity of how others seek to actualize the book's imagery. After all, the power of the book lies precisely in how John was able to actualize his own symbolic heritage within the challenges facing him and his community. Similarly, although I focus on how the text might have been received by its first readers, I do so in order to gain insight into how they might speak to contemporary Christians in light of the future the book expects. Therefore, although I do not do it in this book, enacting the symbolism of the book anew in a new context is faithfulness to the tradition in which it stands. This, though, is not to be mistaken for arbitrary use of the imagery—a new actualisation, if it is to be a Christian one, must be performed within the rules of the semantic game in which the history of the text stands. And if it is to be considered Christian, it must be an actualisation of the imagery within how Christian communities configure the world.

The Referentiality of Texts

If the way I approach Revelation—as well as Moltmann—is justified in the desire to communicate that produces texts, what about my attempt to make the concerns of these two speak to one another? Again, a potential objection to this is most clearly seen when we consider Revelation. If a good reading is one consonant with the semantic field encoded in the text, how can a twenty-first-century question of which it knows nothing be brought to bear on it? How can an ancient text span the ages and speak today?

In addition to experiences of life that transcend time and space and the human capacity for the new, the different,[17] the possibility of texts to span vastly different contexts owes much to their referentiality. While authors and first readers pass away, what they speak about remains. Texts do not survive by drawing attention to themselves but by their capacity to make *something*, a referent, present that otherwise would be absent. Texts are icons that *in-form* the reader's imagination.[18] Texts make present something that cannot be equated with themselves, with the "set of black marks on white paper." When writers encode a text, they do so in the hope that readers will be able to rightly decipher this set of marks, "make sense of it, to read it, to interpret it," and so see what the author seeks to bring to present in the light the author sheds on it.[19] If the text points beyond itself, it always contains more than the communicative desire that shaped it.

If texts are about something other than themselves, they always draw the reader beyond themselves. In order to read well it is not sufficient to only know the text well; one must be opened to and engage

---

17. Anyone who has found themselves in a cross-cultural and cross-lingual context cannot help but be amazed by the human capability to enter a radically new context, despite the initial and often excruciating difficulties of doing so.

18. A possible referent should not be limited to a material object or a historical sequence of events but may just as well be a fictive world, an idea, or a mood. For an excellent essay on this iconic purpose not just of text but of language generally, see Pieper, *Abuse of Language*. He cogently argues that the proper use of language is for the purpose "to name and identify something that is real, to identify it for *someone*" (15). Language is abused when it is primarily used for some other and usually self-serving end than the attempt to convey reality. "The dignity of the word, to be sure, consists in this: through the word is accomplished what no other means can accomplish, namely, communication based on reality" (33).

19. Lash, *Way to Emmaus*, 38.

oneself with that which the text brings into the open. A reading that does not result in engagement with a text's subject matter is a failed reading.[20] If this is the case, a successful reading always engages more than the text, it always goes beyond simply the text's perspective on a subject, in order to make sense of the subject as a whole. If this is the case, a theological engagement with a text is not only possible but also desirable. And, although engagement can be made with the Bible from a variety of contexts, an important interpretive situation must be from within a Christian community that sees itself as predicated upon that which it believes the Scriptures seek to bring to presence.[21]

Since texts speak about *something*, give a perspective on a subject from a particular situatedness, reading a text is not only related to the text but also to its subject matter. The polyvalence of a rich text is not simply due to the multi-layered and complex nature of writing and reading texts, but is also grounded in the rich irreducibility of the referent, that which we speak and write about always contains more than we can convey and see. As texts lead us through themselves to their referent, they also bring us to something that is always only partially grasped. But as such, the referent can also be an important semantic anchor; it gives any reading both elasticity and boundedness, since the meaning of a thing is always a relational matter but never arbitrary.[22] Although

---

20. Although many scholars question Barth's exegetical practices, one of his great contributions is his insistence on the subject matter. He says of Calvin's reading of Romans, "having first established what stands in the text, [he] sets himself to re-think the whole material and to wrestle with it, till the walls which separate the sixteenth century from the first become transparent, i.e., till Paul *speaks* there and the man of the sixteenth century *hears* here, till the conversation between the document and the reader is totally concentrated on the subject-matter, which *cannot* be a different one in the first and sixteenth century" (Barth, as quoted in Stendahl, "Biblical Theology," 420).

21. Says Fowl *Engaging Scripture*, 6: "Christians' convictions about God's providence must include the view that God has providentially provided in their scriptures what Christians require in order to live and worship faithfully before God" (cf. 8–9, 20–21, 30; Watson, *Text*, vii). As such, "Christian doctrine is . . . concerned with the unfolding and uncovering of the history of Jesus of Nazareth, in the belief that this gives insight into the nature of reality" (McGrath, *Genesis*, 74–5, as quoted in Gilbertson, *God and History*, 44).

22. The modern distinction between perception and the "thing in itself" is misguided since the significance, and thus the meaning, of a thing lies always in the relation between perceiver and that which is perceived. This is not to deny the existence of things apart from our perception of them, but it is denying meaning to instances apart from the relationships in which they stand. The animals did exist before Adam saw them, but

its essence provides it with a substantial continuity, its significance, and thus its "signification" is known only in a dynamic and enriching flow of various relations.[23] Any reading of a text will be different than another, for each is done within a particular, non-repeatable context—even when one is exposed to the subject matter from a particular angle within the text, one always makes sense of it from one's own.[24] Gregory of Nyssa was right when he said: "Scripture grows with its readers."[25] Part of this enriching engagement with and through texts is bringing our own conceptual framework, our own ideas, concerns and ways of thinking, to the text in order to see what answers the text may throw at us from its own situatedness.[26] Therefore, if our engagement with the text is to gain insight into that of which the text speaks, it is appropriate to bring our own concerns and perspectives on the subject matter to the text, hoping the text will both enrich and correct our own perspective. The theologian's habit of bringing his or her own concerns to the text is not an inexcusable anachronistic fallacy, but the way everyone comes to texts—we cannot understand the past without grasping our present.[27]

---

they had no meaning in his cosmos before he named them, before he made sense of his perception of them, before he encoded their place in the cosmos he occupied.

23. Gilbertson says, "The rhetorical power of a text like Revelation comes from the interplay of the text and the reality to which it relates: to postulate either the absorption of the world by the text or the text by the world is therefore to assume a false antithesis" (*God and History*, 39). Drawing on Thiselton, Gilbertson goes on to see how this rich and complex relationship between text and referent is seen in how a *promise* seeks to conform the world to the word and how an *assertion* depends on matching the word to the world; "if a promise can have no effect in reality, it has no meaning. If the assertion does not match reality, *it* has no meaning" (40).

24. Because of this, the language of horizons, as e.g. employed by Thiselton, *Two Horizons* and *New Horizons*, seems a better way to distinguish the primary loci of interests usually associated with biblical studies and theology than Stendahl's categories.

25. As quoted in LaCocque and Ricoeur, *Thinking Biblically*, xi.

26. Although a text should not be reduced to propositional statements, most texts nevertheless make certain judgments on the character and nature of that of which they speak. Thus, part of reading well is trying to discern these judgments, a task that necessarily means a 'translation' of the text's judgments from its own conceptual framework to our own, to say the same thing differently (Yeago, "Nicene Dogma," 159, 60). See Yeago's "Nicene Dogma" for an excellent exposition on the continuity between texts like Phil 2 and later trinitarian formulations. Although the conceptual framework and concerns the Fathers worked with were very different from those of the NT writers, the judgments of the former were not inconsistent with those of the latter.

27. Commenting on the irreducible dialectic of existing as historical beings, that our present consciousness is shaped by the history that precedes us, N. Lash says, "If it

If the communicability of texts lies behind the way I read both Revelation and Moltmann, it is the referentiality of texts that holds the dialogue between the two together. I construct a conversation between the two because there is a sufficient overlap in that which they speak about. Although Moltmann assumes a world Revelation could not even imagine, and although Revelation's concerns are far from the context in which Moltmann writes, the reign of God and how it relates to humanity in its social existence as it moves through time and space is central to both. The Kingdom of God binds the conversation together. And, in the final analysis, the texts are windows, iconic venues to grapple with the same concerns with which they grapple. In the end, the fundamental concern of this book is not what Moltmann and Revelation believe, but *that in which* they believe. The goal is not interpretation itself, it is nurturing the symphonies, "the sounding together," with the subject matter, growing in interpretation, so the textured relationship with the referent grows in potentiality and possibility, in truth.

These thoughts on the communicability and referentiality of texts are but a brief endeavour into that incomprehensible sea of modern hermeneutics. It is anything but comprehensive but hopefully it conveys the desire and rationale behind this book: with the help of two loci of textual icons to move further into interpreting the world that assumes there is a kingdom ahead of us which in hidden ways is making itself known among us.

In summary, the purpose of this book is to make one contribution to the larger theological conversation on the Kingdom of God through an appraisal of the function of the kingdom in the work of Jürgen Moltmann, and by exploring how this appraisal may both enrich and be corrected by an interpretation of how Revelation deals with similar

---

is true for us, as creatures of history, that some understanding of our past is a necessary condition of an accurate grasp of our present predicament and of our responsibilities for the future, it is also true that a measure of critical self-understanding of our present predicament is a necessary condition of an accurate 'reading' of our past. We do not *first* understand the past and *then* proceed to understand the present. The relationship between these two dimensions of our quest for meaning and truth is dialectical: they mutually inform, enable, correct and enlighten each other" (Lash, *Way to Emmaus*, 79–80). This does not mean that we are helplessly bound to our present but historically conditioned consciousness, but as Jeanrond, "After Hermeneutics," 96, rightly points out: while one's commitment and purpose of course conditions one's reading, it does not necessarily determine it.

concerns. The particular way I construct this conversation is grounded in the two fundamental assumptions discussed above, that text are written to *communicate*, and to communicate *something*. How, then, will this conversation, be developed?

Approach of the Study

The central discussion of this book commences with an appraisal of Moltmann's view of the kingdom in chaps. 3 and 4. Chapter 3 looks at how the kingdom functions as a symbol of hope for humanity, how this hope is grounded in the way the promise of the kingdom has appeared in the person and history of Jesus, and how this gives shape to a messianic understanding of history and a corresponding historical praxis. Chapter 4 considers what has become increasingly important for Moltmann, the presence of the kingdom in history—how God's "rule" is present to creation, orienting the world toward the future opened up to it in the promise of the kingdom.

Chapter 5 sets the stage for the second part of the book, outlining first the issues in Moltmann's view of the kingdom that will be brought to my study of Revelation, and second, introducing the urgencies that Revelation responds to in its own depiction of God's rule and kingdom. Following the structure established in the appraisal of Moltmann, chapters 6 considers how the future hoped for in Revelation is a "regime change," the time when the powers that now occupy the central geopolitical authority on earth will be replaced by God and his Christ. Chapter 7 turns to how the book depicts God as the sovereign over both heaven and earth, and how he is now orienting the world toward this future, not only in acts of judgment but also through the Spirit-enabled kerygmatic witness of the ecclesial communities that have been constituted by the slain Lamb as a kingdom to God. The latter part of these chapters place my interpretation of Revelation into a dialogue with Moltmann, considering how Moltmann may open up ways of reading Revelation today, and how Revelation may suggest correctives to potential weaknesses in Moltmann.

In a brief concluding chapter I will suggest how I think the dialogue I have proposed here has fared in the body of the work, as well as make a few remark on the importance of the authorial "I" as not outside the dialogue but as an interested and situated partner in it. Anticipating that discussion, I point out that while the dialogue on paper is between Moltmann and Revelation, it is more accurate to describe this book as a three-way conversation, since it is I who construct the dialogue, decide what the two textual voices will speak on, interpret what they say and evaluate my portraits. It is my hope, that the portraits I paint in these pages are trustworthy, but they are still painted with my palette.

By the time astute readers come to the later chapters, they will notice how I consistently privilege the voice of Revelation over Moltmann when the two seem to be in conflict. This pattern is primarily due to the different ways in which Moltmann and I see the place and function the Bible has in the church. Therefore, before we delve into our primary concern, we turn first, in the next chapter, to Moltmann's view on Scripture and how it differs from my own. And since Moltmann's view of Scripture cannot be separated from its place within his theological framework, this chapter will commence with an overview of the basic strokes of his theological approach, including the important role the Kingdom of God plays in it.

2

Witness to the Promised Kingdom
The Bible in Moltmann's Theological Approach

THE PURPOSE OF THIS CHAPTER IS TO EXPLORE HOW MOLTMANN SEES the role and function of the Bible in the church and theology. However, since his view of the Bible is embedded in his theological approach, we must first consider the broad trajectories of his theology, including the pivotal role the Kingdom of God plays in it.

Setting the Stage
The Crisis of Modernity and Messianic Hope

Moltmann's theological journey begins in an experience of crisis, when, as a reluctant seventeen year old recruit into Hitler's failing war effort, his anti-aircraft artillery unit in Hamburg was bombed during "Operation Gomorrah." A fellow soldier standing by him was torn to pieces, but Moltmann was left unscathed; and he asked himself: "My God, where are you?" and "Why am I alive and not dead like the rest?"[1] This deeply personal experience crystallizes for Moltmann what he and much of twentieth-century German theology sought to come to grips with. The two world wars spelt the death knell to Cultural Protestantism and the modern humanist project and its idea of progress.[2] Moltmann was dissatisfied, however, with the response of dialectical theology, especially as seen in Bultmann's existential approach, because of its incapability to speak the promise of the Gospel into concrete historical

---

1. *EiT*, 3–4.

2. While initially the concern for Moltmann was history, his later thought expands this in the concern for economic justice in light of the divide between the First World and Third World, and ecological justice in light of the ecological crisis (*WJC*, 63–69; *CoG*, 202–18; *CrG*, 329–335; *JCTW*, 24–28).

reality.³ Therefore, when Gerhard von Rad sharply criticized Bultmann's "epiphanous" understanding of revelation as failing to pay attention "to the peculiar context of 'revelation' in the biblical traditions,"⁴ Moltmann firmly sided with von Rad in the ensuing debate.⁵

Von Rad argued that from the earliest strands of OT tradition, Israel's confessions about the LORD are "historically determined, that is, they connect the name of this God with some statement about or action in history."⁶ However, in contrast to Pannenberg, who also is influenced by von Rad, Moltmann does not see revelation as history but as "word-history": God reveals himself in his word, his promise that contradicts a given actuality and thus creates history as the history of God's faithfulness to his promise; revelation, then, is "the demonstration of God's faithfulness to his promise."⁷ "It was not in the *logos* of the epiphany of the eternal present," says Moltmann, "but in the hope-giving word of promise that Israel found God's truth."⁸ As we will discuss in a later chapter, Moltmann embeds the person and history of Jesus within this promissory history of the Old Testament, seeing Easter as the possibility-making event of this history, it opens the whole world that otherwise is bound by the horizon of death up to the eschatological promise the resurrection holds for it.

In the way he develops his understanding of history, Moltmann is particularly indebted to twentieth-century Jewish thinkers who were both children of the modern world and also, as Jews, experienced its

---

3. As such, Bultmann's problem is for Moltmann very similar to the pitfall of the often "other-worldly" nature of traditional Christian hope.

4. Meeks, *Origins*, 68.

5. For his own account on the importance of his teachers in Göttingen and A. A. van Ruler in the shape of his own response, see *EiT*, 87–91. For an overview of the "eschatological" milieu in which Moltmann's thought emerges, see Runia, "Eschatology;" cf. Gilkey (*Reaping the Whirlwind*, 227–33), who argues that the "new" historical theologians "pivoted the basic axis of Christian thought and concern from a *vertical* axis relating time and eternity, creatureliness and transcendence, into a *horizontal* axis relating present and future, a godless world of the now with a God whose 'being is future'" (229).

6. Von Rad, *Old Testament Theology*, 121, as quoted in Meeks, *Origins*, 68.

7. Meeks, *Origins*, 72; for a recent exposition on the similarities and differences between Moltmann and Pannenberg, see Gilbertson, *God and History*, 11–19, 143–200; cf. Meeks, *Origins*, 64–73.

8. *TH*, 40–41. Braaten says, "Christian eschatology speaks of the future in utterances of hope based on the history of promise" ("Theology of Hope," 216).

downfall most acutely.[9] As the modern dream of historical progress in European culture was shattered in the first half of the twentieth century, these Jews returned to their own Judaic roots for an alternative understanding of history, and found it in messianism. Rejecting the notions that the human race can be educated toward perfection and that history can bring the world to completion, they reverted to messianic categories of hope and redemption, the possibility of the new rising out of history's ashes.[10] From their heritage they recovered the biblical notion that the true historical force is found in the hope birthed by promise. It is the promise of the future that reveals the evils history produces and offers redemption when history lies in ruin. What we need to seek is not the evolving and progressive meaning of history but rather its redemption. It is after the catastrophe, when the world lies in ruin, that the splinters of redemption shine through it, when the time of the victims has come. T. W. Adorno states:

> Philosophy, in the only form in which it can still be responsibly upheld in face of despair, would be the attempt to regard all things as they present themselves from the standpoint of redemption. Knowledge has no light save that which shines upon the world from the standpoint of redemption: all else exhausts itself in imitation and remains a piece of technique. Perspectives must be created in which the world looks changed and alien and reveals its cracks and flaws in much the same way as it will one day lie destitute and disfigured in Messiah's light. To attain such perspectives without arbitrariness or force, entirely out of sensitiveness towards things—that alone is the aim of thought.[11]

Among these thinkers, Ernst Bloch was especially influential on Moltmann, since it was in his principle of hope Moltmann found the conceptual categories that enabled him to draw together the various ideas that were shaping his theology.[12] Bloch's dynamic materialism, heavily influenced by Jewish and Christian messianic ideas, has a fundamentally eschatological ontology in which matter is incomplete, its

---

9. *CoG*, 29–30, where he mentions several authors, and then goes on to discuss Bloch (30–33), Rosenzweig (33–36), Scholem (36–38), Benjamin (38–41), and Taubes and Löwith (41–44). For the importance of Heschel in Moltmann, see Jaeger, "Heschel."

10. *CoG*, 29–30.

11. T. W. Adorno, as quoted in *TH*, 290–291.

12. *EiT*, 92–93; cf. *TH*, 9; *HTG*, 169.

potential not yet fulfilled.¹³ Matter's potential, its "not yet," is then the power of its future, the force that drives what "is" toward what it can be. This creates a historical dialectic with three fundamental elements: The "Not," the experience of the absence of that which is not yet; "Novum," the realization of matter's potentiality; and "Hope," the aspiration, the search and explication of the possible, the realization of the Novum at the front of the present.¹⁴ The pivotal difference between Bloch and Moltmann is how they understand the power of the future; for the former it is the transcending potential within matter, for the latter the promise of God and the pneumatological presence of this promising God in creation.¹⁵

Although many post-war theologians were reluctant to speak about the kingdom of God in concrete political terms because of the role such language had in Cultural Protestantism,¹⁶ for Moltmann, it is precisely this retrieval of messianic categories and the conceptual framework that Bloch clothes them in that leads him to see the hope for the coming kingdom as pivotal to a theological response to the crisis of faith in the post-war German context.

Moltmann's Theological Approach

A concern for the kingdom colors every aspect of Moltmann's approach to theology. Although Moltmann has often been critiqued for his methodological looseness and is self-confessedly experimental,¹⁷ there are

---

13. For a brief introduction to the basic elements in Bloch's thought, see Geoghegan, "Bloch."

14. The Novum's fulfillment is the humanizing of the world, when nature and humanity become "one in essence" (Chapman, "Jürgen Moltmann," 446). Says Bloch: "The World is not true, but through human beings and through truth it strives to arrive at its homecoming" (as quoted in *CoG*, 33).

15. Bloch believes religious hope "reflects the tension between humanity's present estrangement and its future essence," whose "God" Marxism shows to be the not yet realized ideal of the human essence (Chapman, "Jürgen Moltmann," 438; cf. *HTG*, 169; Eckert, "Zukunft," 130–31).

16. See Runia, "Kingdom of God," for an overview of how the kingdom has been understood in history.

17. It is better to talk of Moltmann's theological approach than his method; although not arbitrary, his theology is not methodologically committed. He says, "I am often asked about my theological method," and continues, "and seldom provide an answer . . . I do not defend any impersonal dogmas, but nor do I merely express my own personal opinion. I make suggestions within a community. So I write without any

some basic trajectories that give shape to his thought. "If I were to attempt to sum up the outline of my theology in a few key phrases," he says, "I would have at the least to say that I am attempting to reflect on a theology which has: a biblical foundation, an eschatological orientation, a political responsibility. In and under that it is certainly a theology in pain and joy at God himself, a theology of constant wonder."[18] First, by "biblical foundation" he means reading "the Bible as witness of God's promissory history and the human history of hope." Second, inherent in the "biblical foundation" is an "eschatological orientation." The task of theology is not the formulation of orthodox dogma or merely making sense of human existence.[19] Rather, it seeks to discern how we can faithfully orient ourselves to the promised future of God and his kingdom in the situations which face us now. Third, since this is a hope that is not limited to the church but includes the whole world, it must be "politically responsible." This means that Christians cannot take a neutral stand vis-à-vis the political realities of the world. Since the promissory history of God witnessed to in the Bible is one of liberation, the church's stance must always be with and among those that now live in bondage. As the church seeks to discern the role it cannot help but have in society, it must be careful not to play into the hands of the powers to be and seek to maintain the status quo that benefits them, but rather ask "about the origin and legitimation of the church in the name of Christ and making Jesus' message of the kingdom of God for the poor the starting point of a politics of consistent discipleship."[20] So, "political theology designates the field, the milieu, the environment, and the medium in which Christian theology should be articulated today."[21]

Considering this three-fold approach, Moltmann's theology is to be seen as one of "mediation," "of relating the Christian tradition and message critically and therapeutically to this modern situation, for only in that way can it communicate the tradition of Christian faith, love and

---

built-in safeguards, recklessly as some people think" (*CoG*, xiii, xiv). Moltmann sets his own account of his theological approach and journey in *HTG*, 165–82 and in *EiT*.

18. *HTG*, 182.

19. Moltmann's continuity with Scripture and tradition is not to be seen "in terms of faithfulness to the past, but faithfulness to promises of the future" (Clutterbuck, "Moltmann," 495).

20. *HTG*, 178.

21. *EH*, 102–3.

hope."[22] It is only as the Gospel of the kingdom is mediated, made present, "in such a way that it falls within the horizons of the understanding of the people of a particular time,"[23] that it can turn contemporary circumstances toward the peace of God's kingdom. This necessarily involves adaptations and even contradictions as times move from the contingencies of one age to another. However, as the Gospel changes its outer garments, its substance must remain the same. In modernity, this does not mean adapting to the Spirit of the age but with the Gospel entering into the suffering of this age, "taking the side of the victims of the 'modern world'" and there finding the potential for this world from the hope of Christ and the coming kingdom.[24] As such, "mediation between the Christian tradition and the culture of the present is the most important task of theology."[25]

"Imagination for the Kingdom of God"

Moltmann's understanding of the kingdom of God is intrinsically bound up with his approach to theology. Indeed, he describes his theology as "imagination for the kingdom of God."[26] The close relationship between the two is evident in one of his earliest essays, *Die Gemeinde im Horizont der Herrschaft Christi* in which Moltmann claims most of his later ideas exist in incipient form.[27]

---

22. *ThT*, 94.
23. Ibid., 53.
24. Ibid., ix.
25. Ibid., 53. See Rasmusson on the mediating method of Moltmann's political theology (*Church as Polis*, 42–48). Bauckham says, "The greatest achievement of Moltmann's theology has been to open up hermeneutical structures for relating biblical faith to the modern world. The strength and appropriateness of these structures lie in their biblical basis, their Christological center and their eschatological openness" (*Messianic Theology*, 140; cf. Hunsinger, "Crucified God. . . , II," 395).
26. *CoG*, xiv.
27. Reflecting at the end of his career on this essay, Moltmann says: "I can see that here all the themes of my later theology are really already sounded: the eschatological horizon of history in the kingdom of God; faithfulness to the earth; new partnerships for the church in the world; and 'the narrow wideness of the cross of Christ'" (*EiT*, 91; cf. "How I Have Changed," 15). For an analysis of the place of this essay in Moltmann's thought, see Müller-Fahrenholz, *Kingdom*, 26–39. If not otherwise noted, my discussion is drawn from him.

Critiquing the singular christological focus in post-war German theology, he argues that we can only truly account for Christ as the center if we at the same time account for the horizon around this center, the horizon being the kingdom of God. First, with Barth and against every attempt to fuse the kingdom with human institutions and achievements, Moltmann emphasises that the kingdom of God is revealed in his word. As God's self-revelation, Jesus is the Kingdom in person; it is in him that God's purposes for the whole world are revealed; in him God has determined himself in favour of all humanity.[28] This manifestation of the kingdom in Jesus is the objective ground for the redemption of the whole world.[29] Second, it is precisely this christological center of the kingdom that indicates that the whole world is the concrete realm of the kingdom, the horizon against which Christ wills to reign. But this "yes" to the world should not and cannot be equated with the utopian progressivism of cultural Protestantism since the basis for the rule of Christ anticipated in the resurrection is articulated in the cross.[30] Therefore, the church can only anticipate the kingdom in the concrete political, social and cultural processes of the world by following the way God's love is revealed in staurological praxis.[31] Third, since the way of the kingdom revealed in the cross embraces not only the church but also the world, the church must seek partnerships for the kingdom with the orders instituted in the world that have their own future in the kingdom. Fourth, this then eventually leads to what Moltmann calls "mut zur weltlichen

---

28. For Moltmann's mature development of the relationship between Jesus and "the coming kingdom" that made itself present in his ministry, see *WJC*, 97–99.

29. "Die in Christus für die Welt gefallene göttliche Entscheidung steht objektiv über allen in der Welt lebenden Menschen; denn Jesus Christus ist auch ihr Haupt und ihr Herr. Alle Menschen sind darum—objektiv, d. h. von Gott her gesehen,—die Seinigen, sein Eigentum, ob sie es wissen oder nicht, und sind eben auf diesen göttlichen Tatbestand *de jure* anzusprechen. Sie alle sind 'potentielle Christen'" (*GHHC*, 12).

30. "Die Erwartung der erlösenden und zurechtbringenden Herrschaft in allen Dingen unserer weltlichen Wirklichkeit von dem gekreuzigten und erhöhten Christus allein vermag uns die Kraft zu geben, das 'Kreuz der Wirklichkeit' auf uns zu nehmen und diese Welt in ihrer ganzen Wirklichkeit *ohne Vorbehalt, aber auch ohne illusion* anzunehmen" (*GHHC*, 21).

31. Note his positive adoption of Blumhart's call that "Christen müssen die Posaune hören, die in der Welt ertönt. Christen müssen diesem Ruf folgen hinein in die Welt," they must commit themselves "im Dienst an der Herrschaft und am dem Leben Christi in der Welt" (*GHHC*, 17–18).

Predigt," (courage for worldly preaching) to a kerygmatic praxis that accords with the centrifugal power of the cross that occupies the church's confessional center. It cannot remember Easter without being drawn into the concrete cultural, political and social realities of the world that constitute the horizon of Christ's kingdom, and therefore it must seek to shape its praxis in the light that the cross sheds on the kingdom. In taking its christological center seriously, the church is led out into the world, into the horizon of the kingdom which encompasses both the world (i.e., it is related to the entire world in its concrete realities) and its history (as hope for the last things).

Not only do we find most of Moltmann's theological concerns in incipient form here but we also see how his understanding of the kingdom is central to the content of his theology, the mirror image of his theological approach. The pivotal part of "the biblical foundation" of his theology is the 'happening' of the kingdom in the person and history of Jesus. This is the event that gives faith confidence because here God proves himself faithful to his own promise for the whole world in one person, in the death and resurrection of Jesus. Consequently, the "eschatological orientation" is how this appearance of the kingdom in Jesus opens the whole world to its own future in the kingdom. Jesus the center is the anticipation of the future that awaits the world, of the kingdom that will extend to the whole world. "Political responsibility" is therefore nothing less than taking seriously that the church's central christological confession does not concern only its own existence but includes all things in the rule of God—the practical outworking of the church's existence is living for the future of the whole world in the kingdom of God.

These are the basic notes of the main theme that characterises Moltmann's understanding of the kingdom from the beginning. As his theology develops, some variations on that theme emerge, the two most important being how he develops the kingdom as a symbol of hope, and how he augments the eschatological focus of his early emphasis with a second relational one.

First, we see an intentional move from the kingdom being *the* symbol to being *a* mediating symbol of hope. In Moltmann's early writings, up to *God in Creation*, the Kingdom of God functions as the integrating symbol of Christian hope, as "the comprehensive Christian horizon of life" and as "the breadth of the horizon of hope opened up through

Christ for Christianity as it lives and suffers in history."[32] As Christ is the center of Christian hope, the Kingdom of God is the horizon encircling it. However, as Moltmann becomes increasingly concerned with the ecological crisis facing the earth because of the anthropocentricity of modernity, he begins to differentiate between hope for humanity and for creation, relating the kingdom to the former.[33]

Although he uses the kingdom of God as the comprehensive symbol of hope in *God in Creation*,[34] he, in the preface to the paperback edition of the book, published some five years later, describes the book as an attempt at "integrating the historical symbol of hope, 'the Kingdom of God', with the natural symbol of hope, 'the new creation of all things,'" just as he had in *Theology of Hope* expanded the personal hope for "eternal life" by integrating it with the expectation of the redemption of humanity in the kingdom.[35] This three-fold differentiation of hope then becomes a structuring principle for the *Coming of God* where he first deals with "eternal life" as personal eschatology (part II), then with "the Kingdom of God" as historical eschatology (Part III), and thirdly with "New Heaven—New Earth" as cosmic eschatology (Part IV).[36] He illustrates the relationship between these as three concentric circles, in which "the Kingdom of God" is the mediating symbol between "eternal life" and "the new creation."[37] While the individual personal hope for eternal life is embedded within the expectation for the kingdom, the hope for the redemption of humanity must itself be seen within the expectation of the transformation of the whole cosmos in the new heaven and earth.[38] In the following chapters our focus will be on this mediat-

---

32. *CPS*, 134, 133.

33. It is in *GiC* that Moltmann first, in a sustained way, begins to consider the future of creation on its own terms.

34. *GiC*, 8; cf. 53–56; cf. *WJC*, 98 where he equates the future kingdom with the "new creation."

35. *GiC*, xi.

36. In *CoG*, he adds another symbol, "Glory," as the divine eschatology the other three are oriented toward (Part V).

37. *CoG*, 132. While the integration of these three symbols is a particular focus of *CoG*, the recent minor work *IEB*, *TH*, and *GiC* can be seen as his main treatises on each of these symbols.

38. While Moltmann is careful to make this distinction when discussing the eschatological 'homeland' of the kingdom, he tends to use it comprehensively in other context, as e.g. when he describes his theology as an "imagination for the kingdom of

ing symbol, seeing the kingdom as referring to the history of God with humanity, the way in which he overcomes the alienation of humanity and reconciles humanity to himself.

Second, while Moltmann has affirmed from the outset of his theological journey that the kingdom has broken into history in the person of Jesus, *Theology of Hope* was singularly focused on what this means for the kingdom as a symbol of hope. However, from *The Crucified God* and onwards, he becomes increasingly concerned with how the kingdom expected is now present in the world in anticipatory form. Noting how βασιλεία ("kingdom") can refer either to the present and actual rule of God in the world (which is disputed and manifests itself in hidden ways) or to the universal goal of divine rule (which is eschatological, universal and undisputed),[39] he, in *The Church in the Power of the Spirit*, makes a distinction between the historical and relational aspects of the kingdom, its future and its presence. Of the inseparability of these two, Moltmann says:

> If we view history, with its conditions and potentialities, as an open system, we are bound to understand the kingdom of God in the liberating rule of God as a transforming power immanent in that system, and the rule of God in the kingdom of God as a future transcending the system. Without the counterpart of the future of the kingdom, which transcends the present system, the transforming power immanent in the system loses its orientation. Without the transformation immanent in the system the future transcending the system would become a powerless dream.[40]

In relation to human history then, the historical aspect of the Kingdom of God refers to the specific hope that the history of Jesus sets out for humanity, and the relational aspect refers to the anticipatory presence of the future of humanity in its social relationship within creation before God. "In history God rules through Spirit and Word, liberty and obedience. But his rule comes up against conflict, contradiction and contention. It is a controversial rule, veiled in antagonism." As such, it is oriented beyond itself to "that future when God will rule uncontra-

---

God" in the very same preface he has taken care to distinguish its function as a symbol of hope (*CoG*, xiv).

39. *CPS*, 190.

40. Ibid.

dicted, and in his glory will be all in all." At the same time however, the future kingdom can throw "its light ahead of itself into this history of struggle" precisely because it is now present in paradoxical and hidden ways. "We therefore have to understand the liberating activity of God as the *immanence* of the eschatological kingdom of God, and the coming kingdom as the *transcendence* of the present lordship of God."[41]

Thus, when we speak about the kingdom of God in Moltmann's thought, we are concerned with human sociality in all its relationships before God and his purposes. It concerns the social, political, economic, cultural and religious processes which constitute human sociality. Living toward and in light of the kingdom is seeking the alignment of these to the will and purposes of God. Then, when we enquire into the kingdom of God in its future fulfillment, we seek to depict the character of human sociality in all its dimensions, as it is brought into the full presence of God and is predicated upon this. And when we enquire into the presence of the kingdom of God in history, we seek to discern how this future reality is present within the era that is predicated on powers that contradict it, and how, by its presence, precisely those relations which now often oppose it are being aligned toward its future. In the following two chapters which constitute our analysis of the place of the kingdom in Moltmann's theology, we will first turn to this historical aspect, how the kingdom is the symbol of hope for humanity, and then to how Moltmann perceives how the divine rule of this kingdom revealed in Christ is present in the world by the power of the Spirit.

But first, as already noted, we turn to how Moltmann's view of Scripture fits within the broad strands of his thought, how I differ from him, and how this difference influences my appraisal of both Moltmann and Revelation.

Moltmann's View of Scripture

For Moltmann, the Bible is the documented expression of the experience of the promissory history, which is trinitarian and covenantal in character, is oriented toward its fulfillment in the coming Kingdom of God, and has Christ as its interpretive nexus.[42] The Bible, as everything

---

41. *WJC*, 97–98.

42. The following discussion is based on "Hermeneutics of Hope" in *EiT*, especially 125–50, Moltmann's most recent and comprehensive discussion on the Bible.

else, must be seen within the open ontology of the promissory history, in which creation is not finished "but all created beings in heaven and earth, appear as *real promises* of their future in the kingdom of glory."[43] God has promised his coming kingdom to the whole community of his creatures, a promise which orients them to their completion in it. And so it is also with the Bible. Moltmann believes the Bible has a unique function within this history, as it documents God's own history with Israel and the fulfillment of this promise in Christ. But the Bible also partakes in the same nature as everything else in this history; it is not finished, not complete. It strives toward its eschatological fulfillment. This has two fundamental consequences.

First, Scripture has an inherent "added value." Since the promise always surpasses the fulfillment the text records, "[t]he 'meaning' of a text is not exhausted either in its own time or in its interpretation in a new kairos."[44] For this reason, Scripture is a well-spring for fresh interpretation, for reading the text's promise anew in our own day; taking our cues from within the text, we carry its promises beyond its original bounds to see how it makes itself felt, present in our own contemporary situations, our *kairos*. But, second, the flipside of this "surplus" is the incompleteness of the text. As the rest of created reality, it too is transitory and partial, and longs for its completion in the kingdom of God. For Moltmann, the Bible is not the infallible text of or for the church but rather the account of the history of promise, first in God's covenant with Israel (OT) and then in the pivotal (but not exhaustive) fulfillment of the promise for all nations in Christ (NT). The Bible, as a part of this history shares both the potential inherent in the promise but also the incomplete and transitory character of historical reality. In its partialness it testifies to how the promise has drawn near in Israel and in the communities gathered around Jesus, but it also reflects the ways in which the promises have not yet been fulfilled. This raises the question

---

43. Ibid., 111.

44. Ibid., 105. Precisely because of the anticipatory nature of all reality, including the promises of Scripture, Moltmann rejects any notion of the Bible as a deposit of conceptual presuppositions (which "presupposes a finished, completed reality") in favour for the language of promise which alone bridges "the historical present and the eschatological future, . . . a promise reaches out beyond what is existently real into the sphere of what is not yet real, the sphere of the possible, and in the word anticipates what is promised" (ibid., 103).

of the status of the Bible in the church, both in regard to its character and to the way in which it is authoritative.

Moltmann rejects both views of Scripture that see it exhaustive from above as the Word of God, a *holy* message dictated from God above, or from below as human words about God, *hallowed* for a particular purpose, claiming that both attempts assume a single monistic subject which determines the whole.[45] Instead he proposes a trinitarian understanding of the Bible in which "God does not just speak; he also hears."[46] Understood in trinitarian terms, the movement from above (in which the sovereignty of God that proceeds "from the Father *through* the Son *in* the Holy Spirit" is revealed to us "from the Holy Spirit *through* scripture *in* the proclamation"[47]) is met with a Eucharistic movement from below (in which our knowledge of God proceeds in movements of thanksgiving but also of lament and doubt, "which proceeds from the indwelling Spirit, through the Son / the eternal Word / the eternal Wisdom, to the Father"[48]). The Bible is the result of this double movement. It reflects a reciprocal relationship between the Triune God and his people, in which the "callings and energies of God's Spirit," and his "suffering and sadness" find expression. This *ex*pression of the experience of the Spirit "follows the traces of *im*pression of God which called the expression forth."[49] Scripture is holy as it contains the revelation of God in the expressions of the Spirit. However, part of this, in fact, the condition in which this revelation can find expression, is the impression this revelation makes on the community of faith, in all its incompleteness, juxtaposition and jarring metaphors. It is this Bible, which testifies to the trinitarian history, which is hallowed by the church to be the witness to this story. The Scriptures are holy, generating faith, as they "they correspond to God's promise in Christ and the Spirit."[50] But this

45. See, ibid., 140–44.

46. Ibid., 143.

47. Ibid., 140. Italics his. Henceforth, if not otherwise noted italics in quotation are original.

48. Ibid., 143.

49. Ibid. This reciprocal nature of Scripture is grounded in the fundamental reciprocity of God's promissory history with the world; it is, so to say, the fruit of the covenant that aligns itself "toward reciprocity, and requires of men and women the conduct which accords with it" (ibid., 96).

50. Ibid., 136. The church then is "the determining subject of scripture" when we consider it as this particular collection of texts, "the written form given to the Word

holiness, that which corresponds to God's promises, which generates faith, is contained within the biblical texts, in all their diversity, even disharmony, and always partialness. These texts are the "disharmonious" witnesses of those who have been caught up in the "harmonies of God" by faith.[51] Therefore, the holiness of the Bible must be distinguished from the biblical witness that have been "hallowed", the texts that are a product generated by faith and are hallowed for use in worship.[52]

Therefore, although Moltmann sees the Bible as the primary depository of the promissory history, he certainly does not think the subject matter of the text can be identified with the text, an error which roots he sees in the Post-Reformation orthodox rhetoric against Catholicism. In its enthusiasm to free the Bible from its ecclesiastical shackles, the orthodox reduced the subject matter of the Bible to the text of the Bible through the "theopneustic" doctrine, making the teaching on Scripture the pivotal dogma on which all hangs.[53] For Moltmann, it is pivotal that the claim that Scripture is its own interpreter does not get reduced to the Bible being "a kind of Protestant pocket-pope, infallible and inerrant."[54] The Bible as a whole is not the authoritative Word of God, without error or fault. The matter of Scripture must be distinguished clearly from the text of Scripture.[55] To profess that the Bible is "self-interpreting" does not mean that the entire text of the Bible is to be taken at face value; rather it refers to the standard by which it is to be read, which is contained in it. The text of Scripture is to be judged by the matter of Scripture. For Moltmann, "the matter of scripture is God's promissory history"[56] as it is testified to in the duality of the two testaments, first in the covenant with Israel and then in "Jesus' messianic history," which opens the history begun with Israel (which still awaits its fulfillment) to

---

of God," but when we consider it with reference to its subject matter "*scripture* is the determining subject of the church," (ibid., 136) determines it to be "the people of God's coming kingdom" that is to act on the emerging promise of God (ibid., 130).

51. Ibid., 143.
52. See, ibid., 135–36.
53. Ibid., 139.
54. Ibid., 129.
55. Moltmann claims that the notion of "verbal inspiration" reduces the efficacy of the Spirit because it limits it to the inspiration of scripture (ibid., 136). This, however, is to build a straw man of the doctrine, for most who hold it would not limit the work of the Spirit to the particular way they see Him at work in the formation of the Bible.
56. Ibid., 129.

"its final eschatological history for the peoples of the world."[57] The matter of the Old Testament, Israel's Tenakh, is God's covenant with Israel, a covenant with promises that both embrace Israel as Israel but also point beyond to all peoples and the whole creation, to universal salvation and peace.[58] The matter of the New Testament is the unequivocal endorsement and enactment of these universal promises "through and in Christ," and the commencement of their fulfillment in the Spirit.[59] The history of promises proclaims in narrative form the relationship within the fellowship of the Trinity which is open to the world.[60] Scripture is its own interpreter as it is interpreted according to this its subject matter. It is this logic of promise and hope, and the relationship between God and the world it conveys that is to guide how we read the Bible. Therefore, it is fundamentally interested in "the power of the future" that is revealed in God's promises and that stirs human hope. The Bible is a witness to how the promissory history of God has repeatedly "liberated people from their inner and outer prisons," whether that is Israel from Egypt or Jesus from death. This is the dangerous but liberating memory from which "we also learn to see critically beyond our own present."[61] It is this that "thrusts and ferments, something which has to come out and must be e-lucidated, because it cannot remain within itself."[62]

---

57. Ibid., 126.

58. Ibid., 135–36.

59. Ibid., 136. Moltmann categorically rejects that the opening up of Israel's promises to all nations in Christ leads to a supersessionist understanding of the relation between the two testaments, that the church in any way takes the place of Israel as God's chosen people. Christianity does not fulfil the Old Testament's promissory history but rather "Jesus' messianic history" and the gift of the Spirit "enters into Israel's promissory history for the peoples of the world" (ibid., 126). Israel's own story is not abrogated, but rather, the nations, in their own way, are opened up to the promises first given to Israel. Rather than making Israel superfluous, this makes the church indivisibly linked to Judaism, and a Christian reading of the Old Testament should always be dependent on how Jews read their Tenakh and should always be developed in dialogue with its Judaic counterpart (ibid., 125). Although the call for respectful dialogue is to be applauded, the dependence Moltmann calls for is not as obvious as he thinks since Rabbinic Judaism and Christianity have emerged in parallel fashion, and current Judaic interpretations of scripture are no less modern or any more immediately in tune with the ancient text than the Christian ones.

60. Ibid., 144; *TKG*, 64.

61. *OHD*, 105, 106.

62. *EiT*, 129.

For Moltmann, then, the criteria by which one reads and discerns Scripture is neither an external ideological framework nor a particular central idea within the Bible, a canon within the canon, but it is the history about which it testifies, and which points beyond itself. The Bible does not have a center but a goal, its point of verification is eccentrically located, in the homeland of God's future to which it points; since "the 'matter of scripture' is God's history of promise, then scripture is part of it, and points beyond itself to the time of its fulfilment."[63] This fulfillment will find place when the present transient time (*chronos*), with its history of death and suffering passes away, is met by the eternal *kairos* of God, when death is no more and the living God will be "all in all" (1 Cor 15:28).[64] This is the coming of God to his creation, the arrival of his Kingdom to the whole created community, and therefore the symbol of "the Kingdom of God . . . becomes the scarlet thread of biblical theology which does not just read the Old Testament in light of the New, and the New Testament in light of the Old, but reads both in the light of God's coming to his whole creation."[65] It is this that "thrust and ferments," what "has to come out and . . . be e-lucidated" in the Bible. Therefore when reading and interpreting the Bible faithfully according to is subject matter, we must do it in "such a way that its hearers are drawn into the event which 'is already in the process of coming.' This happens if in the telling of what is past the future is heralded, so that what is proclaimed is future in the past."[66] This calls for a dialectic of christological reading, in which the scriptural testimony to the promissory history has its interpretive nexus in Jesus and is read within both the socio-historical conditions of its own time but also in light of the experience of the kingdom within the contingencies of our own time. Such reading must allow the testimony within the text to confront our own experience but also be confronted by it.[67]

---

63. Ibid., 129–30. "The Old Testament surplus of promise directs the apprehension of Christ and the experience of the Spirit to the future kingdom . . . the very reason that the biblical histories of promise and gospel can be called historical is that they point beyond *excentrically* beyond themselves into God's future" (ibid., 16–27).

64. Ibid., 99–100.

65. Ibid., 127–28.

66. Ibid., 129.

67. See ibid., 130–33.

Since the purpose of this analysis of Moltmann's view of Scripture is to set out how our respective views of the Bible influence my analysis in the following chapters, I will here only note my differences with Moltmann that have a direct bearing on that analysis. But first a few words on how I find Moltmann's approach helpful.

First, many, and perhaps especially evangelical attempts to defend the authority of Scripture only focus on its veracity—if the Bible is God's word, it must be without error. However, even when such discussions are more than fideistic assertions, they often fail to give an adequate theological account of the Scriptures. Consequently, they fail to sufficiently discuss the place and function of the Bible in the church.[68] And if the question of purpose and function is not clarified, the question of reliability becomes nonsensical, since the reliability of a text is always dependent on its purpose and function. The criteria of sufficient reliability for a post-graduate medical text book on the gastro-intestinal system are vastly different from the instructions on the side of a bottle of laxatives. The question of the Bible's reliability and authority cannot be accounted for before we have made sense of its purpose and function.[69] And while one may disagree with Moltmann's approach to theology and how he accounts for Scripture within it, he nevertheless begins in the right place. He seeks to understand the Bible in light of the place he believes it has in Christian faith and in the life of the church. I disagree with how Moltmann ties the Bible so closely to the promissory history, since it is difficult to see how the text can stand in a critical relationship to Moltmann's construction of its primary subject matter. It seems bet-

---

68. McGowan, *Divine Spiration of Scripture*, 33; cf. 25–30. He notes how the common habit among evangelicals to place Scripture as the first article in statements of faith is problematic since it detracts from God as the determining subject of faith (28–29, 98). For other theologically nuanced and textures accounts of Scripture within the Evangelical tradition, see Bloesch, *Holy Scripture*, and Grenz, *Community*, 379–404.

69. To put it bluntly, if someone is able to convincingly argue that the Bible is inerrant, what is achieved? What makes it different from the manual that comes with a piece of flat box IKEA furniture? It too is inerrant in instructing how to turn a few pieces of wood and metal into a table. However, this does not mean it is a sufficient guide to interpret the world. Little is accomplished simply by a criterion of accuracy. What is needed in a defence of a high view of Scripture is an account of the role and function of Scripture in the church, and whether it can bear such a function, is sufficient in the role it is said to play. See McGowan, *Divine Spiration of Scripture*, 103–13, 119, on the ways in which the notion of inerrancy fails to account for the high view of Scripture it claims to establish.

ter to account for the theological locus of the Bible formally, as e.g. the divinely ordained witness to God and his ways with his creation, which is to govern the faith and life of the church.[70] However, Moltmann, in seeing the Bible within the promissory history, still helpfully reminds us that its authority does not lie in itself but in that which it bears witness to, its referent. This is an important reminder, especially for those of us who have a high view of Scripture, because the more authority we invest into the witness of Scripture, the greater the temptation to divinise the Bible, to make it the locus of the potency for salvation, which we believe God establishes through it.[71] Although the Bible is an epistemic starting point, it should never be the first article in our statements of faith. It is by the grace of the triune God that Christians believe people are reconfigured and incorporated into the people of God, not by a sufficiently accurate view of the Bible, no matter how important that is. Indeed, if we take the words of Jesus seriously, placing one's confidence in one's view of Scripture can be detrimental to faith (John 5:39). The Bible's authority is iconic, its potency, sufficiency and reliability lie in its faithfulness to the referent it seeks to lead its readers to.

Second, Moltmann helpfully reminds us of the empirical fact that often gets lost in defences of the divine origin of the Scriptures, namely, that it contains not only a message from God through his faithful witnesses, but also their response to this message. Yes, in its testimony, the whole Bible is the human response to the revelatory initiative of God.[72] This, although often not noted in evangelical circles, is but stating the obvious. As the depository of this response, the Bible contains both the record of God's revelatory expressions and human responses to it. The Bible contains both the divine proclamation of the prophets and the songs of the psalmists as they praise his presence and lament his ab-

---

70. That said, Moltmann's understanding of the promissory history is nevertheless helpful because of its comprehensive scope. It is rightly centered and takes its bearing in God, but also, at least formally, encompasses the whole horizon of God's relations.

71. McGowan, *Divine Spiration of Scripture*, 28–29, notes an exclusive focus on the Bible's authority as self-sufficient tends to take the focus away from God, in which the salvific message contained in the Bible is accessible apart from a relationship with God—the Bible must never "become mere data to be processed by the theologian, rather than the means by which God confronts and communicates with us" (ibid., 117).

72. This does not preclude that the whole, as well, can be the vehicle through which God reveals Himself faithfully.

sence.⁷³ A high view of Scripture must take account of the reciprocal nature of the biblical witness. If the Bible as a whole is the epistemic venue through which God reveals himself faithfully, this revelation does not only contain God's revelation of Himself and his ways and purposes, but also the multiplicity of ways in which the people of faith respond to him. It is when we have this in mind, that we can employ a more sophisticated *theological* hermeneutic that is able to differentiate not simply between literary genres but also between the *ways* in which biblical statements are canonical, without trying to separate the chaff from imagined kernels. For, if who God is and what his ways with us are is not the only thing revealed in the Bible, but also who we are in the Creator-creature relationship, not all biblical statements are to be seen as revealed command, ideal ways of life, or pedagogic examples of the opposite. It also contains the actual ways in which believers live their faith, without necessarily commenting on whether this is commendable or not. This provides the important theological rationale for how most believers read e.g. the imprecatory psalms. They exemplify how the believer comes before God in raw honesty, expressing both doubt in God and desire for vengeance against the enemy. It is not inappropriate to bring before God one's complaint and deepest desires. But this does not mean that these complaints and desires are normative for how God acts or desires his people to behave. Another type of canonical statements that demand a similarly nuanced and differentiating hermeneutic, is when the writers themselves distinguish between the divine perspective and their own preference, as e.g., Paul does in 1 Corinthians 7.

Third, by rooting the canonical statements in the promissory history, Moltmann provides a healthy metaphor of how the text comes alive in every new generation without simply becoming an arbitrary justification of the community's preferences. The texts' "added value," their capacity for new readings, lies in the potential of their promises, the promises which are oriented toward the fulfillment of the history to which they bear witness. As guided by the Spirit, the reading and

73. God reveals himself to the patriarchs, to Moses, in the giving of the Law, to the prophets, in the proclamation and life of Jesus, and in the visions to John of the Apocalypse. He also communicates indirectly in the Wisdom literature of the OT and the epistles of the NT. But the Bible also records the worship of the psalmists, as well as their sorrows and complaints, the gospels document both the worship and incomprehension of the disciples, and even Paul qualifies some of his statements as his preferene rather than as a word coming from God (see, e.g., 1 Cor 7:6, 10, 12, 25, 40).

proclamation of Scripture is dynamic, surprising and even innovative, it constantly seeks how the force and promise of the biblical witness can engage, enlighten, and transform the present situation.

For Moltmann, the necessary flipside of this trinitarian, reciprocal, and promissory character of the Bible is its incompleteness. If it is truly reciprocal, then it is not only the retainer of how God has revealed himself to his people, but also the partial, and partially faulty, human response to this revelation. And if the fundamental matter of Scripture is the promissory history, it does not only open itself up to the added value of the promises it reports, but is itself also the documentation of the incomplete ways in which the promises of God have been actualised in history. But is this necessary so? I do not believe so.[74]

First, to acknowledge that the Bible is a human product does not necessarily preclude that it has a different character and status than other human products. To claim that God has divinely safeguarded the Scriptures so that they, in their entirety, are a faithful and reliable testimony to his history with his creation, as they are illuminated by the Spirit, does not necessarily entail a dictation view of Scripture that does not take account of the testimony's human character, as Moltmann claims.[75] And it seems Moltmann must at least be open to this possibility. For, if not, neither can he affirm some of his basic Christological commitments.[76] If the Son was truly incarnated in Jesus of Nazareth, and if Jesus is the perfect man, who was not tainted by nor succumbed to sin, then it must be possible for God to so safeguard the composition and collection of a corpus of canonical writings that is a reliable and authoritative testimony to Him and His history with his creatures, able to sufficiently guide the faith, life and hermeneutic of the church. And for it to be this, it does not need to lose an iota of its human character, just as Jesus' humanity was perfected, not negated in the incarnation.[77]

---

74. Here I will only consider where I differ from Moltmann's view as it has a direct bearing on this study. Other disagreements, as how I would locate the Scriptures theologically, which I briefly alluded to above, will not be discussed.

75. *EiT*, 139–49, esp. 140–41.

76. This, of course, neither necessitates that he should see the Scriptures in this way—only that his argument against any form of understanding the Scriptures as infallible does not hold.

77. By this comparison, I am not necessarily endorsing an incarnational view of Scripture. See McGowan, *Divine Spiration of Scripture* 119–21, who also appeals to John Webster, on how the incarnation is only properly related to the meeting of the di-

Second, to affirm that the Bible not only testifies to God's revelatory initiative toward us but also our response to it, does not necessarily mean that it shares in the "disharmonies" of these respondents. This does not imply the Bible only contains what might be called, for lack of a better term, "ideal situations." To claim that God has safeguarded the canon from error does not mean that it only contains reliable portraits of God, of the right faith and conduct of believers, and, negatively, of case studies of the consequences of turning away from God. Within a high view of Scripture, it does contain this, but it is also more than this, is more complex. It seems better to claim that the Bible faithfully testifies to the ways in which believers actually live in their relationships with God, without indicating directly what is admirable or not.[78]

Third, it is simply not the case that the incomplete ways in which God's promises have been actualised in biblical history necessarily entails the partially faulty nature of the promises themselves as they are recorded in the Scriptures. If we make a distinction between promise and actualisation, it is reasonable to claim that the text is a sufficiently reliable record of the promise and a reliable record of the partial ways in which it is fulfilled.

Now, it is given, that nothing I have said here proves the view of Scripture I hold nor necessarily will compel those who happen to disagree with me to change their mind. My purpose is less ambitious, I hope to have merely shown that the kind of critique Moltmann levels against the spectrum of evangelical convictions within which I stand, does not necessarily hold. And therefore I do not think I am compelled to abandon it. Here I will not enter a discussion why I hold this view, merely note that it is a presupposition of this study.[79]

---

vine and human nature in Jesus Christ—it is only he who has both a divine and human nature. I merely claim that if in the incarnation neither the divine nor human nature were compromised, so it must be possible for God to safeguard a scriptural testimony without it losing its fundamental human character.

78. The oppressed psalmist is right in expressing his desire that the Babylonian babies will be smashed against the rocks (Ps 137:9) before they grow up to oppress him. But this certainly does not mean he should do it, or that God agrees with him and condones infanticide.

79. For a good defense of a high view of Scripture that avoids the pitfalls of the inerrancy debate that has dominated the North American evangelical scene, see McGowan, *The Divine Spiration of Scripture*. For a balanced critique of contemporary views of inerrancy, see Bloesch, *Holy Scripture*, 27–28, 33–45, and esp. 104–17. See Grenz, *Community*, 398–403, for a definition of the concept of inerrancy that works inductively from the claims and apparent purposes of the text itself.

How then does my difference with Moltmann on Scripture influence this study? First, although Moltmann takes his cues from Scripture in his understanding of the Kingdom of God, he gives himself license to dismiss strains of the biblical tradition which he believes run counter to the matter of Scripture. I am restrained by my view of Scripture to seek an understanding that can encompass these apparent disharmonies. However, this does not allow me to hold on to certain claims just because the Bible says so. If the authority of the Bible's voice is iconic, lies outside itself, in that which it speaks about, its claims must always be open to falsification by the criterion of that which it bears witness to. Therefore, an appeal to the authority of the Scriptures must not circumvent the responsibility to give a reasonable and coherent account of one's interpretation of the Bible.[80] Therefore, where I disagree with Moltmann in his dismissal or alteration of biblical ideas and themes, I have tried to argue why my own view can be considered coherent, and theologically preferable to Moltmann's. Although not all questions are answered equally well and satisfactorily, I believe I have sufficiently answered them.

Second, because of how I see the canonical texts, I consistently privilege the perspective I see in Revelation to that which I see in Moltmann. Where the two diverge, I side with how I understand Revelation.[81] But again, I have sought to do so in a critical manner, not simply grounding my judgment in Revelation's canonical status, but have sought to show why I believe the perspective I see in the book is a valid alternative to certain aspects of Moltmann's thought. Whether I have succeeded in doing so, or even in reading Revelation well, is up to the reader to judge.

---

80. E.g. one of the fundamental mistake those who seek to argue for the inerrancy of Scripture often make, is to give particular texts authority apart from the kind of claims they make, as seen e.g. in many defences of "literal" readings of Genesis 1–11, etc.

81. In privileging Revelation, I am not consenting to the "baton-passing" relationship between biblical studies and theology, as advocated by Krister Stendahl and others. I do not privilege my analysis of the canonical books because I believe the Bible scholar ought to do the preparatory work, on which the dogmatician must base his or her systematisation. Rather, I privilege what I see in Revelation over what I see in Moltmann because I privilege the canonical texts. Therefore, I do not think that the Bible scholar is the only arbiter of good exegesis. The question is not what theological guild one's study proceeds from, but rather, whether one proposes good readings of the text.

3

The Kingdom of God as Symbol of Hope

Introduction

As discussed in the previous chapter, a basic dialectic is at work in Moltmann's theology, it moves constantly between Christ as the confessional center of the church and the kingdom of God as the universal horizon within which he is the center. Now we turn to the historical aspect of this dialectic, how for Moltmann, hope for the coming kingdom is grounded in the death and resurrection of Jesus—the Christ event makes the eschatological coming of the kingdom possible. Moltmann's view of the relationship between Easter and the kingdom leads him to a) a dialectic understanding of the world (it exists in the contradiction between death and resurrection), b) a view of history that is seen as messianic mediation, and c) an understanding of Christian praxis that is messianically informed. The great strength in Moltmann's messianic understanding of history is the way it helps us to theologically appropriate biblical hope as we seek to make sense of our own world. A basic flaw, however, is the way he transposes the biblical logic of human rebellion and sin into a fundamental and necessary structure in creation.

The History of the Kingdom of God

If the coming kingdom is the horizon that informs Christo-centric faith, how, if this kingdom radically differs from the world as it is known, can it be known? And why should we hope for it rather than dismiss it as a utopian vision? For Moltmann, both its knowability and its "realism" are grounded in the life, death and resurrection of Jesus. The kingdom breaks into history in the ministry of Jesus, and the future of the world in this kingdom is made possible because of Easter: In entering death in the death of the Son, God has broken death's chains, and in the resurrection, Jesus has entered the future that awaits the world. Moltmann develops this by considering how Jesus and his message are embedded in the hope for the kingdom found in the promissory history of the Old Testament and how this hope has been radicalized and universalized in the cross. He then interprets the history of the world in light of Jesus' death and resurrection, seeing a Christian understanding of history as messianically mediated. This in return leads to a praxis based in the hope of the coming kingdom.

The Kingdom in the Person and History of Jesus

Israel's history is driven by the promises of God. In contrast to her neighbours who lived through the cycle of the year with the repeated epiphanies of their seasonal gods, Israel's is the promising God of the nomad.[1] Even when Israel settles in the land, she does not adopt the agrarian deities found awaiting her there. Rather she subsumes their cults to her own history with God. Her neighbours' annual celebrations and rituals, which maintained the cycles of life and held the forces of chaos at bay, become in Israel festivals by which she maintains her history with God, remembering what he has done for her as the God of the Exodus, and anticipating, on basis of this memory, how he will fulfil the promises that are still outstanding.[2] This creates a view of history which is determined by the logic of promise.[3] The people are bound to a reality that does not yet exist but has been opened up to them as a divine possibility in the promise of God.[4] "In the promises, the hidden future already announces itself and exerts its influence on the present through the hope it awakens."[5] Therefore, life is not experienced cyclically but

---

1. *TH*, 96–99.
2. Ibid., 99–102; cf. 40–41.
3. See Rasmusson, *Church as Polis*, 62–65, for a brief description of the logic of promise in *TH* that shows well how it is related to modern future-oriented consciousness but fails to adequately account for Moltmann's strong criticism of progressivism. For a full account of the logic of promise in his early works, see Morse, *Logic of Promise*.
4. *TH*, 103.
5. Ibid., 18.

as a trend from the tension promise creates toward its fulfillment, from the time when reality contradicts the promise till it corresponds to it.[6] History is "viewed as the time period between the Promise and its fulfilment, a time period pregnant with possibility."[7] There are two implications of this. First people's hearts are set "on a future history in which the fulfilling of the promise is to be expected."[8] Since any fulfillment falls short of the expected before the parousia, the promise drives history forward by its surplus. Israel's history is the journey between the promise and its fulfillment.[9] Second, the deferred fulfillment does not end in disillusion because the future it expects "does not have to develop within the framework of the possibilities inherent in the present, but arises from that which is possible to the God of that promise. This can also be something which by the standard of present experience appears impossible."[10]

Initially, the promise is seen only in terms of how the LORD calls his people out of the land of their bondage to inhabit a land rich in every resource for an abundant life, where the LORD will be their God and they his people. However, as Israel's history gets intertwined with the nations around her, the promise is universalized. And as Israel faces her own tragedies, it is intensified. By the time of the prophets, "*the universalizing of the promise finds its eschaton in the promise of Yahweh's lordship over all peoples. The intensification of the promise finds its approach to the eschatological in the negation of death.*"[11] This universalizing of the promise is often driven by the expectation of judgment on the nations that rage against Israel but at times develops into an expectation that God has also a future for the nations just as he has for Israel. Its intensification, eventually bearing fruit in the expectation of a resurrection of the dead, is driven by the need for the vindication of the faithful who did not taste the promise but suffered injustice.

It is within this promissory history of Israel, that Jesus must be understood, especially his death and resurrection. Jesus announced that

---

6. Ibid., 103–4.
7. Cornelison "Reality of Hope," 114; cf. *TH* 16.
8. *TH*, 103.
9. Ibid., 104–6.
10. Ibid., 103.
11. Ibid., 132.

The Kingdom of God as Symbol of Hope 41

the kingdom Israel hoped for was drawing near in and around him; in his proclamation of the Gospel the promise was coming to the unexpected, the sinners, the poor and the godless.[12] This hope was shattered in his death.[13] Not only was he rejected by the religious authorities that should have embraced him and executed by the political power he should have defeated, but he was also forsaken by the God whom he called Father and whose kingdom he proclaimed.[14] However, since it is precisely this God who also raised him from the dead, he and the kingdom he proclaimed are vindicated.[15] Jesus was raised ahead of the rest into the kingdom that awaits all,[16] "into God's future and was seen and believed as the present representative of this future, of the free, new mankind and the new creation."[17] As such, the resurrection of the crucified one is the scandalous "promise" for the world which stands in contradiction to it.[18] However, precisely in the way the promise is fulfilled at Easter, it undergoes two important transformations. First, while Israel's particular hope is not abrogated and still awaits its concrete fulfillment,[19] the promise is now not limited ethnically but the resurrection of Jesus anticipates the vivification of all flesh, since the resurrection is the "conquest of the deadliness of death ... the abolition of the universal Good Friday, of that god-forsakenness of the world which comes to light in the deadliness of the death of the cross."[20] This "is why God's presence in the crucified Christ gives creation eternal life, and does not annihilate it."[21] As the pivotal establishment of God's promise, the resurrection reveals the promise to be God's abrogation of the fundamental condition that faces all, death. He "creates salvation" for the world precisely by suffering

---

12. *CrG*, 126–52; cf. *WJC*, 96.

13. "The death of Jesus is also the death of his eschatological message through which he brought God to utterance and made the kingdom of God immanent" (*CrG*, 122).

14. *CrG*, 122; cf. *TH*, 210–11.

15. *CrG*, 175–76; cf. 153, 168–71.

16. See *TH*, 139ff on how Moltmann interprets the resurrection of Jesus within Israel's promissory history.

17. *CrG*, 168.

18. Ibid., 173.

19. The fulfillment of God's promises to Israel is one of the reasons for Moltmann's millenarianism (*CoG*, 196–99; cf. *CPS*, 138–39, 149–50).

20. *TH*, 211; cf. *CrG*, 189.

21. *GiC*, 91.

the "disaster of the whole world inwardly in himself."[22] Second, precisely in that Christ rose into his own future in the kingdom, the eschatological hope has been made firm.[23] The realism of the coming is grounded in the anticipatory appearance of the kingdom in Jesus.

We now turn to how Easter, because of the way it responds to the universal condition of death, is the sign in which history is seen, how this is to be understood messianically, and how it calls for a particular kind of historical praxis, how "it means following the intention of God by entering into the dialectic of suffering and dying in expectation of eternal life and of resurrection."[24]

History in the Sign of Jesus' Death and Resurrection

> But how, then, can Christian eschatology give expression to the future? Christian eschatology does not speak of the future as such. It sets out from a definite reality in history and announces the future of that reality, its future possibilities and its power over the future. Christian eschatology speaks of Jesus Christ and *his* future. It recognizes the reality of the raising of Jesus and proclaims the future of the risen Lord. Hence the question whether all statements about the future are grounded in the person and history of Jesus Christ provides it with the touchstone by which to distinguish the spirit of eschatology from that of utopia.[25]

By entering his opposite in the death of the Son, God has broken the bondage of the conditions the world lives under, transience that leads to suffering and death, and opens up all creation for its future in God's kingdom. In the cross the history of the world's suffering has been "taken up into this 'history of God.'"[26] In his resurrection, Jesus, as the firstborn of the many, enters into the future of the whole world. In this way the future has broken into the present. Therefore, the world must now be seen in this light, not finally bound to death but the impossible

22. *TKG*, 160.
23. *TH*, 145–48.
24. Ibid., 211, where he notes that this "assenting to the tendency towards resurrection of the dead" is grounded in the "expectant knowledge" of "the event of the resurrection of Christ."
25. Ibid., 17.
26. *CrG*, 246–47.

has been made possible, history has been opened up to life in the kingdom as seen in the resurrection of Jesus. "In that one man the future of the new world of life has already gained power over this unredeemed world of death and has condemned it to become a world that passes away."[27] Easter is a "history-making event;" it is unparalleled in history and as such determines history, orients it toward the possibility of its own future in the coming kingdom.[28] Easter, then, is the epistemological foundation for a Christian understanding of history because it is the ontological foundation of its future. This is "the reality in history" which future Christian hope proclaims.

However, what makes the resurrection a truly history-making event is its unfinished character. Although Jesus entered his own future in his resurrection, Easter nevertheless foreshadows "his eschatologically still outstanding goal and end."[29] Although Easter is the center of the history of God's promised kingdom, its fulfillment is still outstanding, the history of him who rose into the future of the kingdom is not fulfilled before he returns in glory in the coming of the same kingdom to the whole world.[30] If all things had come to their end at Easter, history would cease, but precisely because Jesus entered the future that he eventually will bring to all, Easter "*makes* history in which we can and must live."[31] The fulfillment of the promise in Jesus therefore "makes the reality of man 'historic' and stakes it on history."[32] As such, "the *logos* of the *eschaton* is promise of that which is not yet, and for that reason it *makes* history. The promise which announces the *eschaton*, and in which the

27. Ibid., 171.
28. *TH*, 180.
29. Ibid., 219.
30. *CrG*, 171. It is in this light that Moltmann's assertion that "the resurrection of Jesus from the dead by God does not speak the 'language of facts', but only the language of faith and hope, that is, the 'language of promise'" should be understood (ibid., 173). Against Otto, "Anti-Monotheism," 301 (cf. Otto, "Resurrection," 85) this does mean that for Moltmann Easter is simply a symbol of what occurs in history as people grasp for the potential, but rather that Easter is the eschatological event that opens up history (and all its historical facts) to its own future, it is a "history-making event" (*TH*, 180; *CrG*, 105–6). Although its verification is eschatological its bodylines is essential, "Christ's resurrection is bodily resurrection, or it is not a resurrection at all" (*WJC*, 256–57). It is only as such that it is the basis for the resurrection of all creatures (*WJC*, 256–59; cf. Hunsinger, "Daybreak").
31. *TH*, 181.
32. Ibid., 139.

eschaton announces itself, is the motive power, the mainspring, the driving force and the torture of history." In this way Moltmann has bridged the ditch between present and future, between the historically known and the eschatologically unknown, without collapsing the distinction. The hope for the Kingdom "keeps history moving by its criticism and hope;" criticism, because the light of the kingdom shed from Easter always reveals the unredeemed state of the world, and hope, because this very light is the beginning of the future of the world.[33] Richard Bauckham says of the view of the world that grows out of this:

> The cross represents, and indeed reveals with full clarity for the first time, the plight and the fate of this world. But the same Jesus who was crucified was also raised and sustained in his own person the total contradiction of cross and resurrection. His resurrection is therefore God's promise of new creation for the whole of the godforsaken reality which the crucified Jesus represents. It is therefore an event of *dialectical* promise: it opens up a qualitatively *new* future, which negates all the negatives of present experience.[34]

From Easter, history is seen in the sign of the cross and the resurrection, its present state under the conditions of transience is aligned to the former while its future in the kingdom is aligned to the latter.[35] The cross of the raised one shows how God has entered the deadliness of the history of the world, and the resurrection of the crucified one shows how precisely in doing so he has broken the bounds of death and has oriented the world to its own living future.[36] If this is the case, then the present and the future of the world must be both seen in a radical discontinuity and a radical continuity. Just as Jesus remains the same person in the total contradiction of death and resurrection, so it is precisely the reality that now is bound by the horizon of death (which is its own total annihilation) that awaits resurrection life in the Kingdom.[37]

---

33. Ibid., 165. So, in *CrG*, 1, he notes it is only as people are reminded of the cross that they are both set in a critical relationship to their present circumstances as well as opened to the future that does not grow dark.

34. Bauckham, *Theology of Jürgen Moltmann*, 101.

35. *TH*, 200–203; *CrG*, 160–87.

36. *WJC*, 214. This logic is pivotal in Moltmann's theology, as evident from beginning to end, from *TH* to more recently, *IEB*.

37. Jesus is a revelation of the promised future as Easter reveals what Jesus was and what he will be, and how in all the qualitative differences between these, Jesus remains

By understanding the history of the world in the relationship of the death and resurrection of Jesus to the promised kingdom of God, Moltmann can account for the radical nature of death and suffering without losing hope, and he can develop an understanding of history without seeing it as an evolving progress. Since it is precisely in his death that Christ breaks the bonds of transience, Christian hope is not contingent on historical optimism.[38] While it will always seek to orient the world toward its coming "homeland," it does not lose hope in hopeless situations, whether that is at a death-bed or among the most destitute who possess no power to change their circumstances.[39] Indeed while an understanding of history grounded in Easter will seek anticipations of the coming kingdom anywhere, it will especially seek the most hopeless situations, because it is precisely in these circumstances that it expects interruptions, or conversions,[40] of the kingdom in history.

History is not the development of the world's latent potentialities, but a process that is open to the redemption that is coming to it. "By the raising of Christ we do not mean a possible process in world history, but the eschatological process to which world history is subjected."[41] Jesus' resurrection was not the realisation of a latent potential but something that happened to Jesus when every potentiality had died. Therefore, "the things that are not yet, that are future, also become 'thinkable' because they can be hoped for."[42] So, history, in the sign of Easter, does not ask

---

the same (*TH*, 84). This discontinuity within the continuity of a subject is reminiscent of how Paul speaks about the perishable being clothed with the imperishable, the mortal with immortality in 1 Corinthians 15, a chapter that is one of the main Scriptural influences on Moltmann's theology.

38. In a recent comment on *TH*, Miroslav Volf notes that hope, unlike optimism, is informed by "God's *novum* rather than the *futurum* of latent potentials." As such it is not contingent on human circumstances. "Hope is not based on the possibilities of the situation [but] grounded in the faithfulness of God and therefore on the effectiveness of God's promise" (Volf, "Not Optimistic," 31).

39. It is because of this that Christian hope can go where Bloch's principle of hope cannot, face death squarely, and face it with hope ("Hope and Confidence," 52; cf. *CrG*, 274–78; *GiC*, 92).

40. In *CoG*, 22, reflecting his later emphasis on how God works in history, Moltmann replaces the language of "interruption" with "conversion," since the former simply denotes a disturbance but the latter is concerned with the transformation of things, their re-orientation toward the coming in its anticipatory experiences in history.

41. *TH*, 179–80.

42. Ibid., 30.

first how we can orient the potential toward our own ideals but rather seeks to see every situation, both "its possibilities and dangers," in the light of the redemption that is coming to it.[43] The arrow of modern history has been reversed, progress has given way to the messianic light that both reveals "history's ruins" and is its "star of redemption." As such, "the *word* of the promise itself already creates something new"[44] precisely where every possibility has ceased. It is precisely because of this that a Christian view of history can stand where every other falters, at the threshold of death and final annihilation. Although before the Parousia everything that lives must die, in the resurrection its death is revealed to not be the end since the vivifying power of God even reaches into the realm of death, and it can take that which has lost everything in death and transform it into life in the eternal Kingdom within God's presence.

The Messianic Concept of History

From the various strands developed above, how the kingdom promised to Israel has arrived in Jesus' person and history, how Easter is a proleptic and anticipatory fulfillment of this hope in Jesus, and how history is therefore seen in his death and resurrection, Moltmann develops a messianic concept of history, in which "the eschatological future of the kingdom of God" is now the power that determines the present; he says:

> Through his mission and his resurrection Jesus has brought the kingdom of God into history. As the eschatological future the kingdom has become the power that determines the present. This future has already begun. We can already live in the light of the "new era" in the circumstances of the "old" one. Since the eschatological becomes historical in this way, the historical also becomes eschatological. Hope becomes realistic and reality hopeful. We have given this the mediating name of "*messianic*." The lordship of Christ points beyond itself to the kingdom of God.[45]

---

43. Ibid., 84.
44. *EH*, 49.
45. *CPS*, 192.

The logic of this messianic mediation of history is as follows. First, in his whole person and history, including the relationship between his death and resurrection, "Jesus has brought the kingdom of God into history." Therefore, second, the future, although it has not yet arrived to the rest of the created order, has begun in the raised Jesus. Third, as the future of all has appeared in Jesus, this "has become the power that determines the present," the eschatological hope has broken into history and in this way it renders all history eschatological as it opens it up to its future in the kingdom, "out of violence and injustice is reborn peace and justice."[46] As such, "the resurrection has set in motion an eschatologically determined process of history, whose goal is the annihilation of death in the victory of the life of the resurrection, and which ends in that righteousness in which God receives in all things his due and the creature thereby finds its salvation."[47] "The future of the kingdom of God . . . renews heaven and earth."[48] Fourth, the "lordship of Christ [therefore] points beyond itself to the Kingdom of God."[49] Within this messianic understanding of history what remains constant is the name of Jesus as the one who made the arrival of the kingdom possible on earth and who was raised into it in his resurrection, while the various christological titles are the variables by which we seek to discern the significance of Jesus in every changing context.[50] The kingdom "is the all-embracing eschatological breadth of his future, into which the mission and the love of Christ lead the man of hope."[51] It is as Christians look at how Jesus' history remains fixed in his raising up into the kingdom that they seek to extrapolate who this Jesus is for the world as they orient their praxis in anticipation of that kingdom.[52]

---

46. "Jesus and the Kingdom of God," 13.
47. *TH*, 163.
48. *ThT*, 23.
49. *CPS*, 192.
50. *CrG*, 103–12.
51. *TH*, 222.
52. "It is profoundly significant that the name of Jesus and his history remain fixed, as fixed as his death, whereas the titles of Christ which are a response to his openness are historically changeable with the passing of time, and in fact change history" (*CrG*, 106).

Leaning into the Coming Kingdom

Since Christian hope is for the future of this world in the kingdom and since Easter orients history toward the kingdom, "the *pro-missio* of the kingdom is the ground of the *missio* of love to the world."[53] Of this mission, Moltmann says:

> The coming lordship of God takes shape here in the suffering of the Christians, who because of their hope cannot be conformed to the world, but are drawn by the mission and love of Christ into discipleship and conformity to his sufferings. This way of taking into consideration the cross and resurrection of Christ does not mean that the "kingdom of God" is spiritualized and made into a thing of the beyond, but it becomes this-worldly and becomes the antithesis and contradiction of a godless and god-forsaken world.[54]

This rich passage suggests ways in which the kingdom hoped for shapes Christian existence. First, this hope orients the posture of Christian existence toward the world as it hopes for the future of the kingdom.[55] Christian life is not oriented toward "a thing of the beyond" but to the kingdom that is the "this-worldly...antithesis...of a godless and god-forsaken world." The person who has seen the world as it is in the cross and the hope opened up to it in the resurrection "will never be able to reconcile himself with the laws and constraints of this earth, neither with the inevitability of death nor with the evil that constantly bears further evil."[56] For those infected with hope, who "experience the closeness of the kingdom, 'the chains begin to hurt,'"[57] and they will not be satisfied with anything less than the transformation of the world in the life and righteousness of the coming kingdom.[58] "To believe means to cross in hope and anticipation the bounds that have been penetrated by the raising of the crucified." Since it is in the sign of the cross that

---

53. *TH*, 224.

54. Ibid., 222.

55. "To reimagine the future differently in the light of God's promise is thereby also at once to force a revaluation of the present and its significance" (Hart, "Imagination," 63).

56. *TH*, 21; cf. *CrG*, 101.

57. "Jesus and the Kingdom of God," 12.

58. *TH*, 223–24. "The goad of the promised future stabs inexorably into the flesh of every unfulfilled present" (21).

Christians are to lean into the kingdom, they seek to live it where it is now most manifestly absent, in the cause "of the devastated earth and of harassed humanity."[59] In the dialectic between the cross and resurrection, between Christ's passion and the fulfillment of his resurrection in the kingdom, "there is . . . no transcending of hope without the paradoxical countermovement of the incarnation of love, no breaking out to new horizons without the sacrifice of life, no anticipating of the future without first investing in it. It is in the incarnational movement even unto passion and death that, paradoxically, the kingdom of God can even now be lived and not just hoped for."[60]

Second, as such it shapes the praxis of Christians in the world as they are drawn "into discipleship and conformity to [Christ's] sufferings." The hope for the kingdom does not only provide "consolation *in* suffering" but also "protest *against* suffering."[61] And protest has always a for and an against, it is partial. Although Jesus died *for* all and therefore rose into the kingdom *before* all, he died in solidarity with precisely those who now most acutely suffer the absence of God's kingdom, those on the social, economic and religious periphery.[62] Likewise those who have been infected with hope and therefore commit themselves in "solidarity with the anxious expectation of the whole creation,"[63] do so by seeking the justice for the victims of history.[64] Christians can only be for all by seeking justice for the victims and the conversion of the perpetrators.[65] As Christians are turned toward the world armed with the light of Easter, they will judge the possibilities that face them and only grasp for those that hold a promise to establish the justice that accords to the

---

59. Ibid., 20–21; cf. *CrG*, 321.

60. "Messianic Atheism," 204.

61. *TH*, 21.

62. *WJC*, 112–16. "God has not begun the future of man at the extremities of human progress, but with this humiliated man" (*Man*, 117).

63. *TH*, 223.

64. *CrG*, 101. This is key to Moltmann's political theology; for a brief overview of the political implications of Moltmann's *Theology of Hope*, see Staedke, "Hoffnung."

65. *TH*, 224. In being for the poor, both the rich and poor are given their particular way into the kingdom of God—to the poor. it is preached that the eternal kingdom of the God who has broken the power of death is theirs, and to the oppressor, it is preached that only in repenting from their way of protecting themselves against the power of death by joining the poor will they enter the Kingdom in which death is overcome. Cf. *CrG*, 126–60; 325–38.

kingdom.⁶⁶ In addition to human rights,⁶⁷ Moltmann has particularly emphasized three crises that face the modern world, economic justice, ecological justice and the nuclear crisis.⁶⁸ And although this praxis toward the kingdom is not the kingdom but merely "anticipations," people can be "empowered [by the way the kingdom has dawned in the crucified and raised Jesus] to alter these relationships, to make the world more homelike, and to abolish internal and external slavery."⁶⁹

Third, however, precisely because "the coming lordship of God takes shape in the suffering of the Christians," their "parables of the kingdom" do not only take place where the possible can be oriented toward the promised but also where every possibility has ceased. "The Christian hope, in so far as it is Christian, is the hope of those who have no future."⁷⁰ Since the form in which Christ won the victory for the kingdom was his cross, his followers can enter the darkest place that others fear to tread because they know that even if engulfed by it, the hope of the resurrection will sustain them in the negation of death.⁷¹ Therefore, they can carry the hope of the kingdom precisely into those places where it is most absent; among the crosses of the world they expect the future of the crucified one.⁷²

The Contribution: The World in the History of the Kingdom of God

Aware of the difficulties of God-talk after Kant, Moltmann, from the beginning of *Theology of Hope*, notes that the primary reason that we can know anything about God's ways with the world is grounded in how God has revealed himself and his purposes in the cross and resurrection of Jesus.⁷³ A Christian understanding of history is possible

66. See *HP*, 178–99.
67. *OHD*, 3–58.
68. *WJC*, 63–69; *CoG*, 202–18; *CrG*, 329–335; *JCTW*, 24–28.
69. *Man*, 116.
70. Ibid., 117.
71. *CrG*, 16–17.

72. See ibid., 246–47 on how he sees history in the cross; cf. 57–58, 64–65. See Graham, "Biblical Hope," who argues that Moltmann's Christian vision can better account for a moral praxis than humanism since the outcome it hopes for is not based in the probability of one's own success but in the faithfulness of the God who promises.

73. *TH*, 17.

because the future known in Jesus is known as the future of the whole world in the Kingdom of God.⁷⁴ This is the basic and crucially important theme of Moltmann's understanding of history as he seeks to push the implications of this in-breaking of the future of God for the world in every area of his thought. Although we will dispute what Moltmann sees as the problem the messianic history responds to, it remains that in his consistent and urgent insistence on how the future kingdom has been opened up christologically at Easter and how this calls for a radical reorientation of Christian praxis in the world are lasting contributions to contemporary theology.⁷⁵

First, it overcomes the modern ditch between faith and history in a thoroughly Christian way. In distinction from the escapism often found in conservative circles, Moltmann insists on the continuity between what is and what it will become; therefore, hope can never leave things as they are, for it is hope for them—it cannot leave the world to hell.⁷⁶ Similarly, in distinction from the ahistorical focus of, e.g., the existentialist theology of Bultmann, Moltmann insists that God deals with humanity in history. Albeit in hidden, paradoxical and anticipatory ways, the messianic interruptions of God happen not simply within the human subject but in their real interactions within history.⁷⁷ Moltmann avoids the dangers of the progressivism which characterized nineteenth-century Protestant theology precisely because of the way in which he sees history from the vantage point of how its future goal is anticipated in Christ's entrance into his own future in the resurrection.⁷⁸ A view of history developed consistently from the principle of

---

74. Ibid., 222; cf. *CrG*, 168, 246–47.

75. Bauckham notes that it is his biblical basis, christological focus and eschatological openness which enables Moltmann to make Christian faith relevant to the modern world without losing its central characteristics (*Messianic Theology*, 140); cf. Bauckham, *Theology of Jürgen Moltmann*, 30; Rasmusson, *Church as Polis*, 42; Hunsinger, "Crucified God . . . , I," 395.

76. *CoG*, 153.

77. Bauckham notes that a "highly polemical dialogue with [Bultmann] runs right through *Theology of Hope*" (*Theology of Jürgen Moltmann*, 31; cf. *TH*, 58–69; *CoG*, 13–22).

78. Moltmann's theological project has fought on two fronts, against the progressivism Christian messianism took in its modern form (*TH*, 69–76; cf. *CoG*, 5, 10), and against the disappearance of eschatology in the way dialectical theology responded to this crisis (*TH*, 39–42, 47–69; cf. *CoG*, 6, 13–22). See Gilbertson, *God and History*, 173

the messianic mediation set out by Moltmann ought not end up in the cultural enmeshment that characterized liberal Protestantism's ideal of an evolutionary understanding of the fulfillment of Christianity within the progression of modern European culture.[79]

Second, it is precisely as we consider Moltmann's understanding of history against the backdrop of liberal Protestantism, that we see how it points to a fundamental reorientation of Western progressive views of history.[80] Most modern Westerners orient themselves toward the future in a movement from the particular location and situation they find themselves in toward the future they can construct by using the potentialities of that which is found around them, directing them toward the end they desire.[81] Whether this construction of the future is purely selfish, getting what I want, or highly idealistic, the creation of what we think is the best of all possible worlds, the arrow of history moves from my present context to the future. Moltmann shows how for the Christian it should point in the opposite direction. As revealed in the Christ event, the radical openness toward the future is not the possibility to populate the unknown through manipulating the present according to one's desire, but rather is orienting one's life according to what is made possible in the light of the coming of God's kingdom.[82] This reorientation of the fundamental posture toward history is as urgent today as when Moltmann first set it out. For while the great Modern metaphysical structures and ideals may have crumbled, the fundamental Western orientation toward the future has not, it has only shrunk to the level of individuals, or perhaps small communities,

---

on how Moltmann correlates extrapolation and anticipation in his understanding of history.

79. Against Rasmusson, *Church as Polis*, 57, this christologically informed view of history provides a potential internal corrective mechanism to what Rasmusson rightly points out, Moltmann's over-privileging of certain modern notions, especially of freedom.

80. See *TH*, 230–68 on Moltmann's critique of modern concepts of history; cf. *CoG*, 184–92; "Progress and Abyss," 301–8, where he, as elsewhere sees "progress" as the storm that has left the twentieth-century in ruins (306, 310, cf. *CoG*, 3–6). Josef Pieper grounds this loss in the disappearance of a theological basis for an understanding of history (*Hope and History*, 45–47).

81. The following discussion is based on two essays, "The Falls Angels Attend" and "Book-ended by Creation," I wrote at Regent College, Vancouver, Canada, in the spring of 1999.

82. *TH*, 333–34.

and their particular desires.[83] In many ways this has left us with a generation that has lost any ground of meaning and sense of belonging, a generation therefore characterized by an incredibly strong sense of estrangement.[84] Such a generation will seek a place it can call home, a place that reverberates "yes" to it, where it can know and be known. Bound by the web fear spins, such a generation generates private visions to avoid the nightmare of the unknown, whether that is in the material world offered to it by the current market economy and its cynical marketing structures, or whether that is in some privately structured cosmos of meaning. But such fear binds the fearer and the goal is never achieved as the fearer abuses what is found today to create the tomorrow that does not exist. It becomes an illusory dream that always evades the fearer while holding him or her tightly in its tyranny. Seen in the light the cross and resurrection shed on history, this approach is doomed to failure because it has no true telos, it is not shaped by the created purpose for one's own life nor by life found in one's context. Its posture is unloving because in the selfish illusion of self-making the self tries to shape 'the other' (whether persons or other members of God's creation) in relation to how it benefits the self instead of relating to the true nature of 'the other.' This makes the self both blind to the other (the other is never seen except as its potential for one's own desires) and destroys the possibility for its own future because it severs every true relation to the other one's future is bound up with. The response of Moltmann's vision of history to this peculiar late modern mixture

---

83. Moltmann comments, "Europe has lost its ability to hope for great things. The European spirit is like a landscape of burned-out craters, covered by a dull layer of lava. Ideologies, utopias, hopeful designs, plans for a better future have become caricatures" ("Messianic Atheism," 192). The only public ideal left seems the consumerist wedding of modern democracy and market economics which constitutes "the freedom" George W. Bush has frequently appealed to in his war on terror, as evident in his second inaugural address, where he concludes: "America, in this young century, proclaims liberty throughout all the world, and to all the inhabitants thereof. Renewed in our strength—tested, but not weary—we are ready for the greatest achievements in the history of freedom" (Bush, line 168–71). See Skorupski, "Future," 204, who notes how public bourgeois ideals have shrunk in "a kind of combination of existentialism and populism" that serves the consumerism of liberal capitalism in which "the state has a neutral pragmatic role in providing a rule of law within which this pursuit of personal self-definition takes place and in maintaining and refining the socio-economic and technological engines of prosperity which enable it to continue."

84. *CPS*, 165–68.

of despair and presumption[85] is to abandon every such attempt and be seized by the hope that the real "yes" behind every yearning is found in the future God has in store for his children, in "the inviting horizon of God's future,"[86] that place where heaven and earth are new, when God's yes permeates the whole creation, breathes its vitalizing breath through every eye of his created fabric.[87] This is the future that needs no alternative sun because God shines into every corner that darkens souls of the earth, and it is this future the Christian view of history holds out for humanity to be caught up into.

The third implication, which arises out of the reorientation of the historical posture that comes with a Christian understanding of history, is a particular future oriented praxis. It is a choice presented to the world to stop manipulating its present circumstances and let the present, both our lives and the context in which we live, be shaped by the vision of God's future as it is set out in the person and history of Jesus. Openness toward the future is not the possibility of creating what we want but the choice whether to move in the trajectory of the vivifying future of God or in the trajectory of its rejection, toward death, the absence of the fullness of life before God's presence which he purposes for his creatures.

On the one hand it calls for an abandonment of every orientation toward the future, and any anticipatory praxis toward the future that is fuelled by the fear of death and nothingness. "Anyone who reads the 'signs of the time' with the eyes of his own existential anxiety reads them falsely."[88] The power of the Christ event over history is that its future has dawned within it, and therefore everything can be risked as one seeks to orient one's life toward this future because even in death hope lives and awaits the resurrection. Therefore, the Christian "does not require to preserve himself by himself, in constant unity with himself, but by surrendering himself to the work of mission he is preserved by the hope inherent in that mission." Every role, calling, and responsibility

---

85. See *TH*, 22–25.

86. "How I Have Changed," 15.

87. Malcolm Muggeridge, as quoted in Escobar, "Return of Christ," 258, expresses a similar movement when he says: "So each symptom of breakdown, however immediately painful and menacing in its future consequences, is also an occasion for hope and optimism."

88. *CrG*, 21.

will be judged by "whether and how far they afford possibilities for the incarnation of faith, for the concretion of hope, and for earthly, historic correspondence with the hoped-for and promised kingdom of God and of freedom."[89]

On the other hand, the flipside of abandoning a praxis that manipulates the present in order to stave off death is "the imagination for the Kingdom of God"[90] where we seek out the possibilities of everything in the light of the Kingdom that has been opened up to us in the resurrection. Planning then does not become an irrelevant category. Rather, planning receives its orientation not from the plight of the present but from the hope of the future Kingdom.[91] Having been infected by hope, Christians, if they are to be true to their hope must seek the fulfillment of everything according to what can be known from the cross and resurrection. Therefore, although everyone and all things must meet their death on this side of the parousia, their life is lived with the light that shines from the future beyond their death, and in this way the joy of the Kingdom that awaits them is tasted in anticipatory ways.

The Transposition of the Logic of Redemption in Moltmann

A weakness in Moltmann's understanding of the kingdom as a history-making event that affects his theological project as a whole is the way in which he adapts the fundamental concern Easter responds to, no longer seeing it as sin but as a necessary contradiction in creation, its God-forsakenness and its resultant transience. Here, we will first look at how Moltmann adapts the biblical logic of redemption in his understanding of the cross and in his soteriological understanding of creation, and how this informs Moltmann's understanding of the history of the kingdom. Second, we consider why Moltmann thinks it necessary to modify the tradition and what role sin plays in his innovation of the logic of redemption, no longer seeing it as the basic problem the cross responds to but rather a problem, a particular human instantiation of the fundamental problem of transience. Third, we will consider what

---

89. *TH*, 334.

90. *CoG*, xiv.

91. See *HP*, 182–84 where Moltmann aligns God's promise with the hope for the *novum* and his providence with planning.

seems to be certain crucial weaknesses in Moltmann's transposition of the logic of redemption and pose the question whether his innovation is necessary.

The Cross in Moltmann's and the Bible's Logic of Redemption

It is common for critics of Moltmann's theology to center their questioning on Moltmann's understanding of sin specifically and what it is God accomplishes in the history of redemption generally.[92] In order to come to terms with the problem these commentators sense, we need to return to what Moltmann actually believes God accomplishes in the Christ event since Moltmann develops his whole understanding of the history of redemption from Easter.

According to Moltmann it is in the death of the Son, that God overcomes the fundamental condition of the world by entering the realm of his absence.[93] Although God overcomes sin in the cross, the cross being that 'wondrous exchange' in which the Son takes on the condition of sinful humanity so they may become the children of God, the more fundamental concern is another: the basic transient character of nature, that everything which lives dies because everything which was created to share in the eternal life of God exists in a god-forsaken space.[94] The cosmos is meant for life eternal in harmony with itself before God but is incomplete. In the face of death, it seeks and strives for that newness that will come to it and complete it, but as long as it is within death's grasp it is always the tragic struggle where "everything that wants to live ... has to die."[95] However, in the death of the Son, God enters the fundamental condition in which the whole cosmos exists, god-forsakenness, and by being present to it breaks its fundamental power. Thus, from the cross, hope of life eternal is extended to individual human beings,

---

92. Farrow, "Review," 436–37; Walsh, "Theology of Hope," 62–63, whose argument is close to what I develop here.

93. *CrG*, 217–18, 246–47.

94. Although Moltmann begins to develop his panentheism of the cross in *CrG*, 277, the Blochian ontology he develops in *TH* suggests such a development. His panentheism is most fully developed in *GiC*. For Moltmann's interaction with Bloch, see especially *IGEB*, "Hope and Confidence," and Bauckham, *Messianic Theology*, 3–22.

95. *FC*, 164. This is "the sufferings of the whole groaning creation in this present time" (*WJC*, 152; cf. *CoG*, 91–92, 264–68).

humanity as a whole and the whole order of creation.[96] The cross is the pivot that turns everything toward life in the coming presence of God, and the resurrection "is not merely the endorsement of his death for the salvation of sinners; it is also the beginning of the transfiguration of the body and of the earth."[97]

It is in his doctrine of creation that Moltmann explains why everything that was meant for life in the presence of God is rendered transient—it exists in a god-forsaken context.[98] Since God is omnipresent, God had to vacate a place within himself for there to be room for creation.[99] Into this space he breathed creation by his life-giving Spirit.[100] This results in a fundamental contradiction: everything that was meant to live from the vivacity of God and in the communion of his love exists now in the condition of the opposite, and thus is bound to transience.[101] But this contradiction in the structure of creation is necessary because without God ceding a place within himself there would be no place in which creation could be.[102] As such, Moltmann collapses Genesis 3 into Genesis 1, he moves the fundamental problem which in Genesis is seen in the fall of humanity into the fundamental structure of creation.[103]

From this view of redemption and its corresponding notion of creation, Moltmann sees the whole history of God with his creation as overcoming creation's fundamental contradiction. From how the cross overcomes the fundamental but necessary contradiction in creation arises the hope of the eschatological moment when God completes the movement begun at Easter, when God again fully invades the space he

---

96. See *WJC*, 274–312, where he works this out in his understanding of the cosmic Christ.

97. *CoG*, 93.

98. *GiC* is his primary work on creation; for a recent overview, see "God's Kenosis." For analyses of his doctrine of creation, see especially Bouma-Prediger, *Greening*, and Deane-Drummond, *Ecology*.

99. *GiC*, 87–89.

100. Ibid., 98–103, where he says: "The whole creation is a fabric woven by the Spirit, and is therefore a reality to which the Spirit gives form" (99).

101. See ibid., 87–88, on how creation exists in a context of "non-being" God has ceded within himself.

102. Ibid., 86.

103. Although I question Walsh's claim that Moltmann's problem is starting with soteriology instead of creation, his is a convincing overview of how Moltmann collapses the fall into the structure of creation ("Theology of Hope," 72–73).

ceded in creation and is fully present to his creation, when "he arrives at his rest in all things, and in which all things will live eternally in him."[104] "Redemption, then, is not primarily a restoration of a covenantal relationship broken in history, but a 're-filling' of that space, an overcoming of God's self-limitation by means of an *annihilation nihili*."[105] When the process of creation meets its fulfillment in the arrival of God's presence, all things in each and every of their lived moments will be transformed into what they were meant to be, living in eternal communion with the God who gave them their life, who created them out of his love to live in everlasting communion with him, an end which goes beyond both restoration and transformation to the "deification" of creation in the presence of God's glory.[106]

How then is this logic of redemption related to the historical aspect of the kingdom? The kingdom as symbol of hope is to be seen as the expectation of how the problem of transience as it is manifested in human history will be overcome. The history of the kingdom that is oriented toward this hope is the story of the particular character transience takes in humanity and the way God overcomes it. In the cross God has broken the power of the fundamental logic that drives the misery of human history, the violence perpetrated in the attempt to fend off the anomie of transience, the constant struggle to escape suffering and death by one's own power at the expense of the powerless.[107] In the light the cross sheds on human history, we see that God is not the God of the rulers but of "the poor, the oppressed and the humiliated."[108] Therefore, "the coming kingdom" has "taken the form of a cross in the alienated world. The cross is the form of the coming, redeeming kingdom and the crucified Jesus is the incarnation of the risen Christ."[109] The cry of the crucified one explains why God was present to the blood of Abel, for it is always where the power of godlessness is strongest that God defeats it in being present to it. The future hope of the kingdom is therefore

---

104. *CoG*, 335.

105. Walsh, "Theology of Hope," 75.

106. *CoG*, 272–74. See Cottingham, "Rosen, Moltmann," for a discussion on how Moltmann's cosmic teleology relates to recent theories of a supposedly teleonomic character of biological processes.

107. *WJC*, 99–102.

108. *CrG*, 329; cf. 195.

109. *CrG*, 185.

oriented toward the moment when the redemption that began in the darkest hour of human history, when the hope of the kingdom died on the cross, is fulfilled in the full breadth of human history, when the conditions that now fuel the human history of violence and suffering cease to exist.

It is within this understanding of the Christ event and how it informs Moltmann's understanding of history that we see his pivotal innovation over against a traditional understanding of redemption, an innovation that amounts to a transposition of the basic logic of redemption from being primarily related to God's response to human rebellion and its consequences to being first related to a fundamental contradiction in creation. It is within this contradiction and how God overcomes it that we must see human history, both its trajectory and its redemption. But what then happened to sin in the midst of this transposition

The Place of Sin in Moltmann's Understanding of Redemption

SIN IN MOLTMANN

Although Moltmann is often accused of not giving a sufficient account of sin in his theology,[110] he nevertheless affirms sin as a pivotal part of the human condition and that central to the work of the cross is the question of human guilt.[111] Of the various places he discusses sin,[112] he sets out the basic aspects of his view most clearly in a discussion on the relationship between justifying faith and the cross and resurrection in *The Way of Jesus Christ*. He says:

> We understand by "sin" the condition in which a person closes himself off from the source of life, from God. A closing of the self like this comes about when the purposes for which human beings are by nature destined are not discovered or not fulfilled, because of hybris, or depression, or "the God complex," or

---

110. Kelsey argues that the problem in much modern theology, including Moltmann, is not the disappearance of sin but its migration into a variety of doctrinal loci ("Doctrine of Sin"). He perceptively observes that what "is sensed is not so much a disuse of the concept of sin as it is an abandonment of the concept of divine wrath, for, if there is no need to talk about the wrath of God, then there is not much need to talk about the sin that incurs wrath" (ibid., 178).

111. *TKG*, 52; cf. *CrG*, 69.

112. *TH*, 22–26, 203–8; *CrG*, 194–95. For how he sees the relationship between sin and death, see especially *CoG*, 77–95.

because of a refusal to accept what human existence is about. This leads to the self-destruction of the regenerating energies of life, and thus to death. The self-deification of human beings is the beginning of their self-destruction, and the destruction also of the world in which they live. This death has to be understood as absolute death, because it is not identical with the natural life process. "Sin" in this sense means missing the mark of being, and has to be used in the singular. It is a happening in the created being as a whole, and it precedes morality, although it is the source of the acts and kinds of behaviour which in a moral sense can be recognized as infringing the laws of life—that is, sins in the plural. Because every created being belongs to a social context shared with other beings, "sin" always destroys life in the social sense too. We talk about the trans-personal "power of sin" because sin involves the inescapable structural processes of destruction over which Paul cries out when he acknowledges for himself personally: "I do not do the good I want, but the evil I do not want is what I do" (Rom 7:19). Today everyone can see these processes at work in the developments for which he shares responsibility and at the same time helplessly deplores. Ordered systems which once ministered to life are toppling over into their very opposite, so that they now work for death.[113]

First, sin is "the condition in which a person closes himself off from the source of life, from God." This, whether by ignorance or wilful rejection, is a "happening in the created being as a whole" which results "in missing the mark of being." This is "Sin" in the singular and as such preceded all other "sins" which infringe "the laws of life." Within it humanity exists as "man in pursuit of his own interests, man who in reality is inhuman, because he is under the compulsion of self-justification, dominating self-assertion and illusionary self-deification."[114]

Second, although not stated directly in this passage, Moltmann elsewhere grounds this "happening" as the wrong-headed human response to the reality of transience, which preceded sin and made it possible.[115] Sin is the form the problem of transience has taken in human

113. *WJC*, 184–85. In *FC*, 122–23, Moltmann seems to collapse his understanding of sin into the structure of creation as "closedness to the future."

114. *CrG*, 69.

115. Rejecting a causal relationship between death and sin, Moltmann sees a correlation between sin and death: "The frailty of the temporal creation of human beings is like a detonator for the sin of wanting to be equal to God [i.e. not bound by transience] and to overcome this frailty ... It is the awareness of death which first creates fear for

history. In face of transience, humanity has turned from the inviting horizon of the coming God and turned to its own means to deal with the fear of death. But instead of stemming the tide of transience sin intensifies it.[116] The drumbeat of human history is the escalation of suffering and death as those who have power seek to avert the might of death by violence at the expense of the powerless. As such the question of sin plays an important role in the history of the Kingdom, but always within the larger question of the suffering of transience, a suffering intensified by sin.

Third, this human existence in sin is also fundamentally social because people exist in a "social context," and sin's death is expressed in a social sense. This is the legitimate violence of "political and economic structures" to exploit some in the interest of others, of alienating human beings from one another.[117] This is sin's transpersonal power, people are enslaved in their social practice to a web of systems that "once ministered to life" but "now work for death."[118]

Fourth, in the discussion following this passage Moltmann then goes on to discuss how the work of justification relates to the expia-

---

life, the fear of not getting one's fair share, of not having enough from life, the fear that life will be cut short. This leads to a craving for life, and to greed" (*CoG*, 91, 93).

116. "Death is only the consequence of sin inasmuch as sin exists because of death: we cannot endure mortality, and by killing we can make other people die. The vulnerability of creation-in-the-beginning makes the act of violence against life possible" (*CoG*, 91). It is the craving to be like God, "rich, healthy, invulnerable and immortal," which is the well spring "of the sin that destroys life; not being willing to be what one is, but having to be something different;" as such, "sin is the violence against life which springs from knowledge of mortality" (*CoG*, 93, 94).

117. *CoG*, 95. Moltmann adds insightfully that precisely because of the economic injustice that characterises the relationship between the First and the Third World, "a 'natural death' is rare among" most who live in the Third world: "most of them cannot afford it."

118. Note how there is a subtle shift in this passage. It begins by acknowledging that sin is an offence against God but states it in the rather weak form as closing oneself "from the source of life, from God" and thus focuses on what humanity does to itself rather than its offence against God. By the end of the passage it is simply seen as that which has shifted from ministering to life to working for death. In here lies a weakness of Moltmann's understanding of sin, his primary focus is on what sin does to humanity and usually neglects what it means in relation to God, the outrage it is against the holiness of the God who in grace created humanity to be those who bear his image. Kelsey, "Doctrine of Sin," 175–78, notes that among political and liberation theologians this structural emphasis tends to eclipse the personal (cf. Deane-Drummond, *Ecology*, 217).

tion of sin. With the forgiveness of sin comes the liberation from sin's power and the reconciliation with God which places the believer "in the service of righteousness and justice" as those who have received "the right to inherit the new creation" with the aim of "participation in God's new just world through passionate effort on its behalf."[119] Being freed from the power of sin (the power of transience), the life of the believer is bound to the victory of life won on the cross for the whole creation. "Justifying faith is not yet the goal and end of Christ's history. For every individual believer it is no more than the beginning of a way that leads to the new creation of the world."[120]

The Transposition of Sin

In his understanding of the work of the cross, Moltmann has not changed the way the logic of redemption works but what it most fundamentally deals with. His understanding of how God interacts with his creation follows faithfully the fundamental movements of the biblical story, but he has shifted what these movements first refer to, a fundamental contradiction in creation rather than sin.[121] Moltmann acknowledges this move when in *Trinity and the Kingdom of God*, in a discussion on the problematic nature of simply attributing suffering as punishment for sin, he argues that "the framework of the question of human guilt" plays the central part in the atoning work on the cross as it reveals the logic of the universal significance of the cross. As such, the question of human guilt "is not the whole of it, or all its fullness." "Its fullness" is the way in which the suffering of Christ "belongs to the history of the sufferings of mankind," which in the end is grounded in "the limitations of created reality itself."[122] Walsh argues, "Moltmann insists that an anthropological understanding of sin is superficial because *behind* anthropological guilt is death, 'absolute death and total end.' Rather than understanding the destructiveness of death as the *result* of sin, Moltmann describes

---

119. *WJC*, 189.
120. Ibid., 186–87.
121. *FC*, 121–24; cf. *CrG*, 183–87 for his critique of singularly expiatory understandings of reconciliation.
122. *TKG*, 52, 51.

it in his eschatological view of creation as 'an apocalyptic pressure of affliction for everything that wants to live and has to die.'"[123]

Therefore, Moltmann's fundamental innovation over against the traditional understanding of redemption amounts to a transposition of sin, from being the fundamental problem to being a specific human problem within the larger question of creation's transience—sin is not *the* problem but *a* problem nestled within the fundamental contradiction of creation, and the solution is not first God's response to sin but to the fundamental condition that made sin possible.[124] And so the logic of redemption is reversed, now it is not sin that has catastrophic consequences in cosmic proportions which are overcome as God reconciles humanity to himself, but rather the basic constitution of the cosmos has devastating consequences for humanity and the redemption of humanity is only one part of God's reconciliation with his estranged creation.[125] The difference between Moltmann and the traditional dogma is not the question of the absence of God—fundamental to the work of the cross in both is how God seeks to become present to the earthly realm from which he is absent. The big difference is how this absence is accounted for. For Moltmann it is predicated on a fundamental contradiction in creation made necessary by the kenotic act of God preceding creation, while in the biblical logic it is the result of human sin, which the holiness of God cannot tolerate and from which he therefore must retrieve his presence.[126]

---

123 *FC*, 164. Walsh, "Theology of Hope," 65, says Moltmann "has ontologically structuralized the directional question of sin" and thus fused creation with the fall.

124. So he can say: "God's activity in history consists essentially in opening up systems which are closed in on themselves; and he does this by way of suffering communication" (*GiC*, 211).

125. Similarly to this fundamentally ontological contradiction in creation, Moltmann develops in *CrG*, 25–32, an epistemological necessity for the cross; by the dialectical principle of knowledge God can only be known in his opposite. Cf. *CrG*, 86–87.

126. Even just a casual reading of Leviticus shows how one of the basic concerns of Israel's cult, or more precisely, God's concern with Israel's cult, is the question of how God can be present to his covenantal people without them being destroyed. The elaborate schemes of purification rites and sacrifices are oriented toward that the people, when they enter God's presence, is properly cleansed of the impurity which the holiness of God cannot tolerate. In the coming of God's presence, there are only two options: holy communion or death (Lev 10:1–3).

There is a cluster of related reasons why Moltmann transposes the biblical logic of redemption. First, while admitting that both within the Bible and the tradition of the church sin has been seen as the dominant problem God's story of redemption responds to, Moltmann claims that in light of what we today know about ecological history and about the human condition, all aspects of suffering simply cannot be accounted for by recourse to sin as we see among the Rabbis, in Paul and in the Western tradition.[127] It is impossible to trace all suffering back to sin, and "suffering as *punishment for sin* is an explanation that has a very limited value."[128] Second, the inadequacy of sin as the catch-all for the misery of the world is accentuated by the suffering of the victims of the horrors of the twentieth century, which for Moltmann are primarily symbolized by Auschwitz and Hiroshima. Third, a fundamental problem in the traditional understanding of redemption, according to Moltmann, is an unhelpful restorationism which leads to a fundamental conservatism, i.e. redemption is not a transformation but rather a restoration of an older order that has been perverted.[129] Fourth, the reason Moltmann responds as he does to these concerns is probably to a certain extent due to the Blochian element in his ontology.[130] There is a small step from seeing nature as incomplete matter striving for its future potential to seeing this incompleteness as a contradictory yet necessary condition for creation.[131] For these reasons Moltmann thinks we have to reconsider how the logic of redemption as revealed in the biblical witness is

---

127. *TKG*, 49–52.

128. Ibid., 52.

129. Ibid., 51; *FC*, 168–69.

130. He says: "It is the greatness of Ernst Bloch, whom we are basically following here, that he has developed not only a 'principle of hope' for man, but also an ontology of the not-yet-being, and of possibility in the world process. . . . If we understand reality as the realization of possibility, then this necessitates an ontology of that which is not yet but is possible or stands in possibility" (*EH*, 25; cf. *RRF*, 217). Gilbertson, *God and History*, 17, notes that one of the lasting influences of Bloch on Moltmann is the "unsettled and unconcluded" ontology of the former, resulting in the latter's suspicion of "any epistemology or ontology based on a backward-looking orientation."

131. Rasmusson, *Church as Polis*, 57–60, notes how Moltmann's ontology relates to the often overly abstract formulations in his political hermeneutics—the mediation of the future to the present is fundamentally vague and abstract since what the future is like cannot be concretely known—present actuality is necessarily fundamentally different from its fulfillment.

to be configured if we are to be faithful to the Christian Gospel within the context in which we now live.

However, considering both the importance Moltmann ascribes to biblical tradition as providing the categories in which to think theologically and the consistency of the biblical witness to sin as the fundamental condition God overcomes in the history of redemption, we must ask whether such a move is necessary. Do the benefits Moltmann sees in it outweigh the problems Moltmann's position creates?

Problems in Moltmann's Transposition of Sin

Moltmann's transposition of the logic of redemption has several unfortunate implications: His schema has difficulty in affirming the goodness of creation, it is in danger of anthropomorphising creation, it leads to a necessary universalism that undermines human freedom, and it tends to over-privilege the new.

First, although Moltmann wants to affirm the fundamental goodness of creation, it is difficult to see how he can. Douglas Schuurman rightly regards Moltmann's understanding of creation as "a collapsing of the traditional distinction between creation and fall" leading to "a very negative assessment of the limitations of that creation which ... God called very good."[132] Because the fundamental problem is drawn from the fall into the structure of creation, Moltmann can only affirm creation eschatologically and thus only in what creation will be when radically transformed.[133] If creation can only be affirmed as good at the moment when it is radically transformed, it is hard to see how Moltmann can affirm its fundamental goodness as it is.[134]

Second, Bauckham notes, "one might ... wonder whether Moltmann's understanding of cosmic redemption does not introduce by the

---

132. Schuurman, "Creation," 61; so also Walsh, "Theology of Hope," who believes Moltmann in the end is unable to affirm the goodness of creation.

133. Another implication of this is that Moltmann ends up doing precisely what he rejects, answering the theodicy question by making evil necessary; the deadly context of creation is a necessary consequence of God vacating the space that gives room for creation. For the importance of the theodicy question in Moltmann's theology, see Bauckham, *Theology of Jürgen Moltmann*, 71–98.

134. Bouma-Prediger says, "since creation is essentially faulted, only some new creation can provide an adequate solution to the reality of sin. But to posit the necessity of a new creation undercuts the goodness of *this* creation" ("Creation," 89). See Musfeldt, "Löwe," for the questionableness of Moltmann's use of scientific theories of creation.

back door the anthropocentric view of creation he has been at pains to reject."[135] I would go further, and claim that in his concern to avoid an anthropocentric view of creation, he has anthropomorphized it.[136] By closely paralleling the death and resurrection of Jesus to the nature and destiny of the whole created order, Moltmann has taken what the Bible sees as humanity's particular plight and made it the paradigm for the whole created order. While Paul in Romans 8 sees the particular plight of creation as a consequence of human rebellion and its transformation as dependent on humanity's, Moltmann sees the plight of creation and humanity as fundamentally the same problem, although manifested in two different ways.[137] Therefore, Moltmann in the end anthropomorphizes creation rather than offering a less anthropocentric view of it— the particular kinds of communion God has with humanity, and the particular plight human beings experience, have their corresponding parallels in nature.[138] Creation is painted in the image of the biblical story of human rebellion and redemption.

Third, this transposition of the fundamental problem the cross responds to lends a strong universalist trajectory to his theology. The necessary problem is a fundamental contradiction in creation. The purpose of God's history with creation is to overcome this state of affairs. From this the expectation arises that the accomplishment of God's mission must be the vivification of all that has been granted life. If anything is lost, it is difficult to see how God's purpose can be seen to have been accomplished. In the next chapter, when discussing how Moltmann's transposition affects his understanding of the kingdom in its relational aspect, we will note how this is in danger of foreclosing precisely the human freedom Moltmann is so concerned to affirm.

Fourth, if a danger in traditional understandings of sin is an unhealthy conservative restorationism, Moltmann's problem is often the

---

135. Bauckham, *Theology of Jürgen Moltmann*, 211.

136. In a different line of argument, Lønning, "Schöpfungstheologie," believes Moltmann fails to free himself from anthropocentric view of nature despite his intentions because of a commitment to key elements in German idealist tradition.

137. For Moltmann's interpretation of Romans 8, see *GiC*, 67–69.

138. Thus Moltmann can say: "Creation is saved and justified in eternity in the sacrifice of the Son, which is her sustaining foundation" (*TKG*, 168). Cf. *FC*, 121–24, where he comes close to equate sin and the bondage of creation; see *GiC*, 67–68 for a more careful differentiation between the two.

opposite. Because redemption responds to a fundamental contradiction in creation which is at minimum the indirect cause of the tragedy of human history, Moltmann tends to over-privilege the new and progressive. Justice, righteousness and freedom tend to always be aligned to that which seems progressively new precisely because in Moltmann it is always from ahead of us that the good arrives.[139]

These concerns lead us to question Moltmann's critique of traditional understandings of sin. However, another proposal, including a defence of the traditional view, must be able to account for Moltmann's critique: if sin is the fundamental concern that the history of redemption responds to, how do we account for the suffering and death that cannot so easily be related to sin? Is the traditional understanding of sin not pastorally inadequate? Does not the traditional dogma lead to an inappropriate conservatism grounded in seeing the eschaton simply as a restoration of a pristine pre-fall order, neglecting the expectation for the radical transformation of creation? Does not a singular focus on sin result in an anthropocentric view of creation? We will let these questions stand for now but will pick them up again in chapter six, where we will consider how the expectation of the coming kingdom in Revelation might help us in making an account for these concerns.

---

139. Although Moltmann holds out hope for the past, it is not a hope of the restoration of something in the past but its transformation. Rasmusson links Moltmann's revolutionary commitments to the Postmaterialist ideas of "the New Class fraction" of the upper-middle class (*Church as Polis*, 158–68, 376).

4

The Passion of the Kingdom in the World

Introduction

WHILE MOLTMANN FOCUSES PRIMARILY ON THE HISTORICAL ASPECT of the kingdom in *Theology of Hope*, as his theology has developed he has paid increasing attention to its relational aspect, how the kingdom is paradoxically present in the world as God is turning the world toward its future in the kingdom.[1] In the following analysis of Moltmann's understanding of the relational aspect of the kingdom, we will first look at the broader question of how Moltmann accounts for God's relationship with creation from the cross. Then we will turn to the particular concern of how the kingdom is present in the world as the paradoxical rule of God revealed in Christ and implemented by the Spirit, paying particular attention to how he sees the relationship between the church and the kingdom. We will suggest that the great strength of this development in his thought is how he is able to account for the weaknesses in his earlier eschatological focus without losing its force, showing that historical and relational aspects of the kingdom are intrinsically related and reinforce each other. In the last part of the chapter we will focus our critique around three concerns:

---

1. In *CrG* he looks at what the cross means for God and what the implications of this is both for our understanding of God and of His ways in the world. His account for God's presence becomes explicitly trinitarian in *CPS* and *TKG*. In his mature thought, as is evident in these two works and which becomes a dominant theme in *GiC* and *SL*, Moltmann accounts for the possibility and actuality of God's presence in the world pneumatologically, while he accounts for the content and contour of that presence mainly christologically, as is most eminently seen in *WJC*.

- how Moltmann's kenotic understanding of the relationship between God and creation is the mirror image of the transposition of the logic of redemption that we outlined in the last chapter,
- how this kenotic understanding has some unfortunate implications for Moltmann's understanding of God's rule, and
- how Moltmann does not sufficiently distinguish between the relationship of the church and the world to the kingdom.

Kenotic Perichoresis: God's Relationship to Creation

When we talk about the presence of the kingdom in the world we necessarily speak about God's presence since the kingdom implies his rule. Therefore, before we consider the specific question of the presence of the kingdom, we will first look at how Moltmann understands the relationship between God and creation, how God is revealed from the cross, and how this shapes Moltmann's understanding of the trinitarian history of God.

The Presence and Identity of God as Revealed in the Cross

God's Self-Involvement in the Redemption of Creation

As Moltmann turns from the question of what the cross means for humanity and the world to what it means for God, he argues that God's act in the cross is not exterior to him but one in which he is fundamentally involved as he expends himself in order to become present to his whole creation.[2] Creation exists in the deathly absence of God's life-giving presence. In the radical self-restriction of the Son in his death, which has its counterpart in the Father and the Spirit,[3] God overcomes this creation's contradiction by becoming present to it.[4] In entering his fundamental negation in creation in the death of the Son, God has made possible the full de-restriction of himself in it. He "creates salvation" for the world precisely by suffering the "disaster of the whole world inwardly in himself."[5] The eschatological redemption purposed from the foundation of creation

---

2. *CrG*, x–xi.
3. See *GiC*, 243–49 on Moltmann's trinitarian understanding of the cross.
4. *TKG*, 119.
5. Ibid., 160. See *CrG*, 151–52 on how the cross takes place in the life of God, "is a *stasis* within God."

is revealed and made possible in the cross: because there God enters and suffers the contradiction of creation so he may "live in it; and that means to come to rest in it, and to remain there."[6]

The Identity of God as Revealed in the Cross

Because God involves himself in creation, the cross not only reveals what God does for creation but also who he fundamentally is. For Moltmann, therefore, God's outward acts always correspond to his inward suffering, "from the foundation of the world, the *opera trinitatis ad extra* correspond to the *passiones trinitatis ad intra*."[7] This is quintessentially revealed in the cross because it is the heart, the dead center of the relationship between the Father, the Son and the Spirit.[8] The cross as an event in God reveals God as a perichoretic communion of Father, Son and Spirit who in their common love for one another open themselves to creation, so creation may be drawn into their eternal communion of love.[9] In this way the identity of God is bound up with God's history with the world revealed from the cross; Moltmann says: "The doctrine of the Trinity is . . . nothing other than a shorter version of the passion narrative of Christ in its significance for the eschatological freedom of faith and the life of oppressed nature . . . The content of the doctrine of the Trinity is the real cross of Christ himself. The form of the crucified Christ is the Trinity."[10]

For Moltmann, God revealed from the cross both affects creation "but is also affected by it. God relates to the world as Trinity, experiencing the world within his own trinitarian experience, and so his chang-

---

6. *SW*, 122. This is the goal of the incarnation, and therefore the incarnation always had the cross in view; cf. "God's Kenosis," 141.

7. *TKG*, 160.

8. Philosophical premises, whether notions of a unitary substance or subjectivity, must be abandoned when one encounters God at Easter, one must begin with how God is here revealed as the "event" which is the relationship between the Father and the Son in the Spirit (*CrG*, 245–47; cf. *TKG*, 65).

9. Moltmann's designation of God as "event," which can easily be misleading, is made within the context of the Trinitarian relationship on the cross, in which the term is functionally synonymous with relationship. God is the event of the cross, that is, God is the event which is the relationship between the three persons in the cross (*CrG*, 246–47; cf. 207).

10. *CrG*, 246.

ing experience of the world is also a changing experience of himself."[11] Since this is the case, the history of creation's redemption revealed from the cross is also the trinitarian history of God with creation.[12]

The History of God's Kenotic Perichoresis with Creation

In tracing God's history with creation we will first look at four aspects of Moltmann's view of the God-creation relation:[13] beginning with Moltmann's kenotic understanding of the immanent Trinity, we will move to how God's resolve to create arises from within his eternal communion of love, how this resolve is grounded in the desire for the other who will respond to God's love, and how God self-restricts himself in order to give space for creation as his other. Then we will look at three aspects of God's presence to his creation:

- how God's whole history with creation has a kenotic shape,
- how therefore God's presence with creation must be seen in fundamentally kenotic terms, and finally
- how God's presence in creation is oriented toward the moment when the contradictions in both God and creation are overcome.

THE IDENTITY OF GOD IN RELATION TO CREATION

The Immanent Trinity: A Kenotic Perichoresis. Moltmann sees the perichoresis of the immanent Trinity in fundamentally kenotic terms.[14] He says:

---

11. Bauckham, "Jürgen Moltmann," 217. For a critical assessment of Moltmann's view of the impassibility of God, see Jansen, "(Im)mutability."

12. *CrG*, 207; *TKG*, 112.

13. See Lull, "Trinity," on the place of Moltmann within the revival of trinitarian theology in the latter part of the twentieth century (cf. Jenson, "Jesus, Father, Spirit"). For a concise review of Moltmann's understanding of the Trinity, see McWilliams, "Trinitarian Doxology" (cf. Peters, "Moltmann;" Radlbeck-Ossmann, ". . . in drei Personen"). See also O'Donnell, "Trinity as Divine Community," who is generally positive of social trinitarianism but warns that it is unwise to abandon discussions on substance. For more critical assessments of key aspects of Moltmann's trinitarian thought, see Neuhaus, "Moltmann," and Jansen, "(Im)mutability."

14. In *TKG*, 118–19, he "uses kenosis" first of the God-creation relation, and more recently of the way in which the three persons reside in one another; see, e.g., "God's Kenosis" and *SW*, 111–26.

> Every person exists in both the others—that is, it exists *in* and also *out of* (*ek*) the others. They are its living spaces. It is love which allows them to go out of themselves to such a degree that each is wholly in the others. The Father comes to himself in the Son and in the Spirit, the Son in the Father and the Spirit, the Spirit in the Son and the Father. By virtue of their reciprocal indwelling, the trinitarian Persons join themselves to a unity and differentiate themselves mutually: the Father differentiates between the Son and the Spirit through his different relations to them; and so on.[15]

The unity of the triune God as well as the distinct existence of each of the divine persons is grounded in a "perfect having one's being in the other." The perfect unity of the three is their constitution in each other made possible by their love—they empty themselves radically for each other so they can exist out of each other. Since "kenotic self-surrender is God's trinitarian nature, [it is] ... the mark of all his works 'outwards.'"[16]

The Necessary Resolve to Create. God's resolve to create is neither arbitrary nor simply an emanation but a "necessary resolve" which flows out of the life of perfect love within the Trinity.[17] Fundamental to love is the love for the unlike; therefore, the will to create an "other" is constituent of the fundamental nature of God.[18] The corollary of the perfect communion of love in God is the resolution to create an "other" to whom the Trinity opens itself and invites into its own communion. "This premises that the world of human beings and death does not exist outside God, but that from the very beginning it lies within the mystery of the Trinity: the Father creates the world out of love for the Son—the Son redeems the world from sin and death though [sic] his emptying of himself out of love for the Father."[19]

Creation Purposed for Perichoretic Communion with God. Just as the triune persons dwell in each other, in the space they have ceded for

15. *SW*, 118.
16. "God's Kenosis," 141.
17. In *GiC*, 79–86, Moltmann sets his own trinitarian understanding against the backdrop of the reformed doctrine of divine decrees and emanationist understandings of creation (cf. *TKG*, 105–8).
18. *TKG*, 106–7, 111–12.
19. "God's Kenosis" 141.

each other, so God's purpose in creation is that creation is to have its being in God and God is to dwell in his creation. God's first movement in achieving this is his protological act in creation. God, through alterations in the trinitarian relations, cedes a space within himself in which his creation can exist, and in this way "determines himself to be the living-space for all those he has created."[20] This kenotic act is both necessary for the possibility of creation (since God is omnipresent he has to cede a space within himself if there is to be any room for creation)[21] and it is fundamental to the God-creation perichoresis which is predicated upon the inner-trinitarian perichoresis—"God makes himself the dwelling place for those he has created, and at the same time he enters into his creation in order to make it his own dwelling place."[22]

Since the purpose of the divine restriction is to make creation God's own dwelling, the eschatological counterpart to the protological restriction is the moment when God de-restricts himself and again fills the space he ceded, making the creation which exists in him the home from which he exists. God's double movement of creation is grounded within and accords to the eternal communion of the love of the three. The three who exist in emptying themselves in love for one another throw themselves open for the other, creation, so that it may be drawn into the trinitarian communion of love.[23]

The Contradiction in God. It is as we consider what creation means for God that we see how the fundamental contradiction in creation finds its counterpart in a contradiction in God: The god-forsaken space in which creation exists is a space God has forsaken in himself, the flipside

---

20. *SW*, 120; cf. *TKG*, 111; "God's Kenosis," 141.

21. It is as "God withdraws to himself [that] he can create something whose essence is not divine, can let it co-exist with himself, give it space and redeem it" (*SW*, 119).

22. *SW*, 123.

23. Although noting fundamental problems with his panentheistic account of the God-creation relation, Bouma-Prediger notes how Moltmann is careful to distinguish himself from both Pantheism and Process Theology by accentuating both the difference between the two as well as their mutual communion (*Greening*, 253–55; cf. "Creation," 77–79). "The world lives in God in a world-like way, and God lives in the world in a God-like way. They interpenetrate each other mutually without destroying each other" (*SW*, 123).

of the history of redemption is how God overcomes the contradiction in himself which he voluntarily took on in his love for creation.[24]

The Presence of God with Creation

The Kenotic Shape of the God-Creation Perichoresis. The broad sweep of God's history with his creation is shaped by kenotic retraction and expansion; it is a history that ultimately moves from panentheism toward "theoenpanism," from a contradiction in God and creation which made their perichoretic communion possible to the fulfillment of that communion when this double contradiction is overcome.[25]

The Kenotic Rhythm and Passion of God's Presence in History. Not only this history as a whole but "every act outwards is preceded by an act inwards which makes the 'outwards' possible." A creative act *ex nihilo* is always logically preceded by a divine self-restriction, seen most radically in the cross where God lowered "himself into his own impotence" in order that creation may be freed from the chains of death and opened up to its own future in Him.[26] This paradoxical kenotic rhythm, where "God is nowhere greater than in his humiliation,"[27] underpins two fundamental aspects of Moltmann's understanding of God's presence in the world.

First, it is a real creative presence. Everything that exists and lives is the creative counterpart to God's self-restriction, a fruit of the divine Spirit. In the "unceasing inflow of the energies and potentialities of the divine Spirit," God, "preserves it, makes it live and renews it" as it grasps for its potentialities in the inflow of the Spirit.[28]

However, second, this kenotic rhythm happens in a creation that exists under the conditions of the protological kenosis, in the common passion of both God and creation. Therefore, God's presence in the

---

24. *GiC*, 88.

25. *CoG*, 306–8.

26. *TKG*, 110. "In this sense, by yielding up the Son to death in God-forsakenness on the cross, and by surrendering him to hell, the eternal God enters the Nothingness out of which he created the world . . . [and thus] pervades the space of God-forsakenness with his presence . . . That is why God's presence in the crucified Christ gives creation eternal life, and does not annihilate it" (*GiC*, 91).

27. *TKG*, 119; cf. *CrG*, 245, 277.

28. *GiC*, 9–10.

world is primarily passion,[29] God suffers with the world, and in suffering with it opens it up to its own future.[30] "God acts in the history of nature and human beings through his patient and silent presence, by way of which he gives those he has created space to unfold, time to develop, and power for their own movement." This hidden presence does not reflect a divine lack of interest in a suffering creation but is rather "the highest form of interest in the other;" instead of shaping creation prematurely into his own likeness by force, the long-suffering God constantly "creates possibilities of life for the other" by "attracting, alluring and enticing" creation into a communion with him. In this way, by the power of the Spirit, God gives creation time to become the creation which freely welcomes the creator who comes to dwell in it.[31]

The Eschatological Orientation of God's Presence in Creation. As is evident in this discussion, the presence of God in a world marked by his absence is oriented toward the moment when this contradiction in creation and its corresponding contradiction in God are overcome, the moment when the God-creation perichoresis corresponds to the life of the three divine person, the *kairos* when the creation that exist in and from God becomes the home from which God exists—"creation is destined to be the dwelling space for God."[32]

The Kingdom of Christ in the Spirit: The Rule of God Oriented toward Freedom

Introduction

Having outlined how Moltmann understands who God is in relation to creation and how he is present to it, we now turn to our primary concern, how the kingdom is present in the world as God's rule. Moltmann calls the relationship between the Trinity and the kingdom "the func-

---

29. *CrG,* 277; cf. *TKG,* 118.

30. Moltmann says, "a trinitarian theology of the cross perceives God in the negative element and therefore the negative element in God, and in this dialectical way is panentheistic. For in the hidden mode of humiliation to the point of the cross, all being and all that annihilates has already been taken up in God and God begins to become 'all in all'" (*CrG,* 277; cf. *TKG,* 118).

31. "God's Kenosis," 149.

32. *CoG,* 307; cf. *SW,* 117.

tional problem of the doctrine of the Trinity" and adds, "theology is never concerned with the actual *existence* of God. It is interested solely in the *rule* of this God in heaven and on earth."[33] Moltmann rejects monotheistic accounts where an absolute divine rule is "exercised by a single, identical subject,"[34] an approach which origin is in early Christian apologetics that sought to accommodate Christianity to Empire, and has in European political thought been consistently used to legitimate authoritarian rule in both state and church (one God, one church, one emperor, one people).[35] Rather, one must move from how God is revealed as Trinity in the cross: As a particular story within God's trinitarian narrative with creation, the history of the kingdom is God's history with humanity in all its relationships, in which God's rule is revealed as "the lordships that makes us free."[36]

In the following discussion we will begin by considering both how the kingdom of God is manifested in Jesus and how the Spirit is the mystery of the Kingdom. On basis of this we will consider how Moltmann understands the purpose of God's rule, how he achieves these purposes, and what claim this rule makes on those who subject themselves to it. We will conclude our analysis by considering how Moltmann sees the relationship between the church and the kingdom.

The Manifestation of the Kingdom in Jesus

In the last chapter we showed how Moltmann's messianic understanding of history is grounded in how the future kingdom has broken into the world in the raising of the crucified one. We now turn our attention to what makes the hope for the kingdom possible, namely that the future kingdom is *present* in the raised Jesus, and therefore Jesus is "the present representative of this future, of the free, new mankind and the new creation."[37] Moving from the resurrection, we will ask how the kingdom

---

33. "The question: does God exist? is an abstract one" (*TKG*, 191). In contrast, the Bible asks the concrete question "nach dem Reich Seiner offenbaren Herrlichkeit in der ganzen Schöpfung" ("Antwort," 215).

34. *TKG*, 191.

35. See especially ibid., 192–202, where Moltmann first critiques political and ecclesiastical understandings of God's sovereignty in monotheistic terms (which are hierarchical and as such legitimate unjust and suppressive social structures).

36. Ibid., 191.

37. *CrG*, 168.

is present in the raised and dead Jesus, and how this vision is informed by how Jesus saw the kingdom drawing near in his ministry.

The kingdom Jesus proclaimed to the poor, the sick and sinners "begins with the resurrection of Christ from the dead and the overcoming of the power of death by his resurrection."[38] In him, the goal of the kingdom is achieved, the pivotal victory over transience and its consequences. But, although a real instantiation of the kingdom, the resurrection of Jesus is not its consummation. Rather, as the first among many he has entered the future that awaits all.[39] However, if the resurrection is the first realisation of the kingdom in the world, how is this appearing made possible? If the raising of the crucified one is the first fruit of the kingdom which Jesus proclaimed in his ministry, how is it revealed in his life? And, how does this appearance of the kingdom in Jesus relate to the world that is not yet the kingdom? The first question leads us to a consideration of how the cross is the foundational event of the kingdom. The second and third draw us to how the kingdom is manifested in the concrete history of Jesus in anticipatory ways, and how this informs the way in which the kingdom is present under the conditions of God's absence in history.

Easter as the Foundational Event of the Kingdom

Although the cross-shattered Jesus' proclamation of the kingdom, it is also the event that made its vindication in the resurrection possible, and as such is the true beginning of the kingdom.[40] How so? Moltmann says, "The Father who sends his Son through all the abysses and hells of God-forsakenness, of the divine curse and final judgment is, in his Son, everywhere with those who are his own; he has become universally present. In giving up the Son he gives 'everything' and 'nothing' can separate us from him. This is the beginning of the language of the kingdom of God, in which 'God will be all in all.'"[41]

The absence of the kingdom in the world is due to the absence of God from the world, that it exists under the conditions of God-forsakenness. The cross is therefore the hidden beginning of the

---

38. HTG, 77.
39. TKG, 123.
40. CrG, 123–24.
41. TKG, 82.

kingdom because in the death of the Son God enters the realm of his absence, and so, God, in entering the passion of the Son, becomes present to the passion of the world, the source of all its suffering and evil, its god-forsakenness.

Since God entered the fundamental condition the whole world exists under, a universal hope is opened up for it, the hope for eternal communion with God. However, although the cross extends hope to all, the way in which Jesus died, who he died as, reveals a fundamental partisanship. In his death as a sinner, as a rebel and as the one forsaken by God, Jesus' criticism of the way of the religious elite is questioned, his confrontation with the Roman sword with the olive branch of peace withers, and most importantly, his intimate bond with God as Father dies as seen in the cry of dereliction (Mark 14:35). However, in the resurrection, it is precisely those who inhabit these identifications that are shown closest to the kingdom, the righteousness of the kingdom is the one that justifies sinners, the people of the kingdom are those who suffer at the hands of the powers to be, and most fundamentally the kingdom appears among those who experience the godforsakenness of the world most acutely.[42] Just as the knowledge of God as well as his presence are revealed paradoxically in their opposite in the cross,[43] so the presence of the kingdom is to be found first among the least expected, the sinners who are sinners at the expense of the self-righteous, the poor who are poor at the expense of the rich, and among the masses of the godforsaken on the earth.[44]

The raising of Jesus is the beginning of the kingdom of God in that it is a happening of the future kingdom ahead of time, but the cross is its beginning in that it is the possibility-making event of the kingdom. It is only because of the way God is radically present to the world in its god-forsakenness in the death of the Son that the Father can raise both the Son and eventually all humanity into the kingdom, which is predicated on the life-giving presence and communion of God. The double movement of Easter is the foundation for the presence of the kingdom of God in the world. In the resurrection we see in anticipation what the kingdom accomplishes, and in the cross we see how God

---

42. See *CrG*, 126–59 for Moltmann's discussion on how Jesus dies as a blasphemer, rebel, and godforsaken.

43. Ibid., 27.

44. Ibid., 326–27.

becomes present to humanity, and among whom he first is present. If the kingdom that is made possible and appears at Easter is the one Jesus proclaimed in his ministry, how does the life of Jesus inform us about the kingdom?

The Kingdom in the Person and History of Jesus

The Christian confession in Jesus Christ receives its form in Easter but "its *content* is determined by *the history of Jesus' life*."[45] Applying this basic premise to the kingdom in Christian faith, we see that while it is the central fact of the cross and resurrection that is the foundation of the kingdom's presence in the world, it is the life and ministry of Jesus that reveals the way the kingdom is present. Moltmann emphasises three things in Jesus' proclamation of the dawning of the kingdom in his ministry: Jesus' unique relationship with God as his Father, the anticipatory presence of the kingdom in his ministry, and the way of the kingdom in his proclamation.

Jesus' ministry begins with his baptism by John.[46] As such it must be seen in the context of the expectation of the kingdom in which John's message of repentance is set. In Jesus' baptism, when he received the Spirit "without measure" (John 3:34) and is called the Son of God, he is revealed to be the messianic figure in which the kingdom will appear that John had proclaimed. However, while the language of sonship is consistent with Israel's messianic expectation (cf. Ps 2:7), the way in which Jesus expresses this relationship throughout his life, calling God "Abba," points to a new intimate relationship with the God whose will he believes he is carrying out.[47] This transforms Jesus' proclamation of the kingdom. In distinction from the Baptist he proclaims "the intimate nearness of God the Father," not "the coming of the wrathful judge of the world," where "what rules is *the justice of mercy* for all the weary and heavy-laden. In the kingdom of the Father what reigns is the *liberty of the children of God* in the Spirit." This is not "the 'last days' before the

---

45. *WJC*, 140.

46. See ibid., 87–91, for how Moltmann relates and contrasts Jesus' message of the kingdom with John the Baptist's.

47. *WJC*, 74; cf. *CrG*, 121–22.

judgment," but the nearness of God's kingdom demonstrated in "signs of grace" to the disenfranchised and in miracles of healing the sick.[48]

Moving from the intimate relational context in which the whole of Jesus' life is to be seen, it is within Jesus' mighty deeds that we see how the kingdom appears. Jesus' healings and exorcisms are messianic signs of the kingdom of God in that they counter the fundamental powers under which the unredeemed world exists, they are "the dawn of the lordship of the divine life in this era of Godless death."[49] However, since those who were healed eventually die, and since the terrorising forces that negate life rage on, these mighty deeds are not a fulfillment of the kingdom but rather signs of what creation will be in the coming kingdom of God, just as Jesus himself was "the *provisional representative* of the still absent God."[50] In the gospel "it is already present, but *present* only as the *coming* kingdom," an anticipation of its future under the conditions of transience and death.[51]

Although the raised Jesus has entered a new "reality" that is discontinuous with the world as it is, the anticipatory appearance of this kingdom in his ministry happened in the world under the conditions it still exists in. Precisely because of this, how it appeared around him can be informative of where we see it in our world. Jesus' mighty deeds are "parables of the new creation in the midst of the everyday life of this exhausted world."[52] So wherever the sick become well and the tormented find peace we see real anticipations of the resurrected order and the annihilation of the forces of death in the kingdom of God.[53]

Implied in the anticipatory presence of the kingdom in Jesus' person and ministry is a certain way of life for those who seek to live according to it in a world of death that passes away. Moltmann develops such a messianic ethic in a variety of ways, including the way Jesus radicalises Israel's Sabbath laws and the laws for the year of Jubilee, which amounts to a "real programme for social reform" for the poor and in-

---

48. *WJC*, 90–91.
49. Ibid., 104.
50. *CrG*, 256.
51. *WJC*, 97.
52. Ibid., 99; cf. "Jesus and the Kingdom of God," 8–9, where he notes that these deeds are premonitions of the resurrected order just as sickness and suffering are premonitions of death.
53. Ibid., 105–11.

debted of Galilea. From the way in which the kingdom Israel hoped for appeared in Jesus, ecclesial communities are enabled to practice "the great alternative to the world's present system."[54] Central to this alternative is the proclamation of the kingdom to the poor, which does not "put the poor on the way to becoming richer, which is a way that is always fraught with violence" but rather "puts them on the way to community" characterised by sharing. In this way the violence against the poor is broken, the logic in which the rich maintain their wealth by keeping the poor poor. In such a culture of sharing we find an anticipation of the kingdom of God, where the cycles of violence and injustice break down and the poor are transformed and given dignity as the rightful heirs of the kingdom.[55]

When the apocalyptic expectation of the approaching kingdom fades, so does such an anticipatory praxis. However, when this hope is kept alive, ecclesial communities are enabled to live as the alternative community of the coming kingdom in hope of not only their own future but the future of the whole world. Although "the Sermon on the Mount . . . offers the ethic of a particular community . . . this ethic is directed to the redemption of the whole people (*ochlos*), and claims universality."[56] "Christian messianic ethics celebrates and anticipates the presence of God in history. It wants to practice the unconditioned within the conditioned and the ultimate in the penultimate."[57] Taking his cues from the way Jesus radicalises Israel's Sabbath laws, Moltmann argues that economically this means seeking a just order in which the needs of all people are met, politically it means seeking a form of government where the dignity and freedom of all is maintained, culturally it means an open solidarity between those who are different, and ecologically this means peace with the ravaged earth.[58] These are the sacramental forms of God's presence in history that "at the same time [point] beyond themselves to a greater presence, and finally to that present in which 'God will be all in all.'"[59]

54. Ibid., 119–22.
55. Ibid., 99–101.
56. Ibid., 125; cf. 122–27.
57. *OHD*, 110.
58. Ibid., 110–11.
59. Ibid., 111. For a recent essay that develops the same concerns, see "The Liberation of the Future."

The Spirit as the Mystery of the Kingdom

The Spirit is the mediating link between the kingdom's presence in the concrete person and history of Jesus and its universal presence in the world. Here we will first look at the work of the Spirit as the kingdom drew near in Jesus, how the presence of the kingdom consequently must be seen as pneumatological, how this pneumatology shapes the purpose of the kingdom, and how it is manifested in the world.

THE SPIRIT AS THE MYSTERY OF JESUS

The Spirit who is "God's own power of creation" is also "the divine saving *power*" by which the messianic kingdom Israel anticipated will be established.[60] It is precisely because everything in Jesus' life, who he is and what he does, is predicated on the efficacy of the divine Spirit that the Kingdom is appearing in Jesus.[61] "The presence of the Holy Spirit," says Moltmann, "is to be understood as the earnest and beginning of the new creation of all things in the kingdom of God."[62] The resurrection as a proleptic event of the future is not limited to itself, since the same Spirit by whose power Jesus was raised is the power in which he now is present in the world in anticipation of the parousia.[63]

THE PNEUMATOLOGICAL PRESENCE OF THE KINGDOM OF GOD

Because the Spirit present in Jesus is the same Spirit at work in the world, the concrete presence of the kingdom in Christ is intrinsically bound to the universal presence of the Spirit in the world.[64] But how is it so bound?

---

60. *WJC*, 91–92.

61. Ibid., 73. See 91–94 for the basic facets of Moltmann's Spirit Christology; cf. *THG*, 84.

62. *CPS*, 191; cf. *HTG*, 77; *WJC*, 73, 92.

63. See *WJC*, 241–45, on how Moltmann understands this as the process of resurrection.

64. The presence of God in the Shekinah that rested with Israel in the land and journeyed with her in exile is in trinitarian terms the Holy Spirit whose Shekinah presence is seen most radically in Jesus where "the Shekinah is manifested as God's self-surrender, and the Shekinah itself becomes capable of suffering and death," revealing how God has entered his creation "so as to live in it, and that means to come to rest in it, and to remain there" (*SW*, 122).

First, the concrete relationship between the two is grounded in the ascension and exaltation of the Son. Jesus, who in his earthly life existed from the power of the Spirit, sends, as the ascended Lord of the Kingdom, the same Spirit into the world so he may be present to the world in the Spirit.[65] Therefore, the presence of Christ and of the kingdom that appeared in him "is experienced in the Spirit who is the giver of life."[66] In this way the kenosis of the Spirit in the particular person of Jesus results in the expansion of the Spirit to the whole world; the kingdom that appeared in Jesus in the power of the Spirit is now present in the world through the same Spirit.[67]

Second, this movement from a pneumatological christology to a christological pneumatology of the kingdom must not be separated from the fact that the Spirit that appeared in Jesus is the same Spirit by whom God has given creation life and through whom he is present in it.[68] Therefore, the history of the kingdom that appeared in Jesus must be understood within the whole history of how God is present to the world by the Spirit. While the history of the kingdom in Jesus makes God's purposes for humanity possible, it is itself set within the large story of how God created humanity and all nature for communion with Him and keeps them open to this future by the Spirit. Within this larger picture, the kingdom is present to the world in hidden and paradoxical ways in the power of the Spirit, turning it toward its future in God's life-giving communion. Therefore, "the kingdom of glory does not come unexpectedly and without any preparation, it is already heralded in the kingdom of the Spirit, where it already has power and is present."[69]

THE PROCESS OF RESURRECTION IN THE SPIRIT

As Moltmann considers the centrality of the resurrection as an event accomplished in the Spirit, history is not simply seen in the light of the resurrection but also as a process of resurrection. He says:

> Seeing history in the perspective of resurrection means participating through the Spirit in *the process of resurrection* . . . It

---

65. *HTG*, 84.
66. *WJC*, 41; cf. 77.
67. Ibid., 85, 86, 93; cf. 94.
68. Ibid., 91–94.
69. *SoL*, 11.

> means participating in the creative act of God. A faith of this kind is the beginning of freedom ... Understood as an event that discloses the future and opens history, the resurrection of Christ is the foundation and promise of life in the midst of the history of death ... In talking about Christ's resurrection we have therefore to talk about a *process of resurrection*. This process has its foundation in Christ, its dynamic in the Spirit, and its future in the bodily new creation of all things. Resurrection means not a *factum* but a *fieri*—not what was once done, but what is in the making: the transition from death to life.[70]

The resurrection shows that God's final purpose for all life that now comes to a deadly end is an eternal life-giving communion with him. Since the resurrection is wrought by precisely the power that is keeping all life open for this future, it is a process. While "death acts on this life and in it as the power of division and isolation ... the resurrection actively penetrates life too, by virtue of hope, and cancels the results of death's power."[71] The future the Spirit orients the world towards is made possible in the resurrection of Jesus. In the appearing of the kingdom in Jesus, the way in which the Spirit is opening the world up to its future is made visible. In the power of the Spirit of the resurrection, men and women can participate in the process of resurrection. Seized by this process, they seek to live the kingdom according to how it appeared in Jesus in anticipatory form.[72]

The Pneumatological Manifestation of the Kingdom of God

When Moltmann turns to the presence of the Spirit in the world, he sees it "wherever life here is quickened and its living energies awake."[73] Precisely because of this, the presence of the kingdom is not to be limited to the spheres in which Christ is confessionally known and where there is a community that intentionally follows him. The future of the kingdom is made possible by how it appeared in Christ by the Spirit, but since the Spirit that was at work in him is also the Spirit at work in the world, the presence of the kingdom is not to be limited to where he is

---

70. *WJC*, 240–41; cf. *JCTW*, 75–80.
71. *WJC*, 264.
72. *JCTW*, 75, 79–80.
73. *WJC*, 264.

known and proclaimed, but must be seen "in everything that ministers to life and resists its destruction."[74] Therefore, those who confess Christ cannot lay claim to be the only heirs of the kingdom, but rather, with the knowledge of the kingdom they have received in their confession, they are to seek precisely those places and movements in which the power and presence of the Spirit of life are evident. Those who seek the kingdom must therefore join themselves to everything where "mortal life" is "quickened and its living energies" is unreservedly affirmed.[75]

The Rule of God as Oriented toward Freedom

It is on basis of how the Trinity is revealed in the relationship of the Father, Son and the Spirit at Easter that Moltmann develops his understanding of divine rule, what its purpose is, how its purpose is achieved, and what claim it lays on people.

THE PURPOSE OF THE RULE OF GOD

God created creation within himself so that one day it may be the dwelling from which he exists, resulting in a perichoretic communion between God and creation that corresponds to the inner-trinitarian communion of God. If this is the case, then the rule of God does not exist at the expense of human freedom but is oriented toward the liberation of all for their mutual communion with God. In Easter, the purpose of God's rule is revealed in negative terms as the redemption from death, from the bondage to transience, and in positive terms, anticipating how the Spirit preserves people for glory, as drawing people into the fellowship with the Father.[76]

Because in his rule God "calls the freedom of men and women to life, ... the trinitarian doctrine of the kingdom is the theological doctrine of freedom. The theological concept of freedom is the concept of the trinitarian history of God: God unceasingly desires the freedom of his creation. God is the inexhaustible freedom of those he has created."[77] Therefore, God's liberation of humanity does not result in enslavement

---

74. *SL*, xi; cf. *CPS*, 196; *WJC*, 91; 253–54.
75. *WJC*, 264.
76. *TKG*, 209–10.
77. Ibid., 218.

to God; rather, God's "sovereignty" is nothing other than his "sustaining fellowship with his creation and his people."[78]

The Character of the Rule of God

As soon as we talk about the purpose of God's rule, what he aims to accomplish in it, we must also talk about the means by which he will accomplish this, i.e. what is the power by which God accomplishes his purposes. From the purpose of God's rule it is evident that its means cannot be coercive power. Rather, as most radically seen in the paradoxical power of the cross, "God acts in the history of nature and human beings through his patient and silent presence, by way of which he gives those he has created space to unfold, time to develop, and power for their own movement." It is by this suffering with creation that God in the presence and power of the Spirit gives creation freedom to come into its own and in this process keeps it open for this future by unceasingly creating the possibilities for its life.[79] In opposition to the despots of the world, "it is his passionate, passible love that is almighty, nothing else," "[t]he sole omnipotence which God possesses is the almighty power of suffering love."[80]

Adapting Joachim of Fiore's trinitarian doctrine of the kingdoms,[81] Moltmann links the kingdom of the Father with the creation of the world and its preservation through God's patience, the kingdom of the Son is linked with the liberation of humanity from "their closed-in-ness," and the kingdom of the Spirit with how all living things are kept open to their future communion with God.[82]

Corresponding to these strata of the kingdom is a stratified understanding of freedom. The freedom of the Father is the freedom to be a servant; those who are God's "property" as his creatures are exalted to be his servants who, dependent on this Lord, are "completely free from other thing and other powers." However, in the kingdom of the Son, while the outward form of being a servant is preserved, "its in-

78. *GiC*, 241; cf. *TKG*, 203ff.
79. "God's Kenosis," 149; cf. *SL*, 42.
80. *TKG*, 197, 31.
81. Rather than seeing the kingdom of the Father, Son and Spirit as three historical ages, he sees them as strata of the one history of the kingdom of God that have a forward thrust. For the importance of Fiore in recent theology, see Conyers, "Revival."
82. *TKG*, 212–13.

ward quality is changed. The servants of the Lord become the children of the Father." Having gained a filial relation to the Father, they are no longer his property but "joint owners of the father's property." In the kingdom of the Spirit, the inward quality of freedom changes again, as "the servants of the Lord and the children of the Father become God's friends." This freedom of friendship received by the indwelling Spirit and experienced in friendship is what the freedom of the servant and of the child is oriented toward. God desires his servants and children to become his friends, so "the distance enjoined by sovereignty ceases to exist," and "the boldness and confidence of friends, who share his rule with him" emerges. It is this friendship, "a conversation in the freedom of love, that shares and allows the other to share," that will characterise the coming kingdom and is now anticipated in prayer.[83]

The Demand of the Rule of God

If the freedom that the rule of God is oriented toward is now experienced as "the intimacy, in which we call God 'Abba' . . . and know ourselves to be his child and friend," Christians must adopt a way of life that corresponds to this and commit themselves to "wherever this future *happens* in history—wherever, that is, God gives his future of the kingdom *in advance*."[84] Their life, then, must correspond to the forward thrust of the rule of the Father, the Son, and the Spirit.[85] Living under the rule of the Father, they resist every other formative power and conform to the way God orients creation toward himself. As those who have become God's children in the Son, this way of life is experienced in the intimacy of the relationship between parents and children, and is oriented toward becoming the friend of God, sharing in his life in the power of the Spirit. These strata of freedom correspond to the movement of the kingdom of God.[86]

---

83. Ibid., 219–21.

84. "The Liberation of the Future," 266, 279.

85. An experience of freedom is an experience of being the servant, the child, and the friend of God but also a trend from the first to the last, because the freedom of the servant in its incompleteness strives toward the freedom of the children, and both push toward the freedom of friends; as "strata in the concept of freedom" they are on the one hand "transitions . . . present in every experience of freedom," but also a trend in "the process of maturing through experience that are continually new" (*TKG*, 221, 222).

86. Ibid., 222.

The Church as an Anticipation of the Kingdom

The above discussion has focused on the character of God's rule, and on the christological and pneumatological logic of its presence. Now we move to the concrete question of how the church is related to this rule, looking at how the church of Christ exists for the kingdom, how as such she is an event, "a happening" in the promised presence of Christ, how on basis of this we are to understand the creedal confession of the church, and how this shapes her mission.[87]

The Church between Christ and the Kingdom in the Spirit

Christ, who "represents in this transitory era of the world the God who is to come" in his Lordship and glory, is the eschatological foundation of the church.[88] Because of this, "every statement about the church will be a statement about Christ."[89] Everything that is true about the church is only so because it is first a predicate of Christ and everything we know of Christ is of importance for the church and her life in the world. As such, the church is "the present realization of the remembrance and hope of Christ."[90]

However, while the church is christologically determined, she does not exhaust who Christ is but rather finds her existence within his broad mission for the coming kingdom. As such, the church lives in the dynamic between Christ as her foundational center and the horizon of the kingdom toward which she is oriented.

The existence of the church then is intrinsically bound up with the kingdom of God because the church's reason for existence, what defines who she is, what she is to seek and how she is to live is predicated upon her existence in Christ's mission of the kingdom. As the church of Christ, "the community of the cross," it identifies with the suffering of the world that Christ entered into in his cross. From there it exists as "the fellowship of the kingdom" that in its exodus toward the kingdom "spreads the feast without end." The church, if it is to exist at all, exists "as a factor of present liberation, between remembrance of his history and

87. *CPS*, 122.
88. Ibid., 70–75.
89. Ibid., 6.
90. Ibid., 144.

hope of his kingdom," and as such is an anticipation of the kingdom.[91] However, she can only exist as such in the power and the presence of the Spirit. Every facet of the church's identity and existence is marked by how the Spirit keeps the world open to its future in God, "the whole being of the church is marked by participation in the history of God's dealing with the world."[92]

The Church as Event in the Promised Presence of Christ

If Christ is the foundation of the church that exists for the coming of his kingdom in the power of his Spirit, it can only exist where Christ is present in the world in the Spirit as the Spirit keeps the world open to its own future in the kingdom of Christ. As such, the church is not a self-determining entity but exists only as the "event" that binds itself to Christ where he has promised to be present in the Spirit. For Moltmann, the three "spheres" in which Christ promises to be present is in the apostolate, among the poor and in his parousia.[93]

The Church in the Apostolic Presence of the Exalted Christ. When discussing Christ's presence in the apostolate, Moltmann understands the Apostolate as "the medium of the proclamation through word and sacrament, as well as the persons and community of the proclaimers."[94] Since the Apostolate is not only the kerygmatic proclamation but also the community which proclaims the kerygma, it is not simply a message but an existence patterned after Jesus, it "has the bodily and social dimension of the passion, and the power of the resurrection."[95] However, this is not an intrinsic quality of the church but only what it receives as the apostolate takes "place in Christ's presence."[96] This 'happening' of the church is made possible in the Spirit who is the fundamental sacrament of the church. It is in the Spirit that the church experiences the presence

---

91. Ibid., 75; cf. 24–26, 34, 191–92, 196.

92. Ibid., 65.

93. Ibid., 122–23; cf. Bauckham, *Theology of Jürgen Moltmann*, 130.

94. CPS, 123.

95. This is especially seen in The Lord's Supper and Baptism, the former is "the feast of his presence . . . surrounded by the remembrance of his death and the expectation of his coming," and in baptism people are "baptized into his death, so they may walk in new life, just as Christ has been raised" (ibid., 124).

96. Ibid., 125.

of her exalted Lord, and it is by the power of the Spirit that the church is empowered for an apostolic existence in the world.[97]

In the church's uniting with Christ's pneumatological presence in the apostolate, we see the particular identity of the church in relation to the kingdom. The church's identity as the church of Jesus Christ is defined by its kerygmatic role in the world, as the community that testifies to how the kingdom of God has appeared in the world in Jesus, and how the fulfillment of this kingdom is what awaits the whole world. This kerygmatic role of the church is sacramental in character and does not simply refer to her message but forms her existence, the kerygmatic church takes "on the form of Christ's destiny."[98] As Christians proclaim the Christ of the Kingdom and the hope for the kingdom, they suffer with the world in its passion; they do so in expectant hope for the future they have in common with the world in the kingdom of God.

The Church and the Presence of Christ among the Poor. However, the church can only unite itself to and exist in the apostolic presence of the exalted Christ when it unites itself with those among whom the crucified one has promised to be present, with his hidden presence among the poor, only perceptible "in the path of suffering of the one who told the story: the way to Golgotha trodden by the hungry, thirsty, naked prisoner, the Son of man from Nazareth."[99]

It is only as such that the church can really be the church because "then . . . with its mission" the church is "present where Christ awaits it, amid the downtrodden, the sick and the captives. The apostolate says what the church is. The least of Christ's brethren say where the church belongs."[100] Although traditionally often separated, the vitality of the church is dependent upon that Christ's kerygmatic presence in word and sacrament takes place in Christ's hidden but anticipatory presence among the poor because "if the church appeals to the crucified and risen Christ, must it not represent this double brotherhood of Christ in itself, and be present with word and Spirit, sacrament, fellowship and all

---

97. This dual emphasis is the structuring principle for the final two chapters of CPS.

98. Ibid., 124.

99. Ibid., 126; see 126–30 on Moltmann's view of Christ's presence among the poor.

100. Ibid., 129.

creative powers among the poor, the hungry and the captives."[101] For the church to be the church its active apostolic mission, its proclamation of the world in the future of the risen Christ, must be united precisely with how, in the power of the Spirit, the kingdom is present in the sign of the cross among the victims of the world.

Thus, while the apostolate sets out the particular identity of the church in the world as it is based on Christ and exists for his kingdom, Christ's presence among the poor shows how the church exist for the future of the whole world in a partisan way. It can only seek the welfare of all by seeking the justice for the victims with whom Jesus identified on the cross and among whom he is now present as the eschatological judge.[102] It is precisely here that the church unites itself to the places where the Spirit enters the fundamental contradiction of the world in order to keep the whole world open to its future in the kingdom.

The Church Oriented toward Christ's Parousia. Christ's promised presence in the apostolate and among the poor is his identification in history with something other than himself, both of which anticipate his promised presence in the parousia, when he comes in glory and is universally manifested in his own person.[103] Although this coming in glory cannot be conceived of since it has not yet occurred, it can now be anticipated since it will be the fulfillment of what is experienced in the apostolate and among the poor.[104] The church's apostolic proclamation among, with and for the poor receives its shape from the hope for the kingdom; as it unites itself with how Christ is present in the world, it is oriented toward his coming in the kingdom which is anticipated in his

---

101. Ibid., 129.
102. *CrG*, 53.
103. On Christ's parousia, see *CPS*, 130–32.
104. It is crucial for Moltmann that the future coming in glory is anticipated both in the apostolate and among the poor because without the latter the church "would not be able to expect the one who was crucified in the coming Lord" and without the former "the church would all too easily wait for the coming Lord as an apocalyptic angel of revenge on behalf of those who are oppressed on earth. The fellowship of Christ lives simultaneously in the presence of the exalted one and of the one who was humiliated. Because of that it expects from his appearance in glory the end of the history of suffering and the consummation of the history of liberation" (*CPS*, 132).

presence in history, and as such exists as "fragments and anticipations of his kingdom."[105]

This places the church in a dialectic relationship to the future coming of Christ. On the one hand, the provisional nature in which Christ is present to the church exists in a dynamic that is oriented toward his coming glory. On the other, precisely because of this, the coming one is present in an anticipatory sense in the apostolate and among the poor. In this way the church is always rendered in relation to the coming one but is also a real anticipation of his coming. And precisely because it is oriented toward this future, it cannot limit its mode of activity to its own interests and preservation but must seek the places where the Lordship of Christ is experienced and the activity of the Spirit is manifested. As such the church that receives its shape from the hope of the coming of Christ and the transformation of the world by the Spirit,

> finds itself on the path traced by this history of God's dealings with the world, and it discovers itself as one element in the movements of the divine sending, gathering together and experience. It is not the church that has a mission of salvation to fulfil to the world; it is the mission of the Son and the Spirit through the Father that includes the church, creating a church as it goes on its way.... If the church understands itself, with all its tasks and powers, in the Spirit and against the horizon of the Spirit's history, then it also understands its particularity as one element in the power of the Spirit and has no need to maintain its special power and its special charges with absolute and self-destructive claims.[106]

The Apostolic Church of the One, Holy and Catholic Kingdom. The relational identity of the church, both her communion with Christ in the Spirit and the various relationships in which she stands in the world as she exists for the coming of his kingdom shape Moltmann's interpretation of the confession of her as "the one, holy, catholic and apostolic church."

Emphasising the location of this confession in the creed, Moltmann argues that the church receives her attributes from the activity of Christ in the working of the Spirit. These attributes then are first christological

---

105. Ibid., 132.
106. Ibid., 64–65.

and intrinsically related to his mission.[107] Therefore, they are also statements of hope, anticipating what the church is becoming as the Spirit opens her to her future in the kingdom, as well as statements of action, what the church seeks as it lives toward both hers and the world's future in the kingdom.[108]

The first three are eternal designations of the coming kingdom. As such, they are not self-contained characteristics of the church but of the destiny of the whole world in the kingdom. Therefore, the church can only be the *one* true church as she, in solidarity with the poor, builds partnerships with others for their common future in the kingdom. The church is one when she is united in the fellowship of Christ and strives for the coming unity of the world in the kingdom of God. Therefore, she can only be *catholic*, whole, in partisan partnerships. Since her mission is one element in the broader mission of Christ, she must build partnerships with others other in her life for the kingdom, first with Israel, on whom her relationships with all others is patterned. But precisely because of the way the Lordship of Christ is now present among the poor in the power of the Spirit, these must be partisan coalitions with and on behalf of the poor and oppressed. It is precisely in this life with the poor that the *holiness* of the kingdom becomes manifest in the church. As a *communio peccatorum* the church confesses her sin and guilt that are grounded in the world that is passing away, but as the *communio sanctorum* it is oriented toward the redemption of the world, the time when it will be predicated on the holiness of God.[109] As such, the church is holy in her poverty. As the church confesses her own poverty and engages herself among the poor, she is oriented in hope toward the holiness of God that will redeem the world.

While the unity, catholicity and holiness of the church are predicates *of* the kingdom, the apostolate is a designation *for* the kingdom.[110] As such, as we have already noted, it is a designation of the church's particular role toward the kingdom. It is her apostolic charge that defines her unique relationship to the kingdom. Her mission is, in her praxical witness, to reveal to the world how its future lies in the coming

---

107. Ibid., 338.
108. Ibid., 339–40.
109. Ibid., 342–47, 350–52, 354–55.
110. Ibid., 357.

Lordship of the crucified one who was raised; following the fundamental movements of her own Lord in the world, she shows the world how its coming Lord is already being manifested in it. Precisely because of this, the church can never be the triumphalist partner of the victors of history but is always inescapably lead "into tribulation, contradiction, and suffering." As such, she is not only determined by the hope of the coming of the raised one but also in the actual discipleship of the crucified one.[111]

The Church in the Mission of the Kingdom

The unique role as well as the church's partnerships in the mission of the kingdom is especially well seen in Moltmann's understanding of inter-religious dialogue. In distinction to the church's quantitative mission, planting churches and bringing people to the Christian faith, Moltmann emphasises what he sees as its qualitative mission.[112] In the latter, the church attends to "the qualitative attention to life's atmosphere."[113] This happens in the church's dialogue with the religions, where the purpose of this dialogue is not to convert but reciprocal cross-fertilisation of potentialities for the Kingdom. Since Christianity is only one movement toward the coming kingdom, her dialogue with other religions recognizes the "creative need for the other";[114] only as our eyes are opened to the relationships of each other to the kingdom can we attain to our common future in it. In this dialogue, as the church of the crucified one, the church will always seek to speak from the context of the vulnerable and the poor, those on the social margins. The particular role of the apostolic church in this dialogue is to find ways in which it is reasonable for others, within the framework of their own religions, to embrace faith in Christ. However, since the religions have their own future in the

---

111. Ibid., 361.

112. Ibid., 152. Although he does not emphasize it, Moltmann cannot abandon this quantitative mission of the church. In a later essay, Moltmann first notes the tension he experiences between the life found in other religions and his own commitment to Christ (*GSS*, 226), and seeks to resolve this by proposing an inter-religious dialogue that is oriented toward discerning the possibilities for life in each others' religion, but, and this is not entirely clear, in such a way that each, within their own religious context, "is called by Christ, and loves life, and helps to work for the kingdom of God" (243).

113. *CPS*, 152.

114. Ibid., 159.

kingdom, the church will seek to do so without trying to make them the church. In the same way it will seek to incorporate other religions' potentialities for the kingdom without denying its own concrete relationship to the kingdom.[115]

Drawing these strands together, what can we say about the church's relationship to the coming kingdom and its paradoxical presence in the world? First, for Moltmann, the church cannot be seen *as* the presence of the kingdom in history but rather *within* the anticipatory forms the kingdom takes where the hidden presence of Christ and the Spirit is experienced. Second, in order to exist as such, the church must not only unite itself to the presence of the exalted Christ in the apostolate, but must carry out the apostolic charge with and on behalf of the poor among whom the crucified one is present. Third, as such, the church exists in the dialectic of Christ and his kingdom; she finds her identity in Christ as her eschatological foundation and therefore finds her whole existence oriented toward the coming of his kingdom. Fourth, since the church is only one of many movements of the kingdom, she can only attain to her confessional identity as she enters in partnerships with others who seek the justice of the kingdom in the world. Fifth, her unique relationship to the kingdom is the way in which the promised hope of Israel is revealed to the whole world in her praxical witness.

Conclusion

Of Christian ethics, which of course cannot be seen in separation from the kingdom, Moltmann says that it is "christologically founded, eschatologically oriented, and pneumatologically implemented."[116] Using this template, we will try to bring the various threads of the preceding discussion together.

If the cross revealed that God's lordship over the world must be seen as the paradoxical power through which God orients the world toward its freedom in communion with himself, then the actual lordship is experienced in the present as the reign of Christ. It is in the incarnation of the Son that the kingdom arrives in the world, and in history it is then experienced as the lordship of Christ. Therefore, in history, those who have been

---

115. Ibid., 162–63. See 163–89, on how he develops the church's relationship to other political, social and cultural entities and movements in a similar way.

116. *OHD*, 109.

infected by the kingdom, align their life according to the remembrance of how the kingdom appeared in and around Jesus. The Christian ethics of the Kingdom is founded christologically precisely because the reign of God in history is the reign of Jesus as the risen Lord.

The kingdom of God is present in the world eschatologically. This does not only mean that it is oriented toward its own future, but that its very presence is eschatological, i.e., it is not present as it will be but only as an anticipation of how it will come. "These anticipations, however, are not identical with the kingdom of God, but point beyond themselves to an always fuller presence of God and to the final eschatological fulfilment when God will be all in all."[117] Thus, the dialectic between the future of the kingdom that cannot be identified as anything in the world, and a real anticipatory presence of it in the world is absolutely fundamental to Moltmann. Since it is a real anticipatory presence, we already experience the kingdom now in love "and creative discipleship. But as long as the dead are dead and we cannot achieve justice, love remains fragmentary. All its works remain in need of redemption."[118] Therefore, an ethics based in the kingdom is always restless, constantly seeking new ways of actualising the ultimate in the provisional. As such, Christian ethics is fundamentally eschatologically oriented, because it is predicated on the eschatologically oriented kingdom of Christ.

The presence of the kingdom is pneumatologically implemented. It is by the Spirit that God can be present to his absence as revealed in the relationship between the Father and Son on the cross. This is the pneumatological pivot that defines the kingdom's anticipatory presence in the ministry of Jesus. If the cross was in God from eternity, then the paradoxical and anticipatory presence of the kingdom in the world is from beginning to end implemented by the Spirit of life who turns creation toward eternal life in God. Christian ethics is therefore fundamentally pneumatologically implemented and universal in its scope, because it is predicated upon the way in which God's reign, his presence to his kingdom in the world, is pneumatologically implemented.

The presence of the kingdom of God in the world then must be seen within the "eschatological history of God," that history "which is aligned towards the future through God's calling and election" which

---

117. Rasmusson, *Church as Polis*, 86.

118. *OHD*, 109.

finds its fulfillment in "the coming redemption of the world . . . in the universal messianic kingdom of peace."[119] The future of this kingdom is free and reciprocal freedom in God, and its presence is the rule of God that makes men and women free from every conceivable bondage and orients them toward this eschatological freedom. To be caught up in this rule is to be seized by the process of resurrection where

> to act ethically in a Christian sense means to participate in God's history in the midst of our own history, to integrate ourselves into the comprehensive process of God's liberation of the world, and to discover our own role in this according to our own calling and abilities. A messianically oriented ethics makes people into co-operators for the kingdom of God. It assumes that the kingdom of God is already here in a concrete, if hidden, form. Christian ethics integrates suffering and ailing people into God's history with this world; it is fulfilled by the hope of the completion of God's history in the world by God himself.[120]

Contribution: The Presence of the Coming Kingdom in History

Some of the significant contributions of the relational aspect of the kingdom in Moltmann's thought emerge when one considers how they overcome recurring critiques levelled at the singularly eschatological focus of the *Theology of Hope*. First, if God is not "in us or over us but always only before us,"[121] then, Moltmann's critics note, God's future and his Kingdom are now only present in the exalted Christ while the world still exists in the cross, characterised by his radical absence.[122] Although Moltmann affirms in *Theology of Hope* that the kingdom has broken into history in Jesus,[123] it is as he turns to its relational aspect that he shows how the kingdom is present as the hidden, paradoxical and anticipatory reign of God in the world. The cross does not only reveal the fundamental absence of God in the world, but also, precisely in do-

119. *WJC*, 70.
120. *OHD*, 111.
121. *TH*, 16.
122. Schuurman, "Creation," 46; Morse, "God's Promise," 144–46; Fries, "Spero ut intelligam," 368–75. This is also a common critique in two collections on his early thought (Marsch, *Diskussion*; Herzog, *Future of Hope*).
123. *TH*, 212, 216, 222.

ing so, reveals God's paradoxical presence in it as he turns it toward its redemption.[124]

Second, a closely related critique questions whether any real Christian praxis is possible if there is a radical discontinuity between the future and the present.[125] Moltmann accounts for this critique in his pneumatological understanding of God's presence in the world. In the Spirit, the force that will transform the world is already present in it and is orienting it towards it transformation in the arrival of God's uninhibited presence. Therefore, Christians who anticipate the future kingdom can actually 'plan' for it within the possibilities that are opened up by the presence of the Spirit. The praxis that finds its foundation in the hope revealed in the resurrection is also a participation in the process of resurrection that transforms the world.

Third, a common critique levelled against Moltmann is his often abstract understanding of Christian ethics that tends to see leftist political ideals as self-evident.[126] Although this is a weakness that runs through most of Moltmann's writings, his discussions on how the kingdom has appeared in the person and history of Jesus provide an important internal corrective, since this christological strand in his theology informs ethics from the concrete biblical narratives.[127]

In Moltmann's mature thought, the historical and relational aspects of the kingdom are intrinsically related. The hope for the kingdom as the goal of history is "the rule of God in the kingdom of God as a future transcending the system." This hope is what gives the divinely opened possibilities within the system their orientation and thus gives Christian praxis its direction. The kingdom's presence is the redemptive force of God within history that turns creation toward this future, "the kingdom of God in the liberating rule of God as a transforming power immanent in that system." Without this the future hoped for would be

124. *CrG*, 276–78; cf. "Homecoming," 279.

125. Although Moltmann claims in *TH* that the resurrection leads to a praxis that is oriented toward its future (223), he does not sufficiently account for how this is possible (Gilkey, *Reaping the Whirlwind*, 234–35; Rasmusson, *Church as Polis*, 66; Morse, "God's Promise," 149).

126. Chapman, "Hope and Ethics," 458–59; Rasmusson, *Church as Polis*, 66–68.

127. See, e.g., *WJC*, 126, on how he relates the Sermon on the Mount to Christian ethics. So Rasmusson, *Church as Polis*, 70, although he is unduly sceptical about how this confessional strand in Moltmann's thought is able to function as an internal corrective.

but "a powerless dream." Thus, prayer and doxological anticipation for the future of the kingdom is inseparable from the obedience of faith that resists anything in history that counters the kingdom, its "godless and inhuman relationships."[128] Moltmann illustrates this dynamic in the image of a seed:

> Being a seed, it is also *the object of hope*, but a hope firmly founded on experience and remembrance: the seed wants to grow, the one who has been found wants to return home, those who have been healed want to rise from the dead, and people liberated from some compulsion want to live in the country of freedom. Just because in the companionship of Jesus the kingdom of God is experienced in the present, its completion is hoped for in the future.[129]

Precisely in placing the church in this dialectic of the kingdom, seeing Christ, in whom the kingdom appeared, as her central foundation, and seeing the kingdom's future fulfillment as the horizon the church exists toward, Moltmann is able to develop a dynamic ecclesiology in which the church is always christologically shaped but also constantly reformed by the hope for the kingdom. Since she receives her identity from another and her reason for existence is other than herself, she can never be self-serving or self-contained. Rather,

> all inherent interests of the Church itself—maintaining the status quo, extending influence—must be subordinated to the interests of the Kingdom of God, otherwise they are unjustified. If the spirit and the institutions of the Church correspond to the Kingdom of God, then it is the Church of Christ. If they contradict the Kingdom of God, then the Church loses its right to existence and will become a superfluous religious community. The Kingdom of God orientation of the Church today consists of proclaiming the gospel of the Kingdom of God to all people and first to the poor in this world in order to awaken faith which lifts up and makes certain.[130]

---

128. *CPS*, 190.

129. *JCTW*, 19.

130. "Jesus and the Kingdom of God," 16. It is within this dialectic that Moltmann's political theology is to be placed. Since the church exists for the future kingdom, it cannot pledge its allegiance to any earthly kingdom; rather, as the church of the crucified one who identified himself with the victims of history, she must see her place "in the framework of the divine history of liberation" (*CPS*, 18). For an overview and critique

Questioning Moltmann's View of God's Kenotic Rule in the World and the Church

There are some basic weaknesses in Moltmann's account of the relational aspect of the kingdom. We will first consider how the flipside of the transposition of the logic of redemption we observed in the last chapter is the kenotic way in which Moltmann relates God to his creation. Next we will consider how this has some unfortunate implications for his understanding of God's rule. We will conclude with certain flaws in how Moltmann relates the church and the kingdom.

Deepening of Transposition

As we turn to how God is present to his creation we see that the flipside of the transposition of the biblical logic of redemption is the kenotic way in which Moltmann accounts for God's relationship to creation. The god-forsaken place in which creation exists is a space God has ceded within himself. The contradiction in creation finds its counterpart in God's own kenosis for creation.[131] The history of redemption is therefore the way in which God overcomes this double contradiction, how he who made communion with creation possible by ceding a space in himself for it orients himself toward the fulfillment of that relationship, when creation is transformed to be able to give God the space from which he will exist.

This has some significant implications for the problems we noted in Moltmann's transposition of the logic of redemption. First, the universalist trajectory in Moltmann's theology becomes a necessity. Since all creation exists in God and its life-force is the Spirit of God, if anything is lost, then something within and of God is lost. And then God cannot be fully God.[132] So, if God is to remain fully the God he is, in his coming, all that has ever lived must be vivified to its every lived moment.[133] In addition to the weak biblical and traditional basis for a necessary universalism, to make what is hoped for a necessity seems to rob humanity of precisely the freedom that Moltmann is elsewhere eager to

---

of Moltmann's early political theology, see Hunsinger's two articles on *The Crucified God* in *Heythrop Journal* vol. 14.

131. *GiC*, 88.
132. *CoG*, 132.
133. Ibid., xiii, 294–95.

protect, it forecloses the possibility of the unthinkable, to reject grace. Therefore, although Moltmann rightly points us to the universality of the hope born out of the cross and resurrection of Christ, it is equally necessary to maintain that men and women can ultimately reject the hope opened up in the Christ event.[134] But in the way Moltmann postulates the God-world relation, this is a possibility that cannot be left open without God ceasing to be God.

Second, because the status of God as God is dependent upon his overcoming of the contradiction that he freely endures for the sake of creation, it is difficult to see how God is not in need of redemption and therefore contingent upon his creation. Although Moltmann at times shies away from this,[135] he elsewhere seems to affirm this is the case.[136] God, in order to be God, is contingent on the future of his creation. If this is the case, it becomes difficult to see how God's history is rooted in the freedom of God's love primarily and not at least equally fundamentally in God's own need. Moltmann seems to acknowledge this when he says that creation is "bound up with the process of God's deliverance from the suffering of his love."[137] Since Moltmann, within his kenotic understanding of God's relation to his creation, can at best, claim that this need in God is rooted in God's own deliberation, he cannot affirm God's freedom from creation unreservedly, that God remains God whether creation exists or not—or will exist or not.

This results in certain other problems as well. First, it is difficult to accommodate God's need of redemption, even if a voluntarily adopted condition, to any kind of notion of God's perfection. Just as Moltmann is unable to affirm the unqualified goodness of creation, so he cannot affirm God's perfection without qualification, since God's eschatologi-

---

134. O'Donnell, "Saved by Hope," 78–79, notes how von Balthasar strikes this balance by both affirming that in Christ's death for all the possibility of hell is taken away, "hell has been emptied", and yet "the frightening possibility of rejecting God's only Son" remains and therefore hell is a possibility. "God takes our freedom seriously and it is possible to say no to Christ. But we must hope that no one has done this. We must hope that all men and women are saved. So Balthasar does not teach that hell is empty but he does affirm that we must hope that it is."

135. "God's Kenosis," 148.

136. E.g., in *CoG*, 333, he says: "If the necessity of sanctifying his Name springs from God's primordial self-restriction, then God has made himself in need of redemption through human beings."

137. *TKG*, 60.

cal perfection stands in contrast to and overcomes how he now exists in a contradiction.[138] Second, the distinction between God and creation which Moltmann affirms seems to be diluted when the being and identity of God are dependent upon the fate of his creatures.[139] Third, in the kenotic way Moltmann interprets God and his relationship to creation from the cross, he so emphasises the passive way in which God suffers in solidarity with his creation that the at least equally strong emphasis on God's transcendent holiness that at times is actively set against the world is lost; he says,

> God acts in the history of nature and human beings through his patient and silent presence, by way of which he gives those he has created space to unfold, time to develop, and power for their own movement. We look in vain for God in the history of nature or in human history if what we are looking for are special divine interventions."[140]

This may indeed be one of the ways God acts but if the history of salvation takes its cues from the biblical witness, this is hardly the only way he acts, a mere glance of Israel's history with her God bears abundant witness to that!

The Disappearance of God's Sovereignty

Moltmann has been critical of language of rule and obedience throughout his authorship. From early on he has set his own social trinitarianism in stark contrast to what he sees as a "monotheistic-monarchistic cosmology" where the one heavenly monarch corresponds to the one

---

138. A related question is whether the way he correlates the contradictions in God and creation renders God both co-temporal and co-spatial with his creation. On other problems in relation to space and time, see Torrance, "*Creatio ex Nihilo*."

139. A related concern is how one can account for creation in the eschaton. If God has to cede a space within himself for creation to exist, then how can there be any place for it in the eschaton? Would it not cease to exist or be absorbed into God? If one follows Moltmann's logic, it is difficult to see how the God-creation relation he affirms (cf. *GiC*, 89, 184) can be maintained. Bouma-Prediger, "Creation," 80, says: "While Moltmann claims that the eschatological kingdom 'does not imply a pantheistic dissolution of creation in God' (*GiC*, 89), it is not evident that his doctrine of creation actually allows him to preserve the otherness of God or affirm the integrity of creation" (cf. Walsh, "Theology of Hope," 75).

140. "God's Kenosis," 149.

emperor and his universal rule.[141] And although demand and obedience have a positive role in *Trinity and the Kingdom of God*, they do so only as the provisional form it takes in the freedom of the servant. It serves a temporary function in the relationship between God and his people, which is oriented toward the experience of mutual friendship. In later writings, reflecting an increased sensitivity especially to feminist and ecological critiques of power, he has increasingly substituted such language for ideas of reciprocity and mutual communion.[142] Thus, in his later work, although the Kingdom of God remains a pivotal symbol in his thought, talk about God's sovereignty and human obedience have all but disappeared.[143]

These concerns are certainly not without biblical precedent. Israel's kingship was initially seen as a compromise of the ideal of Israel's existence as God's people (1 Sam 8:1–9), a critique that functions to relativise the idea of kingship throughout the Old Testament (Deut 17:14–20). In the New Testament, before any functional structuring of the community, churches are first a band of brothers and sisters gathered around Jesus in which there is "no longer Jew or Greek, there is no longer slave or free, there is no longer male and female; for all of you are one in Christ Jesus" (Gal 3:28) and where hierarchical titles as Lord and Rabbi are abandoned (Matt 23:6–9).

However, this diminishing of God's sovereignty in Moltmann's theology has some significant problems of its own. First, although it can

---

141. Moltmann is heavily indebted in his critique of monotheism to Erik Peterson's "Der Monotheismus als Politisches Problem" (Peterson, *Theologische Traktate*, 45–147), whose basic thesis he adopts, that monotheism is fundamentally problematic because it functions to justify monarchical political power ("Dem *einen* König auf Erden entspricht der *eine* Gott, der *eine* König in Himmel und der *eine* königliche Nomos und Logos" [91]). Peterson claimed that this view of God was not native to Christianity but developed as an apologetic accommodation to the Roman empire, seen most clearly in Eusebius (89). The formulation of trinitarian thought, especially as seen in the Cappadocians, forms an important corrective to this trend. For a brief introduction to Peterson's thesis, see Ruggieri, "God and Power," 17–18. For Moltmann's indebtedness to Peterson, see *TKG*, 192–97 (cf. "Christian Theology"; "Inviting Unity," 50–57; cf. O'Donnell, *Trinity and Temporality*, 158).

142. See, e.g., his very personal account on his interaction with feminist theology in *EiT*, 268–92; for his ecological concerns, in addition to *GiC*, see *GSS*, 92–116, where he emphasises the link between modern notions of God's sovereignty and the present ecological crisis.

143. See e.g. *SW*, 64–66.

account for the egalitarian trajectories in Scripture, it does so in a very different way. The biblical vision of the community of the free, perhaps envisioned most strikingly in Rev 22:5 as a community in which all have become rulers and none are ruled, is precisely predicated upon the absolute sovereignty of God. The critique of monarchy in 1 Sam 8 is based in God as Israel's only true king.[144] Any form of human leadership is provisional and functional precisely because the position of absolute monarch is already filled by God. Similarly, the prophets severely criticised the tyrants of their own day on basis of God's sovereignty.[145] This is the same logic we find in the preaching of Jesus when he instructs his disciples—they are not to call anyone Rabbi or Lord because God is the only true Teacher and the only true Lord. This seems also to undergird Paul's logic in his statement of the abolition of the privileging that is based in social, cultural, ethnic, and gender distinction; now all have equal status because they are one in the Christ who is the sole ordering authority of the community.[146] The Scriptural witness does not fit into and thus questions the dichotomy Moltmann sets up between oppressive structures warranted in God's absolute sovereignty and the 'democratic' communion informed by God's almighty love.[147]

---

144. Otto, "Anti-Monotheism," 296, also notes that the reverse was the case, that although Israel's neighbours were polytheistic they had strong monarchical social systems. Otto, however, wrongly accuses Moltmann of seeing God as a "regulative idea to spur the transformation of contemporary inhumanity into future community" ("Anti-Monotheism," 303, 302; cf. Otto, "Resurrection," 86; Gilbert, "Theological Method," 172, 78). Although Moltmann is perfectly capable of such demythologising (see e.g. "Zwölf Bemerkungen"), he never does so in regard to God, Christ and the resurrection.

145. O'Donnell, "Trinity as Divine Community," 22.

146. In Gal 3:28, the social stratification implied in Paul's list is rendered invalid because "all of you are one in Christ Jesus."

147. On the problems of Peterson's thesis that Moltmann relies on, see Ruggieri, "God and Power," 18–20 who notes that K. Hungar's and A. Schindler's extensive study on Peterson (Schindler, *Monotheismus*) has devastated his thesis, "of Peterson's historical argument, hardly one stone remains on another" (Ruggieri, "God and Power," 18). The most fundamental flaw in Peterson's thesis, Ruggieri argues, is that historically there simply is no easy divide between how monotheism and trinitarian theology have been used politically, the latter has also been used to justify the use of state power, and the former to precisely critique the absolutisation of political power, as seen both in Islamic mystical tradition and in thinkers as Buber. Wanting to retain the urgency of Peterson's concern, Ruggieri, 20, notes that Eusebius' problem was not his monotheism but his over-realized eschatology, that the hope of the prophets was seen to be fulfilled in the Roman empire, and that "it is not monotheism as such, but a particular *use* of

Second, while Moltmann's vision of the way God's rule is oriented toward the freedom of humanity rightly emphasises how Jesus radically turns notion of power and rule on their head in his proclamation and own example,[148] this, neither in the Gospels or elsewhere in Scripture, negates the fact that God not only asserts the right of a sovereign but also exercises this right in decisive acts of judgment and redemption. For the biblical witnesses, the revelation in Christ that God's rule is fundamentally oriented toward the fulfillment of human freedom does not negate that it nevertheless is a rule in which the sovereign King orders the realm over which he rules according to his purposes, whether that is in judgment or salvation. For them, the center of the divine rule as servanthood does not negate the universal horizon of that rule as the undisputed claim of a holy God to sovereignty over his creation. In chapter 7 below I will try to show how the centrality of the Passion and the sovereignty of God that demands obedience are not irreconcilable but belong intrinsically together.

Third, while Moltmann's account of freedom in the kingdom of God can account well for the provisionality of any form of authority and how such authority ought to function for the liberation of people, it cannot easily account for the actuality of this authority. That is, if God's

---

it that makes it a function of a view of society in which order and the common good are assured by a sovereign will (whether this be of a ruler, a group or a class)." Precisely because of this, no conception of the Christian God is immune from any ideological framework that seeks to tear it "from its mystical horizon and functionally" tie it "to an ethical outlook" (21). Ruggieri suggests that it is precisely through an apophatic corrective to our understanding of God that such reductions are avoidable. One wonders whether some of Moltmann's problems are precisely due to an over-confidence in what we can know of God's immanent nature. For example, in "Inviting Unity," 57–58, he suggests that in the revelation of the Trinity from the communion of Father and Son "the one-sided patterns of domination and subjection are replaced by forms of community based on free agreement." Now this may be an admirable ideal, but if we pose *our* ideal as a necessary corollary to what we believe is the case of Trinity we are close to the same problem that Moltmann critiques, we have rooted a historically contingent human ideal that may seem self-evident to us (and who today dares critique democracy?) in the nature of God.

148. Consider, e.g., how in the context of his own approaching death, Jesus, in Luke 22, points to himself as the example of how the disciples are not be like the rulers of the world, but rather as Jesus, the one who is placed high is the servant of all. The radical nature of Jesus proclamation here is contextually emphasized as Luke places this teaching around the very table where Jesus has just anticipated his own death as a death for them.

rule in the end is simply reduced to his passion, his patient waiting for the other, it is hard to see how the conferral of any functional power to a provisional authority can ever be legitimate.

Fourth, the way in which Moltmann grounds the ideal of a reciprocal community in the inner-trinitarian communion of God, seems to imply a necessary correlation between God and his creatures. However, if one views creation as the free creation of God and not as an emanation or necessary counterpart to God, then such a correlation between the inner life of God and the human community is not self-evident. What human beings are is not predicated first upon *who God is* but whom *he has purposed them to be*. Human beings, as all other creatures, are embodied intentions. This is not to deny that there are correspondences between God and humanity, the language of the *imago dei* calls for that, but it is a claim that these correspondences are not necessary; rather, they are grounded in God's resolve. If the relationship between God and humanity, and with the whole created order, is grounded first in His purposes, then the fundamental relationship between God and creation must be seen in the economy, not first in the immanent Trinity.[149] In chapter 7 of this thesis we will return to these questions, trying to show how the sovereignty of God can be emphatically affirmed without a diminishing of human freedom if we ground the God-world relation in the relationship between the two natures of Christ rather than in the inner-trinitarian communion.

The Non-Exclusive Relationship of the Church to the Kingdom

Although it is crucial for Moltmann that the church of Christ exists as an anticipation of the kingdom, it is equally important for him not to link the church with the kingdom in an exclusive way. As the Spirit of Christ is at work both within and outside the church, the kingdom is not limited to the church, but is present in the world just as it is present in the church.

---

149. In a similar vein, Deane-Drummond notes that Moltmann "tends to indulge in too much speculation about the inner life of the Trinity in a way which does not seem to take account of the limits to our use of analogy in describing these relationships" (*Ecology*, 223).

A primary motive for Moltmann's emphasis on the non-exclusive relationship between the church and the kingdom is the devastating triumphalism that this has often led to.[150] In order to overcome this Moltmann argues that rather than seeing a sharp division between the Spirit's "world-sustaining operation" and his "activity in redemption," the two should be closely linked together. If this is recognized, "co-operation with people of different religions and secular ideologies" is made possible with neither the loss of the church's identity nor the need to draw up lines of demarcation.[151] Although Moltmann's concern to overcome Christian triumphalism in both ecclesial and secular realms is laudable and important, his proposal has some fundamental problems. Here we will consider how these are evident in his understanding of mission.

First, there seems to be a fundamental tension between what Moltmann labels quantitative and qualitative mission. In its qualitative mission the church ought not to draw people into the church, since this would fundamentally both compromise the nature of the inter-religious dialogue and deny the religions' own particular relationship to the coming kingdom. However, in its quantitative mission, this is precisely what the church does, call people away from their former ways to let their life be fundamentally reoriented in a commitment to Christ within ecclesial communities gathered in his presence. While Moltmann's understanding of qualitative mission may seem comprehensible in places where the church is already established, it seems to negate the validity of the missional approach that actually established the church there.

Second, if the church consists of those who have come to faith in and commit themselves to the way of Christ, then how, as Moltmann also claims, can those of other religions who within their own frame of reference become convinced of faith in Christ not become part of the church? The iconoclasm of the cross that Moltmann so rightly aims at the church must have the same devastating but redemptive effect on the religions as well. While there may be much in them that is retained and which may enrich the church as it spreads in the world, any religion that

---

150. See his criticism of political and clerical monotheism in *TKG*, 192–202, and of ecclesial millenarianism in *CoG*, 178–84.

151. *CPS*, 192.

finds faith in Jesus dies to itself and rises from the waters of its baptism into the living community gathered around Jesus, which is the church.[152]

Third this leads us to a fundamental tension in Moltmann's christological and pneumatological accounts of the kingdom. Christologically he argues: "The peculiar feature of his proclamation of the kingdom lies in the fact that nearness to, entry into, and inheritance of, the kingdom are bound by him to the decision of the hearers and their attitude to his own person. The future of the divine lordship is immediately bound up with the mystery of his own presence."[153]

This stands in tension to his pneumatological account where the kingdom is found in "everything that ministers to life," and therefore among all who do so.[154] It seems that if Moltmann is to maintain his position he needs to do some major adjustments to some of his core christological confessions, since if these are maintained, it is hard to see how the church as the kerygmatic community committed to him is not also the only community that can lay an exclusive claim to be those who now constitute the anticipatory presence of his kingdom.

---

152. See Bauckham's critique (*Theology of Jürgen Moltmann*, 146–50); he concludes, "in gaining this messianic direction, why should they not also, without forfeiting their distinctive potentialities for the kingdom, come to believe in Jesus as the Messiah of the kingdom? But then, as liberating movements of the Spirit, oriented to the kingdom and confessing Jesus Christ as Lord, they will, by Moltmann's definition, be his church."

153. *TH*, 217–18.

154. This fundamental tension can even be seen within particular passages in Moltmann. E.g., in *CPS*, 153–54, he says: "Outside Christ no salvation. Christ has come and was sacrificed for the reconciliation of the whole world. No one is excluded. Outside the salvation that Christ brings to all men there is therefore no church. The visible church is, as Christ's church, the ministry of reconciliation exercised upon the world. Thus the church is to be seen, not as absolute, but in its relationship to the divine reconciler and to reconciled men and women, whatever religion." Although Moltmann rightly points out that the salvation those have found that are in the church is not the church's but Christ's, this passage contains some fundamental logical problems: 1) If Christ was sacrificed for the reconciliation of this world, 2) and if the church is the ministry of reconciliation exercised on the earth, then 3) how can there be reconciled men and women in religions outside the church? Moltmann may reply that the fundamental ministry of reconciliation in the church is the kerygmatic proclamation that Christ reconciles the world to himself. However, if this reconciliation means bringing those near who otherwise are far off in sin, how can such a reconciliation be seen apart from entrance into the community gathered around Jesus? The church's proclamation of reconciliation to the world necessarily implies the movement into the sphere in which that proclamation is pronounced from.

Fourth, however, as Moltmann rightly observes, the Synoptic gospels, not only tie the approaching kingdom to Jesus but also see entrance into the kingdom as dependent upon the reception or rejection of Jesus' message.[155] Although the rest of the New Testament seldom uses the language of the kingdom of God, it reflects the same kind of exclusive relationship between Jesus and those gathered in his name. Redemption is only found in Jesus and is only experienced in the communities that consist of those who have heard and received the message about him. If we understand the fulfillment of this redemption as "the kingdom of God," this would suggest that the church now is the people that experiences his kingdom and are a part of it. They are the "sphere" in which the kingdom is present in anticipatory ways, the "sphere" where Christ is the Lord who is present with them in the Spirit.

Thus, biblical tradition and even fairly important strands of Moltmann's own theology seem to go against his own view of the respective relationships of the church and the world to the kingdom. Precisely because of this it seems that the qualitative mission of the church must always have a quantitative element to it, not because the church believes it is something superior in itself, but precisely because it believes that the relationship it stands in, and the only one in which it can stand and be the church, is qualitatively different in its relationship to the kingdom than any other relationship.

We are then lead right back to what Moltmann fundamentally wants to reject, that the church, as the congregations of believers that are gathered around Jesus and committed to and shaped by his person and history, stands in a qualitatively different relationship to the kingdom than any other human institution or social structure. But can such an exclusive relationship between the church and the kingdom be affirmed without relapsing into the triumphalism Moltmann so rightly critiques? If the church is the only "sphere" in which the coming kingdom is present, why should it not seek to enforce it now? And if the kingdom is only experienced in the church, is it not impossible to affirm anything outside it as the workings of the Spirit that orients the world toward its redemption? In our discussion on the relationship between the church and the kingdom in the book of Revelation, we will suggest that such lines of enquiry indeed can account for some of the excesses Moltmann

155. *WJC*, 94ff.

5

The Crisis of the Kingdom and the Book of Revelation

Crisis and the Kingdom of God in Moltmann

CONSIDERING OUR DISCUSSION ON THE POST-WAR CONTEXT THAT forms the backdrop for the origins of Moltmann's theology, we can discern a two-fold crisis to which he develops his understanding of the kingdom in response. First is the devastating failure of modern Protestant notions of the kingdom and their secular counterparts.[1] The dream that the kingdom of God was progressing to its fulfillment in European civilisation went literally up in flames in the two world wars. The enlightened dream of establishing the kingdom on earth with the newly found powers of humanity turned into a nightmare, showing what happens when the hope for the kingdom of God migrates to the powers to be. Moltmann responds to this crisis by the way he develops the historical axis of the kingdom. The future of the world in the kingdom of God is not seen at the head of the progress of civilisation but in the resurrection of the crucified one. As such it is a hope in the ruins of history and hope for the victims of history. Second, the flipside of the demise of the kingdom of Cultural Protestantism is the apparent absence of God in the relentless suffering of the world. Where is the God of the kingdom when fire rains on Hamburg, when Hiroshima blows up in an atomic blaze, and when the first people of the kingdom are systematically exterminated in Auschwitz? Theology must come to terms with that "the suffering of a single innocent child is an irrefutable

---

1. In the introductory discussion we saw how Moltmann's particular response to this was also responding to the often "other-worldly" hope of traditional Christianity and the disengagement from history in existential theology.

rebuttal of the notion of the almighty and kindly God in heaven."[2] For Moltmann, as is evident from our discussion of the relational aspect on the kingdom, the answer is found in God's paradoxical presence in the cross of Christ. As God has overcome the fundamental condition of the world by entering death on the cross, God is seen to be present in the "crosses" of history. He is present with the victims of history and precisely in being present to them, opens up the history of the whole world to its eschatological fulfillment in the coming of his kingdom. The coming of the kingdom of glory is anticipated in God's presence in the passion of the world.

Crisis and the Book of Revelation

Early Christianity and a Crisis of the Kingdom

Despite the obvious social, cultural and historical differences between the two, Revelation reflects a similar two-fold crisis of the kingdom as seen in Moltmann.[3] First, the emergence of Christianity occurs within an escalating crisis of first century Judaism which resulted in the cataclysmic events of AD 70.[4] If Revelation was written toward the end of the first century, as most commentators assume,[5] then John writes after

---

2. *TKG*, 47.

3. In the following introduction to Revelation, I will only touch on critical issues of date, authorship, historical setting and genre as they relate directly to the concerns under consideration here. For recent and thorough discussions on various introductory matters, see Beale, *Revelation*, 3–177; and Aune, *Revelation 1–5*, xlvii–ccxi. For a briefer introduction that also contains a current overview of important works in Revelation research, see Witherington, *Revelation*, 1–64. On the history of interpretation, see Wainwright, *Mysterious Apocalypse*; Rowland, *Revelation* (NIB), 528–556; and Kovacs and Rowland, *Revelation*. For a recent survey of methodological developments in the study of Revelation, see Prigent, *Apocalypse*, 1–22. Another question circles around whether the book is a unitary whole. Here I assume the unity of book, a position I believe is sufficiently established in readings and interpretations of the book that focus on the way themes and symbols are used throughout the book (see, e.g., Bauckham, *Climax of Prophecy*).

4. "The impact of the fall of Jerusalem in 70 CE on Christians as well as Jews rivals the issue of the Delay of the Parousia as a catalyst for the interpretation of early Christian writings" (Rowland, *Christian Origins*, 296).

5. Of the two most common proposals, placing the book either toward the end of Domitian's reign, around AD 95, or shortly after Nero's death, around AD 68–69, I prefer the former. However, although a Neronic date would change some of the particular ways I will develop my argument, its basic thrust would remain the same. For a succinct

the last vestiges of the physical manifestation of Israel as the geopolitical people of God have been demolished.[6] Although some would interpret the devastation of Jerusalem and the subsequent dispersion of Palestinian Jews as judgment, the question remained why God would allow a Pagan empire to first occupy the promised land and eventually destroy its religio-political institutions. On one level this crisis was resolved for the early Christians as they believed that Jesus had anticipated the fall of Jerusalem because the city had rejected him, and since they believed that the kingdom was now centered in Jesus and was awaiting its earthly manifestation in his parousia.[7] But on another level, this resolution also intensified the crisis for Christians. If Jesus was the Messiah who had won the pivotal battle of the kingdom at Easter, if he, as this one, was the one through whom the rule of God was exercised, and if the believers in Jesus were the people of this kingdom, why did they repeatedly find themselves on the religious and political margins of society? Second, and closely related to this concern, is the question of the apparent absence of the rule of God. The reason why the early Christians do not find themselves in the socio-religious center as befits those who have pledged their unyielding allegiance to the ruler of the cosmos is the lack of any geopolitical manifestation of the divine rule on earth.

Although the modern context Moltmann speaks from and responds to often states this question abstractly or conceptually (how can we believe in a God in the midst of suffering?), it is not that different

---

overview of the main proposals for the date of Revelation, see Collins, "Revelation, Book of," 700–701; for the Domitian date see Witherington, *Revelation*, 4–5; and for recent extensive considerations of the question, see Aune, *Revelation 1–5*, lvi–lxx; Beale, *Revelation*, 4–27.

6. Although Rev 11:1–2 is most likely to be read metaphorically, it probably also harkens back to the events of AD 70, a fact that may be suggested in how Jerusalem is identified as Sodom, another city that was destroyed for its sins (Witherington, *Revelation*, 4). Richard, *Apocalypse*, 90, suggests that John with the measuring of the temple signifies that the Christian community receives what the temple hierarchs were not able to do, "save the community." Although the memory of the collapse of Jerusalem is likely in the background here, I find it unlikely that the imagery should be read in the overtly literal terms proposed by certain preterist interpretations of the text (see, e.g., du Rand and Song, "Partial Preterist").

7. The transformation of Jerusalem into "Sodom and Egypt" in Revelation 11 is closely associated with the death of Jesus in the city, perhaps suggesting that the judgment on Jerusalem is for rejecting Jesus as her Messiah (cf. Luke 20:41–46; 21:5–36).

from the concrete question of the absence of an actual manifestation of God's kingdom. Both are deeply concerned with how we can affirm our confession about what we believe is true about God in the midst of a situation that seems to suggest otherwise. In Revelation, the deep pathos of this incongruence is seen in the cry of the martyrs: "How long, Sovereign Lord, holy and true, until you judge the inhabitants of the earth and avenge our blood?" (6:10).

Crisis and Kingdom Language in Revelation

Adela Yarbro Collins says "it was the tension between John's vision of the kingdom of God and his environment that moved him to write his Apocalypse."[8] This claim is confirmed when we consider how the book employs both the βασιλεία ("kingdom," "rule," "political authority") word group[9] and other political language.[10] "Kingdom" language is used of two distinct groups, God and his kingdom and the kingdom whose ultimate source of authority is the primordial enemy of God, Satan.[11]

From the outset of the book God is assumed to be the Creator who is enthroned in heaven[12] and we are told that Jesus is "the ruler of the kings of the earth" (1:5). This picture is sustained throughout: Jesus is the king of kings (17:14; 19:16) whose ultimate rule over the earth alongside God is anticipated from the outset and is most fully described in the final visions (21:1—22:8).[13] Although the eschatological kingdom

---

8. Collins, *Crisis and Catharsis*, 106.

9. βασιλεία (1:6, 9; 5:10; 11:15; 12:10; 16:10; 17:12, 17, 18), βασιλεύω (5:10; 11:15, 17; 19:6; 20:4, 6; 22:5), βασιλεύς (1:5; 6:15; 9:11; 10:11; 15:3; 16:12, 14; 17:2, 9, 12 (x2), 17:14, 18; 18:3, 9; 19:16, 18, 19; 21:24), βασίλισσα (18:7).

10. Not only do the titles and depictions of God and Christ have strong political overtones, as we will discuss later, but central to the whole book is a battle between God and the Dragon over the sovereignty of the earthly realm. See Bauckham, *Climax of Prophecy*, 210–37 for an insightful discussion on the book as a Christian war scroll.

11. βασιλεία and its cognates are almost exclusively used either of God, Christ and the saints, or of the Dragon and its cohorts. The only exceptions is 9:11 where we find ᾿Αββαδών/ ᾿Απολλύων as the king of the abyss who obviously is not seen as part of God's court but yet is the ruler of the army who inflicts God's punishment on God's opponents.

12. Revelation 1:4 anticipates the fuller depiction of God as the sovereign creator of heaven and earth in ch. 4; cf. 15:3.

13. That 21:1—22:5 depicts the ultimate reign of God and the Lamb is apparent in 21:24 where earthly kings acknowledge God's sovereignty by bringing their glory into the city that is defined by and lives from the occupants of the throne at its center.

covers the whole earth, the only ones who are identified with it in history are the churches to whom John writes: the ἐκκλησίαι ("churches" or "congregations") of Jesus' followers are created in his death to be a βασιλεία ("kingdom") to God (1:6; 5:9–10), and as God's kingdom they are destined to rule the earth (5:10). Although the saints' rule is not to be seen in the same terms as the co-regency of God and the Lamb, it nevertheless is seen as sharing in Christ's dominion over the earth (3:21; 20:4–6; 22:5).[14] Thus, Jesus as the co-regent of God is the king of all earthly authorities, and his followers both constitute a kingdom to God and are destined to share in his sovereignty.

However, the picture of the sovereignty of God and the churches as the people of God's kingdom stands in an unbearable tension to a rival kingdom that now holds sway over the whole world and whose ultimate authority is the arch opponent of God, Satan. This is assumed from the beginning of the book, and from chapter 12 onwards John gives a firm picture of this opposing power. The Dragon, the imagery used of Satan in Rev 12, has established his rival authority on earth by raising a beast, cast in his own image[15] from the chaotic sea and has conferred his own authority to it (12:18—13:2). Through this beast the Dragon is able to gain authority over the whole world (13:3b–4a), and through a second beast, raised from the earth, it solidifies its authority through a religious mystification of its power. The second beast deceives the inhabitants of the world through various miraculous signs to worship the first beast (13:12–14) and forces them to exercise all their commerce within the context of their allegiance to the first beast (13:16–17). Refusing to submit to this blasphemous usurpation of the honor and authority that rightfully is only God's comes at the risk of one's own life (13:15).

It is this beastly order that now holds the βασιλεία, the political authority, over the world (cf. 16:10). The book identifies its geopolitical center as Babylon. This is the great city that rides on the Beast (17:3), who identifies herself as a queen (18:7), and as the center of geopolitical authority has a βασιλεία over the kings of the earth (17:18). While these vassal kings and their ruling elites fornicate with this queen-city

---

14. That the saints remain God's subjects when they exercise their rule is clearly seen in 22:3–5 where it is precisely the δοῦλοι of God who λατρεύσουσιν him, who also are those who βασιλεύσουσιν.

15. Note the strong parallels between the depiction of the beast in 13:1 and of the Dragon in 12:3.

as they enjoy her unjust wealth (17:2; 18:3, 9), the people who have pledged their allegiance to the Christ who is King of Kings and Lord of Lords (19:16; cf. 1:5) are killed by her (17:6).

This is the fundamental "tension between John's vision of the kingdom of God and his environment" that Revelation responds to. While John paints the opposition the followers of Jesus face in the mythic language of Dragon, Beasts and Babylon, there is little doubt that he has Rome, its imperial power and cult in mind as the current manifestation Satan's draconic power. Since the publication Leonard L. Thompson work, *The Book of Revelation: Apocalypse and Empire*,[16] the claim that there was systematic persecution of Christians during the reign of Domitian has been challenged. More recently, however, some scholars have questioned the more benevolent picture of Domitian Thompson proposes, arguing that there indeed was a hardening of attitudes toward Christians during his reign.[17] Considering this and the important religio-political function of imperial cults in Asia Minor,[18] the congregations John wrote to probably "experienced local harassment, ridicule, discrimination and oppression in the early 90s for their religious beliefs and customs," even if there was no centrally orchestrated persecution.[19] Whatever the case might have been, Barr rightfully points out that "Pliny's letter to Trajan shows that that situation in Asia Minor soon lived up to John's worst expectations."[20] John saw clearly that the Christian rejection of calling anyone but Christ Lord and Savior is on a head on-collision with the imperial cult that claimed the same for the emperor.[21] In the end, whether Revelation was written in the context

---

16. Thompson, *Revelation*; cf. Collins, *Crisis and Catharsis* and "Vilification."

17. See Witherington, *Revelation*, 5–8 for a review of recent critiques of Thompson's hypothesis.

18. See Friesen, *Imperial Cults*; he argues that John may indeed have used the common opposition of the entire congregation to the imperial cults to address specific disputes among them (Friesen, "Satan's Throne"). See also Kraybill's extensive study of the Imperial cult in Revelation; for him the New Jerusalem is the final counterpart to the decadence and injustice of Rome and its imperial cult, and "John is willing to pay any social, political or economic price to be true to his Lord" (*Imperial Cult*, 221).

19. Slater, "Social Setting," 241, as quoted in Witherington, *Revelation*, 8.

20. Barr, "Apocalypse," 41.

21. Beale, *Revelation*, 5. Witherington, *Revelation*, 5–6, points out that although it is at times questioned whether Domitian called himself *dominus* and *deus*, the evidence points in the direction that he did.

of actual or anticipated persecution, what remains is that it "represents a view from those who do not have access to political or economic power,"[22] and that "from John's perspective, 'Eternal Rome' could only translate as 'Eternal Oppression.'"[23] And what John anticipates "is an impending battle between the Lamb and the monster," between, from the perspective of earth, a handful and often disunited and compromised churches and "the political power and economic splendor of 'the great city that holds sway over the kings of earth' (xvii. 18)."[24]

To link the symbolic imagery of Babylon and beasts with Rome and the nature of Roman imperial power in the latter half of the first century, however, does not mean that the one is the other,[25] but rather that for John, Rome is the present manifestation of what Babylon represents, the prostitute "is Babylon transferred to Rome."[26] As such, the image of Babylon helps us to understand the true nature of what Rome is, and how John clothes Rome in the image of Babylon further develops the character of Babylon as the topos of the power that is antithetical to the kingdom of God. Babylon was first the prime enemy of Israel. As Babylon became the enemy of God in the way it took his people captive, this city was transformed into a primary symbol of God's opposition on

---

22. Gilbertson, *God and History*, 72.

23. McDonough, *YHWH at Patmos*, 199, referring to Kraybill, *Imperial Cult*, 57–101. John "is not giving an objective evaluation of the accomplishments of Rome" but makes "clear-eyed" observations as he expresses "a radical and complete rejection from the perspective of the lowest and most tangential classes, that is from the perspective of the victims" (Wengst, "Babylon," 196, 197, 196).

24. Caird, *Revelation* (2nd ed.), xiii.

25. N. T. Wright is in danger of doing this. Building on Caird's observation that the mythic language used in Revelation was employed in both Jewish and Greco-Roman circles "for the interpretation of history in the interest of religious or political debate" (Caird, *Revelation* [2nd ed.], xi), Wright claims that apocalyptic "uses 'cosmic' or 'otherworldly' language to describe (what we think of as) 'this-worldly' realities, and to invest them with (what we think of as) their 'theological' or 'spiritual' significance" (*Jesus and the Victory of God*, 513). Elsewhere he claims "apocalyptic language uses complex and highly colored metaphors in order to describe one event in terms of another, thus bringing out the perceived 'meaning' of the first" (Wright, *The New Testament and the People of God*, 282). Although Wright, like Caird, *Revelation* [2nd ed.], xv, does not deny that the referent of apocalyptic symbolism may go beyond its historical referent, he so focuses on this referent that the larger cosmic conflict the historical reality is set in at times gets lost, thus binding the mythic symbol too tightly to one of its particular historical manifestations.

26. O'Donovan, "Political Thought," 83.

earth. When John employs the language of Babylon for Rome, he then both casts Rome in the role of God's arch enemy but also, precisely in doing so, expands the semantic field of the symbol itself. In this way, the symbolic imagery of the book is best seen as open and bounded at the same time.[27] Its referent is not arbitrary but must be read within the tradition of the symbol as it takes form in John's text. And this picture is enriched by how John likely related the symbolism of Babylon and beasts with the religious and political situation of his own day. But precisely because John did not identify Rome as Rome but employed the imagery of Babylon and beasts, the imagery cannot be confined to his own day but is always ready to be employed anew in new manifestations of the old evil in its conflict with the ways of God. What we noted about texts generally in the introductory chapter is especially true of the pensive symbolic world of John's vision, its imagery grow with the journey of its history in the world. While the porous boundaries of such language may frustrate the analytic mind, it extends a wealth of wisdom to those willing to receive it since

> like the newspaper cartoons which make a political comment more tellingly than any editorial, however skilfully written, the resources of apocalyptic imagery can conjure in the imagination a grasp of reality and offer an instrument to understand reality with the result that the reader is stimulated to change it. It is a mode of discourse which taps deep wells of human responsiveness among those who through the experience of struggle, persecution and death have learnt what it means to wash their robes and to make them white in the blood of the Lamb.[28]

As Israel in exile had to come to terms with what it meant to be God's people when held captive by the enemy of God, so John seeks to show how the people of the messianic Lamb can make sense of their own situation when oppressed by the power that fills the shoes of Babylon in their own day. In this way, he equips his hearers to persevere in resistance to it. In the next two chapters, we will consider how John does this in his employment of kingdom language, ideas and imagery. But before we proceed, we will first look at how both the generic ele-

---

27. Humphrey reflects the same sentiment, noting that while the symbolism is "evocative, polyvalent, allusive and sometimes elusive" and thus is open to a range of readings, this does not mean "it can mean anything and everything" (*Ladies*, 20–21).

28. Rowland and Corner, *Liberating Exegesis*, 134–35.

ments of the book as well as its use of spatial and temporal categories are fundamentally oriented toward resolving the tension the crisis of the kingdom John and his readers experience, while at the same time intensifying this experience.

The Formal Character and Spatio-Temporal Expansion of Reality in Revelation

The next two chapters frequently employ the language of spatial and temporal expansion developed by Michael Gilbertson in his study, *God and History in the Book of Revelation*. Since Gilbertson ties his own study closely with how he understands the composite generic form of Revelation, we will conclude this introduction to Revelation by considering both how Gilbertson believes the generic elements of the book and its use of spatial and temporal categories function in the overall purpose of the book.

As most recent commentators do, Gilbertson notes how apocalyptic, prophetic and epistolary features are combined in Revelation,[29] and he argues that this reflects a twofold dynamic: as "temporal and spatial horizons are expanded *outward*" there is also a "heavy *inward* concentration on the meaning of the text for the present."[30] Its apocalyptic features give the book "a universal scope of history and ultimate temporal and spatial perspectives."[31] However, that this is not the pessimistic escapism that apocalyptic at times has been accused of[32] is reinforced by

---

29. For other excellent studies on the generic elements in the book, see Bauckham, *Theology of the Book of Revelation*, 1–23; Beasley-Murray, *Revelation*, 12–29; "Revelation," 1025–27.

30. Gilbertson, *God and History*, 79.

31. On apocalyptic literature and related concerns, see especially Collins, *Apocalyptic Imagination*. While Collins adapts his earlier work (cf. vols 14 and 36 of *Semeia*) in light of Rowland's critique that apocalyptic and eschatology are "two separate issues in Jewish Religion" (Rowland, *Open Heaven*, 48), he still maintains that eschatology ought to be at least one basic elements in generic discussions on apocalyptic literature (*Apocalyptic Imagination*, 10).

32. Consider, e.g., von Rad's sweeping generalization of apocalyptic as a degeneration of Israel's prophetic tradition which dispenses "with the phenomenon of the contingent" (as quoted in Gilbertson, *God and History*, 74). Rowland offers a more measured assessment when he says: "The attitude towards the present age, such as we have it in the apocalypses, arises not so much from the conviction that the present world was too corrupt for the establishment of God's kingdom, but from the frank admission that without God's help the dominance of Israel and the coming of the new age could never

its claim to be a prophecy and by its employment of epistolary features. These relate the apocalyptic horizon of the book to the present situation that John and the ecclesial communities he writes to face. As a prophecy of the "inauguration of the end-time in the Christ event" it calls its hearers to situate themselves according to the light this event sets the world in,[33] and as an apocalyptic-prophetic vision wrapped in a letter[34] it calls its readers to interpret the large, sweeping and universal language of the vision within their own concrete situations. As such, Revelation does not provide its readers with a chronology or philosophy of history but rather gives them a key to the dynamic of history, sets the difficult situation they find themselves in within a larger perspective that also spans past, present and future.[35]

In order to do this, John sets his readers' present situation within a wider reality through a visionary expansion of both space and time. Noting especially Rowland's claim that apocalyptic literature opens up a transcendent reality in order to meet the needs of the community it is written for, Gilbertson argues that in John's spatial expansion of reality, John first places the present earthly experience of the churches (chs. 2–3) in tension with what is confessed in heaven (ch. 4).[36] The rest of the book then sets out to resolve this tension in a set of movements from heaven to earth which culminates in the descent of the

---

be achieved. . . . The eschatology of the apocalypses may have looked to God at work in history as the only means of final salvation, but their authors expected a vindication of their righteousness within the world of men, not in some intangible, existence beyond the sphere of history" (Rowland, *Open Heaven*, 38). This aptly describes the situation John and his fellow believers face vis-à-vis Roman imperial power. Although, Revelation, as such, is deterministic in its expectation of the final accomplishments of God's purposes in judgment and redemption, it leaves radically open who will fall on what side of the eschatological judgment. How one will fare is contingent upon how one orients oneself toward the coming kingdom of God in history.

33. Gilbertson, *God and History*, 79. See Schüssler Fiorenza (*Justice and Judgment*, 133–56) on a plausible context for Revelation in early Christian prophetic tradition. She argues this tradition was rooted in "early Christian apocalyptic experience and conviction" and that for John it was "his belief that the end time has been inaugurated in the death and resurrection of Jesus Christ [which] constitutes the heart and inspiration of his prophecy" (138).

34. See Karrer, *Johannesoffenbarung als Brief* on the epistolary features of the text.

35. For a good discussion of how history has been read in the book, see Gilbertson, *God and History*, 45–57.

36. Ibid., 81–82.

New Jerusalem to the earthly plane. However, John does not conclude his book with the resolution of the spatial dissonance in 22:5, but in his epistolary epilogue draws his readers back to the concrete situation they find themselves in. He calls them back to their situation where the dissonance between heaven and earth is acutely experienced. It is here they are to remain faithful to the vision they have heard. Thus, "the text has the effect of locating the present earthly experience of the reader within a framework of ultimate reality. It also, however, refocuses back to the hard realities of earthly experience, now seen in the light of that ultimate perspective."[37]

Gilbertson argues that the book accomplishes basically the same in the way it employs temporal categories. Although the sequence of the book cannot be set within any tight temporal scheme, whether chronological or as recapitulation, it still displays an irreducibly temporal view of reality.[38] John places the present situation of his readers within a temporal framework that encompasses the primordial past, runs through the recent past, and expects the penultimate future that will usher in the ultimate future. Rome might claim to be the eternal kingdom but God and his Christ are the only ones who truly span all temporal categories. God's claim to sovereignty is based in his status as the creator of the cosmos and in the certainty of his *de facto* rule on earth as established in the paradoxical victory of Easter. The penultimate eschatological events of the establishment of this kingdom are immanent for John's readers and are already making their coming presence known in the

---

37. Ibid., 108; similarly Beale, *Revelation*, 151, argues that how the vision of "the sovereignty of God and Christ in redeeming and judging [which] brings them glory" intends to motivate the readers to persevere in worshipping God and in obedience to his word.

38. Gilbertson, *God and History*, 109. Rather than presenting a chronological sequence of events, the book employs a variety of ways to place the present of the reader in the light of the ultimate and penultimate past as well as the ultimate and penultimate future. In expanding the temporal situation of the reader both backwards and forward, John seeks to refocus his readers' on their present, in the dissonance between their present and their ultimate future in the New Jerusalem (114). Similarly, Schüssler Fiorenza notes that "Revelation does not describe . . . a continuous development of events . . . Rather Revelation consists of pieces or mosaic stones arranged in a certain design, which climaxes in a description of the final eschatological event" (*Justice and Judgment*, 47). For a helpful overview of the basic implied narrative of Revelation, see Garrow, *Revelation*, 103–17.

suffering they experience.³⁹ Although these penultimate events mean an increased conflict between the people of God and his enemies, they find their ultimate resolution in the final victory of God and his Christ in the descent of the New Jerusalem, which geopolitical center is the throne of God and the Lamb.

The spatial and the temporal expansions of reality work together to accomplish John's theological-pastoral purpose. The resolution of the spatial tension set up in Rev 2:1—4:11 is from ch. 5 onwards seen as a long process where this dissonance is first intensified before eventually being resolved in the descent of the new city, which in return is "also a starting point, from which the readers of the text must work as they face once again the present reality portrayed in the earlier visions."⁴⁰ Although critiquing how Thompson sees the unitive vision of the book, Gilbertson quotes him in order to show how the intrinsic relationship between the book's temporal and spatial categories never allows the readers to escape to a heaven above them or a future in front of them. Thompson comments:

> A radical transcendence which could sever heaven from earth is tempered by the future transformation of earthly into heavenly existence; and a radical transcendence which could sever this age completely from the age to come is tempered by the presentness of the age to come in heaven. Thus, the presence and interplay of spatial and temporal dimensions in transcendence prevent a thoroughgoing dualism in which the revelation of transcendence would become a separate set of forces without present effect on everyday human activity.⁴¹

Considering how we already have discussed the kingdom in Moltmann along similar lines, these temporal and spatial notions are a helpful way to organize the book's understanding of the kingdom. In the next chapter we will do this by looking at how the book envisions the ultimate future as a regime change that turns the readers' vision of

---

39. Rowland, *Revelation* (Epworth), 61, notes that "what must soon take place" in 1:1 and 22:7 "may refer to the imminent expectation of the end of the age, but more likely concerns the imminence (indeed reality) of the *presence* of the whole eschatological process in the midst of which the readers need to be aware that they are now standing."

40. Gilbertson, *God and History*, 109.

41. Thompson, *Revelation*, 31. On the interlacing of temporal and spatial categories, Gilbertson also refers to Howard-Brook and Gwyther, *Unveiling Empire*, 120ff.

the world upside down and calls them to live in light of the future where God and his Christ will assume the position of geopolitical authority that now is in the hands of the beastly order whose power is centerd in Babylon. In chapter seven we will look at how this expectation is grounded in the vision's spatial expansion of reality where God, as creator, is revealed to be the true sovereign over both heaven and earth, how he and the Lamb already are established as the authoritative center of the heavenly realm, and how the paradoxical victory of the Lamb on earth is now being extended to the world through the kerygmatic witness of the church in the power and presence of the Spirit. In the latter part of these chapters we will enter into a dialogue with our discussion of the historical and relational aspect of the kingdom in Moltmann respectively.

6

The Future as Regime Change

Introduction

HOPE DRIVES THE BOOK OF REVELATION. FROM THE OUTSET IT SETS the present in the context of the urgency of the future[1] and it moves relentlessly toward the eschatological climax of the descent of the New Jerusalem (21:1—22:5).[2] God is depicted as the coming one (1:4, 8; 4:8) and the book expects the arrival of Christ from the beginning (1:7). Obedience and perseverance are encouraged with the promise of future rewards[3] and evil and disobedience come with a warning of punishment.[4]

Revelation 11:15-19 is the most succinct statement of the book's eschatological hope and it will form the basis of this exposition of how Revelation sees the future as a "regime change," the time when the powers that now have usurped the position of authority in the world will be defeated, the time when God will occupy the authoritative center in the earthly realm that is rightfully his. In our analysis of this passage, we will begin by looking at how the martyrs' prayer for vindication (6:9-11) is a central theme in 8:6—11:19, and how the whole section anticipates the seventh trumpet (11:15-19) as containing the fulfilment of God's final

1. However one interprets ἃ δεῖ γενέσθαι ἐν τάχει in 1:1 and similar phrases (1:19; 4:1; see Beale, *Revelation*, 152-70, 181-2, 216 on various views), it alerts the reader to something that is coming and impinges on his or her present situation.

2. Note how both 20:1-10 and 21:5ff are anticipated in the addresses to the churches (2:7, 11, 26; 3:5, 12, 21; cf. 7:14-17; 15:4).

3. 2:7, 10b, 11, 17, 26-29; 3:4-6, 9-13, 20-21; 7:14-17; 14:13.

4. 2:16, 21-25; 3:3b; 3:16; 14:9-12; 16:5-6, 19; 17:11; 18:2-8, 20. As sure as the establishment of God's eschatological purposes (10:6-7; 15:11; cf. 16:5, 7, 15; 19:9) is the inevitability of his judgments (20:11-15; cf. 21:7-8; 22:11, 12, 14).

eschatological purpose. Then, in a detailed analysis of 11:15–19, we will consider how the seventh trumpet depicts this fulfilment as a regime change in which "our Lord and his Messiah" will replace the powers that now occupy the central position of geopolitical authority on earth. On basins of this analysis, we will both consider how central themes in 11:15–19 are developed in the rest of the book, and place our exposition of "regime change" in Revelation in dialogue with the kingdom as symbol of hope in Moltmann.

The Seventh Trumpet: Heralding a Regime Change

The Function of the Trumpet Sequence

With the blowing of the seventh trumpet in 11:15–19 we reach the conclusion of the trumpet sequence that commences in 8:6. As in the sequences of the seals and the bowls, the seven trumpets focus on God's judgment on the earth.[5] While the seals are likely an overture to the following visionary complex as a whole[6] and the bowls depict God's final eschatological judgment of his opponents on earth (15:1), the seven trumpets are concerned with God's acts of judgment on the world in history.[7]

First, we note two things: the prayers of the martyrs play an important role in the heavenly commissioning of the angels who blow their trumpets,[8] and the first six trumpets are patterned after the plagues

---

5. Beale, *Revelation*, 611. For the main views of the relationship between the three numbered series and how they function in the overall structure of the book, see Beale, *Revelation*, 117–317 who argues for a "structure of recapitulation" but with a thematic intensification of the book's basic themes (cf. Beasley-Murray, *Revelation*, 31); Bauckham *Climax of Prophecy*, 8, suggests that while the seventh of each series refers to the end, each new series approaches this end "from closer range, as it were."

6. Bauckham, *Theology of the Book of Revelation*, 80; cf. Beckwith, *Apocalypse*, 263–64; Campbell, "Findings," 71. Against some commentators who see the content of the scroll being unfolded with the breaking of the seals (Charles, *Revelation*, vol. 1., 161; Aune, *Revelation 6–16*, 392), see Bauckham, *Climax of Prophecy*, 250.

7. Bauckham, *Theology of the Book of Revelation*, 82 (cf. Beasley-Murray, *Revelation*, 156; Caird, *Revelation*, 112); similarly Beale, *Revelation*, 472 but he sees the judgments wholly in negative terms.

8. The incense of the censers in 5:8 is the prayer of the saints. In 6:10 we see these are the martyrs' prayer for vengeance on those who have slain them. While 6:12–17 briefly anticipates the divine response, 8:1–5 makes clear that the trumpets will flesh out this concern, since the prayers play a significant role in the preparation for the blowing of

brought on Egypt.⁹ Since the prayers of the slain saints in heaven is for vindication (6:9-11) and since the purpose of the plagues on Egypt was to punish Pharaoh for his persistence in oppressing Israel and to liberate Israel, the trumpet punishments are probably meant to vindicate the saints and prepare for their final liberation from their oppressors.[10] However, second, Richard Bauckham has convincingly argued that an equally important function of God's judgments in history is to bring the nations to repentance.[11] Thus God's punishment does not have solely a negative purpose vis-à-vis the world but is administered in the hope that it will bring the nations to repentance, that they too will be followers of the Lamb in the pilgrimage to the promised kingdom.

However, we are faced with a problem: at the end of the sixth trumpet, the inhabitants of the world, despite the severe punishment of God, "did not repent" of their idolatry and injustice (9:20-21). The sequences of intensified judgments are perhaps broken off here precisely because of the futility of punishment alone to bring repentance.[12] Instead, John is shown the place the church has in the task. It is as the churches are faithful in their role as witnesses, even to the point of death, that what the trumpets failed to do is accomplished: the resurrection of the two martyred witnesses brings the nations to repentance, "the survivors were terrified and gave glory to the God of heaven" (11:13).[13] This brings us

---

the trumpets (Aune, *Revelation 6-16*, 512-13; Bauckham, *Climax of Prophecy*, 9, 55, 71, 75-76; Beale, *Revelation*, 454-55; Beasley-Murray, *Revelation*, 150-51; Harrington, *Revelation*, 104; Witherington, *Revelation*, 138-39) See Heil, "Fifth Seal," 220-43 on the pivotal role of 6:9-11 in the book.

9. For the use of the Exodus plagues in Revelation, see Aune, *Revelation 6-16*, 499-508; cf. Harrington, *Revelation*, 107; Prigent, *Apocalypse*, 305-6.

10. Beale, *Revelation*, 620 notes that in 1 Chr 16:4; Num 10:10 and Psalm 150 trumpets are blown to call Israel to thank God for how he has dealt graciously with them in the past. If this is part of the background to John's usage, it is perhaps in anticipation of how God will again save his people.

11. Bauckham, *Climax of Prophecy*, 257-58, 273-83; cf. 993a:82-88; Aune, *Revelation 6-16*, 628; Sweet, *Revelation*, 189.

12. Bauckham *Climax of Prophecy*, 259.

13. Ibid., 273-83; cf. *Theology of the Book of Revelation*, 84-88, 98-104; Harrington, *Revelation*, 124. Beale, *Revelation*, 603-07, questions this interpretation, noting that fearing God in the OT is not always used of repentance. However, I follow Bauckham in seeing it as referring to the possibility of real repentance. This, however, does not mean that Bauckham argues for a kind of universalism in Revelation (so Schnabel, "John"). He makes very clear that John uses universal language of both judgment and salvation,

to the seventh trumpet, but before we examine it in detail, let us consider how it is anticipated in the text.

The Anticipation of the Seventh Trumpet

First, we are told in 8:13 that the last three trumpets signal woes on the inhabitants of the earth. Between the blowing of each trumpet we find statements about the woe that is passed and an anticipation of the woe/s that are still to come (9:12; 11:14). Considering this, we are led to expect that the third and last trumpet, as the last of the three woes, will deal, at least in part, with God's judgment on his enemies. Second, we are also led to expect it to contain the establishment of God's final purposes since the great angel in 10:4 has announced that "there will be no more delay! But in the days when the seventh angel is about to sound his trumpet, the mystery of God will be accomplished" (10:7).[14]

The Seventh Trumpet

When considering the parameters for the passage or passages that cover the content of the seventh trumpet, we run into two problems, one minor and one quite significant. First, in the debate on whether the passage starts at 11:14 or 11:15,[15] it is perhaps preferable to see 11:14 as a janus statement signalling the end of what has preceded and anticipating what is coming.[16]

Second, it is unclear how far the seventh trumpet is to extend. There is a definite break between 11:19 and 12:1, making 11:15–19 a

---

"without qualifying one by the other," in order to leave the two eschatological outcomes open (Bauckham, *Theology of the Book of Revelation*, 104). This confusion may be due to that Bauckham, in his major essay on the issue, *Climax of Prophecy*, 238–337, does not sufficiently clarify what he means by his assertion that the vision of salvation holds "theological priority" (so Mathewson, "Destiny," 142). Bauckham, *Climax of Prophecy*, 11–12, suggest the first two woes signal how God's judgments in history alone do not bring repentance, something they can only do in connection with the witness of the church.

14. The trumpet is "a projection into the future, when the kingdom has been established and the heavenly host offers praise in response" (Beale, *Revelation*, 611).

15. Caird, *Revelation*, 140; Harrington, *Revelation*, 125, commence at 11:15 while Beasley-Murray, *Revelation*, 187–88, includes 11:14.

16. Similarly Beale, *Revelation*, 609, sees it as a transition.

pericope.[17] However, this does not solve the problem as to how far the content of the seventh trumpet extends since 11:19 is not followed by a statement signalling the end of the third woe. A likely explanation for this omission may be that while John has concluded his discussion on the first two woes (9:12; 11:14), he has more to say on the third woe.[18] Although the seventh trumpet and the third woe are closely linked, the woe is only briefly indicated in 11:15–19 and is developed in much greater detail from ch. 15 onwards, culminating in the portrayal of the cataclysmic fall of Babylon in Revelation 17–18. And it is precisely in Revelation 18 that we again find the language of the woe, when those who have grown rich with the city, the kings of the earth, the merchants and the sea traders, sing their woes over Babylon (18:10, 16–17, 19). Their three-fold repetition of οὐαὶ οὐαί ("woe, woe") over the city that persecuted the saints but whose privileges these rulers and merchants enjoyed marks the conclusion of the third woe announced in 11:14. Those who grew fat with Babylon who slays the saints and destroys the earth, are also destroyed with her when she tastes the final judgment of God. Thus, although the content of the seventh trumpet is probably to be confined to 11:15–19, John's discussion of the woe it announces is not completed before the end of Revelation 18.

In 11:15–19, as at the beginning of each trumpet passage, we are brought back to the heavenly throne room where the seven trumpet angels are located and see the seventh angel blow his trumpet (v 15a),[19] but unlike the other trumpets it does not exhibit the same kind of

---

17. Against Aune, *Revelation 6–16*, 660–61, who sees a major break between 11:18 and 11:19ff, I follow most scholars in seeing the theophany of 11:19 as the conclusion of 11:15–19 (so Beale, *Revelation*, 618–20; Beasley-Murray, *Revelation*, 190–91; Beckwith, *Apocalypse*, 274; Caird, *Revelation*, 144; Harrington, *Revelation*, 125; Witherington, *Revelation*, 160).

18. Most commentators link the third woe with parts of the following visionary complex although they disagree to exactly what. Aune, *Revelation 6–16*, 495, 524, who links it generally to the seven bowls and specifically to 12:12, also notes the link to the three-fold woes in 18:10, 16, 19 (cf. Beale, *Revelation*, 610 Beckwith, *Apocalypse*, 274, 606–8; Beasley-Murray, *Revelation*, 187–88). Here I build on a suggestion G. D. Fee has proposed (Fee, "Lectures"), linking the third woe with the songs of lament in Revelation 18.

19. The introduction of the blowing of each trumpet is identical: καὶ + number (1st, 2nd, …) + ἄγγελος ἐσάλπισεν (8:7 [ἄγγελος not stated but implied], 8, 10, 12; 9:1, 13; 11:15).

action from heaven to earth as they do.[20] It consists of a proclamation of heavenly voices (v. 15b), a response of praise by the 24 elders (vv. 16–18), and a concluding heavenly theophany (v. 19).

The Transferral of a Kingdom (11:15b)

Immediately after the seventh trumpet is blown, a heavenly choir proclaims (v. 15b): "The kingdom of the world has become the kingdom of our Lord and of his Messiah and he will reign forever and ever." This serves as a summary statement of what the rest of the passage will describe in more detail.[21] In the next chapter we will discuss the importance of this and the following verses for the book's understanding of God's sovereignty and its high christology, but here we focus on how it envisions the eschatological purpose of God as a regime change in which the central position of authority in a socio-political order is transferred from the powers to be to "our Lord and his Christ."

The first clause indicates a radical discontinuity between the coming and the present as is seen in the two genitival modifiers, τοῦ κόσμου ("of the world") and τοῦ κυρίου ("of the Lord") but it also suggests an underlying continuity since the genitives modify the same noun, ἡ βασιλεία, which often is simply translated "kingdom" but which semantic field is much wider, being able to refer to both the realm of a political entity, the position of political authority, and the exercise of such rule.[22] Since βασιλεία signals the continuity between how things are and how they will be when God accomplishes his purposes, it is pivotal to determine what it signifies. It could simply signify the "realm"

---

20. The spatial distance may indicate the temporal dislocation, the proleptic nature of the seventh trumpet. The action toward earth that is likely implied in the earthquake is not depicted before 16:20–21.

21. This is so for several reasons: 1) The following verses narrate both God's eschatological judgment and reward (v. 18) as well as the revelation of his presence (v. 19); 2) the expressed reason for the 24 elders song of thanksgiving is ὅτι εἴληφας τὴν δύναμίν σου τὴν μεγάλην καὶ ἐβασίλευσας (v.17); 3) the structure of the songs of this passage is very similar to what we find elsewhere in the book, where subsequent songs are an elaboration of an initial song or revelation (this causal link is explicitly expressed in 4:11; cf. 5:9). On the structure of 11:15–18 as a "two-part responsory hymn" see Aune, *Revelation 6–16*, 635.

22. Aune (*Revelation 6–16*, 633) suggests the noun is elided in the predicate position for stylistic reasons. Whether this is the case or not, the elision emphasises that the referent is the same in both nominative and predicate position.

which is being ruled. Although we will later show that Revelation assumes such a continuity, several factors, not least the close relationship between this passage and 12:10, suggest that "rule" is more likely in view here.²³ However, this cannot simply be limited to the *activity* of ruling since this is precisely what changes.²⁴ It may be better to see it as rulership, "rule" as an *actual* position of authority over a concrete realm rather than simply as an *activity*.²⁵ As such, the position of authority cannot be separated from its relationship to the realm of which it is the ordering center. If this is right, what is emphasized is that the position of geopolitical authority over the human community on earth that now is in the hands "of the world"²⁶ will be handed over to "our Lord

---

23. Not only does 11:15b continue καὶ βασιλεύσει, but 12:10, a thematically and structurally closely related passage, places ἡ βασιλεία after ἡ δύναμις in a list of things attributed to God that now have been established in heaven, and ἡ βασιλεία τοῦ θεοῦ ἡμῶν is paralleled with ἡ ἐξουσία τοῦ χριστοῦ αὐτοῦ; cf. 5:10; 16:10; 17:12, 17, 18.

24. The identification of the subject with the predicate by the elision of the noun in the predicate position indicates it cannot simply be the reign of a particular authority. In that case there would be two βασιλείαι under consideration, ἡ βασιλεία τοῦ κόσμου that is now experienced in the world and ἡ βασιλεία τοῦ κυρίου that will replace it, but the text accentuates that only one βασιλεία is under consideration.

25. This more "substantive" understanding of βασιλεία as a position of geopolitical authority seems to account well for how the term is used elsewhere in the book: The people who are constituted as a βασιλεία to God (1:6; 5:10a) are those who are destined to rule forever (5:10b); as such they are those who having taken the journey of Christ's assumption to a position of sovereignty will be exalted to positions of authority on his throne (3:21), an expectation that finds its final fulfillment in 22:3–5 (cf. 20:4–6). It is precisely by seeing βασιλεία as referring to a position of authority that can make sense of the juxtaposition in 1:9: precisely in sharing in the θλίψει and ὑπομονῇ which are in Christ, they also share in the present paradoxical rule of Christ on earth. This stands in contrast to how Babylon now occupies the βασιλεία over the kings of the earth (17:18), how the beast confers positions of authority to its vassal kings in 17:12, 17. Note also the relationship between βασιλεία and throne language in 16:10—it is as the fifth bowl is poured on the θρόνος of the beast that its βασιλεία is darkened.

26. The other two occurrences of κόσμος in Revelation (13:8; 17:8) refer simply to a realm. However, since in those verses it is part of a stock phrase καταβολῆς κόσμου (cf. Matt 13:35; 25:34; Luke 11:50; John 17:24; Eph 1:4; Heb 4:3; 9:26; 1 Pet 1:20; Rev 13:8; 17:8) it should not necessarily govern the meaning of the term here. Since it stands in a parallel construction with τοῦ κυρίου . . ., which obviously is a subjective genitive, it more likely refers here to "the human world that had been in opposition to God and in conflict with his purposes" (Aune, *Revelation 6–16*, 638, who appeals to a similar phrase in Matt 4:8, αἱ βασιλείαι τοῦ κόσμου, and the rabbinic expression אֻמּוֹת הָעוֹלָם, "nations of the world"). The Scriptural allusions found here seem to point in the same direction. Beale, *Revelation*, 611, points out that Daniel 7 is one precedent

and his Christ," who then will commence their rightful and everlasting reign on earth.[27] As such what 11:15 depicts is a "regime change." Here it is proleptically announced in a terse formulation but in the following chapters we are first shown how this is accomplished in the heavenly realm (12:10) and Revelation 15 and following then vividly describe how the powers of the world are removed from the position of authority and how God assumes this position that is rightfully his.

The discontinuity which 11:15 anticipates is then between the ruling elite that now holds the political power on earth and the one that will,[28] as well as the radical consequence the exercise of this office has for the whole world in which it is exercised.[29] This discontinuity is pivotal to the book: it is what turns every appearance on its head: it promises vindication to those who have suffered and died at the hands of evil, and it resolves the dissonance between the churches' experience on the unjust periphery of Roman power and the confession that landed them there, that only God is κύριος ("Lord") and that they are his true βασιλεία. But the power of this discontinuity lies in its underlying continuity, the central position of a geopolitical leadership remains. The implication of this is, as we will see below, that although transformed, there is a basic continuity between the irreducibly socio-political character of humanity in history and in the eschaton. If the central position within a politically ordered reality remains, so must the realm of which it is the ordering center.

---

to this passage, in which the "kingdoms" that antagonise the saints will be replaced by "the reign of the Son of man and the saints."

27. Rowland, *Revelation* (NIB), 643, suggests that ἐγένετο should perhaps be simply translated "was" here, indicating that "the kingdom of this world has never belonged to anyone other than God." Since I am not persuaded that γίνομαι can be consistently translated in Revelation as "was" or "is", I follow Aune, *Revelation 1–5*, 638, in seeing the aorists in this passage as relating to the proleptic nature of the trumpet and therefore functioning as the *perfectum propheticum*. Similarly Moltmann describes the fall of Babylon in Revelation as "an anticipation of something that has not yet happened, but it is an anticipation in the mode of the narrated past of what must pass away" (*CoG*, 141). However, this "need not mean that God did not reign as king previously; rather it could mean that his kingship has only now become effective over the world" (Aune, *Revelation 6–16*, 643).

28. As we will discuss below, this power is depicted in the imagery of Dragon, beast and Babylon whose "authority," βασιλεία, is referred to in 16:10; 17:12, 17, 18.

29. Compare chs. 17–18 and 21–22.

Taking a Kingdom (11: 16–18)

The Victory of the Coming God. Revelation 11:16–18 make it clear that the seventh trumpet is located in the heavenly throne-room. As the 24 elders responded to the four living beings in 4:8–11 and proclaimed God the creator as rightful sovereign, they now respond to the heavenly voices and proclaim how God the Almighty has realized this sovereignty.[30]

In 11:17 the 24 elders first repeat basically what the great voices have already told us, thanking God that he has exercised his power and begun to rule. Of special interest to us is first how what is anticipated in 1:4, 8 and 4:8, in the tripartite title of God as the one who is, who was and *who is coming* is here fulfilled: the God who is the undisputed sovereign of both heaven and earth comes and establishes his rule on earth. Just as this passage identifies the purposes of God as the realisation of God's kingdom, so the tripartite title anticipates the dawn of his reign on earth.[31] Second, we see a close relationship between this verse and the doxologies in chs. 4–5. Revelation 11:17a repeats the titles for God found in 4:9, and it lists them in the same sequence: "The Lord God," "the Almighty," and "the one who was and the one who is and the one who is coming," the only difference being the omission of ὁ ἐρχόμενος ("he who is coming") in 11:17a. In this way what the inner court proclaimed about God's rule in chs. 4–5 is now realised, a point underscored by 11:17b.[32] What the elders proclaimed that God was worthy to do in Revelation 4 because he is the creator who sustains all creation, they now praise him for having done. The elders here announce that the regime change proclaimed in 11:15 is nothing other than the realisation of what is ascribed to God in the doxologies of Revelation 4 and anticipated in Revelation 5.[33]

---

30. "Their hymn is an amplification of that of v. 15" (Beckwith, *Apocalypse*, 609).

31. See the discussion on the tripartite title in the next chapter.

32. Note the parallels between 11:17b (λαβεῖν τὴν . . . τὴν δύναμιν) and 4:11 (εἴληφας τὴν δύναμίν σου τὴν μεγάλην).

33. See the next chapter for how the doxologies of chs. 4–5 anticipate the expansion of God's rule.

The Dual Act of the Fulfilment of God's Kingdom.

In v. 18 the elders continue their praise by describing how God has accomplished this, saying:[34] "that is,[35] the nations exercised their wrath but[36] your wrath came and thus[37] the time[38] to judge the dead, to give rewards to your servants, the prophets, the saints and those who fear your name, both small and great, and to destroy those who are destroying the earth" (my translation). Up till now the fulfilment of God's purposes which 10:6b-7 said would accompany the seventh trumpet has merely been pronounced; here the elders' song explains how this will happen, an explanation dominated by God's acts of eschatological punishment and reward.[39]

THE FINAL DEFEAT AND PUNISHMENT OF GOD'S OPPOSITION. God's *lex talionis* punishment on the nations forms an inclusio in 11:18. The verse begins with how God meets the nations who exercise their wrath with his own wrath and concludes with how God destroys those who destroy the earth. The third and final woe which has been anticipated since 8:13 (cf. 9:12; 11:14) is now set before us.

First, as also anticipated in 10:6, this third woe on the earth forms a part of the accomplishment of God's final purposes on earth, of which divine punishment plays an important part. The nations who oppose him have amassed the fullness of their final fury but God meets them with his own fury.[40] While the purpose of God's judgment in history

---

34. This verse is one of the more complex sentences of the book and has faced commentators with some thorny exegetical issues (Beale, *Revelation*, 615–18; Beasley-Murray, *Revelation*, 189–90). We will deal with the exegetical issues that are of particular relevance to us as we come to them in the following discussion.

35. Taking the initial καί as epexegetical, indicating that what is coming describes how God has taken his great power and begun to reign.

36. Contrastive καί.

37. Epexegetical καί.

38. καιρός governing all three genitives (so Aune, *Revelation 6–16*, 637), τῶν νεκρῶν being a genitival object of κριθῆναι.

39. Beale, *Revelation*, 615 notes that v. 18 can either be seen as temporally preceding vv. 15–17 or "as the first expression of God's beginning end-time reign." The latter seems preferable, v. 18 explaining both the negative and positive aspect of what it means when God inaugurates his reign.

40. "The culmination of Gentile wrath against God ... is everywhere in apocalyptic writings a feature of the last fierce assault made upon God's power by his enemies; in our book it appears in 16:13ff, 20:8f" (Beckwith, *Apocalypse*, 609; cf. Beale, *Revelation*, 615).

was to bring the nations to repentance, the purpose of his eschatological judgment is their destruction, proleptically announced here and depicted in chs. 15ff.[41] If the *telos* of God's sovereignty is its full establishment on earth, the *telos* of the world in opposition to him is its destruction.

Second, however, this judgment is not arbitrary but the exercise of measured justice—*lex talionis*, punishment which accords with the crime: the nations who have exercised wrath meet God's wrath, the destroyers of the earth are destroyed.[42]

Third, as the prayers of the martyrs in 6:10 are answered with the arrival of the ὀργή ("wrath") of God and the Lamb on the inhabitants of the earth (6:15–17), so now the answer to their prayers is seen in how God's ὀργή meets the nations that ὠργίσθησαν ("exercise wrath").[43] The full depiction of this is found in the destruction of Babylon. Although this is punishment for all their evil ways, it is the slaying of the saints that the book sees as the apex of the evil endeavours of the nations.[44]

Fourth, however, by delaying the answer to the prayer for vindication to now, John is able both to satisfy the expectation of justice as vindication, and to alter this anticipation by placing its fulfilment after his exposé on the purpose of the churches vis-à-vis precisely those who now oppose them. Although the martyrs' prayer for vindication plays an important role in how God's justice is accomplished, this is not to

---

41. 14:10 anticipates how all who persevere in allegiance to Babylon will also drink what she will drink, the wine of God's ὀργή, an anticipation fulfilled in the depiction of the final destruction of Babylon in 16:19 and the treading of the winepress in 19:15. In this, Revelation picks up a later Jewish tradition which has its most likely roots in Psalm 2 (a psalm Revelation alludes to at pivotal points), Ps 99; Exod 15:14 and other similar OT passages, and juxtaposes "the two motifs of the rule or reign of God and the tumult of the heathen" in the final eschatological scenario (Aune, *Revelation 6–16*, 643).

42. See Hirzel, "Talion," 407–480 on the origins and history of the notion of *lex talionis*.

43. In the only other occurrence of ὠργίζω in Revelation (12:17), we see that behind the raging of the nations is the Dragon who rages against the followers of the Lamb. The outpouring of God's and the Lamb's ὀργή (6:16, 17; 11:18; 14:10; 16:19; 19:15) is then not the outpouring of unmeasured and brute force but the proper and just response to the draconic wrath of the nations.

44. It seems unjustified to equate τὴν γῆν with God's people as Beale does, *Revelation*, 615, since the reference to the destruction of the earth should not be limited to Jer 28:25 but also includes Gen 6:11–12. While the slaying of the saints reveals the true nature of evil (cf. 18:24), the destroying of the earth reveals evil's universal scope.

be the focus of the church on earth. In heaven the martyred saints who have suffered the ultimate injustice pray for vindication, but although the saints on earth await the justice of the martyrs, they are now to apply themselves to the task given them by God, their prophetic witness that can convert the nations.

Fifth, in depicting this universal judgment as destroying "those who destroy the earth," the author likely alludes to Jer 51:25 (LXX Jer 28:25). In Jeremiah the destroyer of the whole earth is Babylon, and in alluding to this passage John anticipates how he will later depict the prime power under consideration as the arch enemy of God, Babylon.[45]

Sixth, since the third woe, being part of the trumpet sequence, is closely linked to the vindication of the martyrs, and to the laments of Revelation 18, the final answer to the prayer for vindication is likely to be seen as the fall of Babylon. And so, the rest of the book first identifies the demonic power that makes war with the saints as two beasts that most likely representing imperial power and the imperial cult (Revelation 12–13). Then, after the role of Jesus in the eschatological complex is anticipated in ch. 14, chs. 15–18 are a tour de force of God's final punishment on Babylon. And so, as Babylon lies in ruins, the saints, apostles and prophets are called to rejoice because "God has judged her [Babylon] for the way she treated you" (18:20). The vindication the martyrs prayed for in 6:10 has been accomplished.[46]

In summary, the third woe is to be identified with God's final defeat over his enemies as he claims his right as sovereign over the earth. This defeat is also the final and just judgment of these enemies in which their punishment fits their crime. This just judgment is also the fulfilment of the slain martyrs' prayer for vindication (6:10). Since John only puts the prayer for vindication in the mouths of the slain saints, and since he postpones the proleptic description of this fulfilment until after his exposition of the role of the ecclesial communities in history,

---

45. Beale, *Revelation*, 615–16, notes the strong parallels between the phrase here and as found in LXX Jer 28:25 and MT Jer 51:25. If this then can be linked to Gen 6, then Babylon in Jeremiah and Rome as the power that plays the role of Babylon in Revelation are associated with the primordial generation that had so utterly destroyed the earth that the only thing God could do was to flood it, cleanse it off its evil and begin anew.

46. In 6:10 the saints pray for God to judge (κρίνεις) on their behalf, and in 18:20 God is praised for having done so (ἔκρινεν ὁ θεὸς τὸ κρίμα ὑμῶν ἐξ αὐτῆς) (cf. Collins, "Eschatology," 65).

he qualifies the desire for vengeance. Although there is an appropriate place for vengeance, this is not what the followers of the lamb are to set their eyes on now. Leaving the prayer for vindication with the martyrs and its actual execution with God, the church is to seek the redemption of her enemies just as God seeks to bring them to repentance through his penultimate judgments on them.

The Final Reward to God's People

The Vindication of the Saints. Although 11:18 is dominated by God's final punishment on his opponents, we see that God's eschatological judgment is not seen as wholly negative, but also includes the final rewarding of God's people. This final reward has been anticipated so far in the addresses to the seven churches,[47] in 5:10 and in 7:15–17 as the gift of life and sovereignty over the earth, and in 6:10–11 as the vengeance for the martyrs' blood.[48] Since the trumpets are linked with the prayer for vindication, Rev 11:18 probably accentuates this last aspect by sandwiching the reward to God's people between his judgment on the nations. Although not limited to vindication,[49] it nevertheless is an important part of the reward since Revelation repeatedly emphasizes that Babylon is judged because of her treatment of God's people.[50]

---

47. Revelation 2:7, 10b–11, 17, 25–27; 3:4–6, 12, 21.

48. For an examination on the background for Revelation's understanding of vengeance, see J. N. Musvosvi, *Vengeance*, who emphasises the legal context of vengeance in Revelation.

49. μισθός is only used here and in 22:12 in the book. While in 22:12 it may be construed positively or negatively, here it "is an umbrella term referring to the salvific benefits that God will bestow on the faithful in the eschaton" (Aune, *Revelation 6–16*, 644; on μισθός, see Smith, *Tannaitic Parallels*, 54–73).

50. 16:5–6; 18:4–8, 20; 18:21–19:2. The close tie between the destruction of Babylon and the martyrs' prayer for vindication in 6:9–10 is especially evident in 16:5–6. Note the repetition of words and semantic parallels between these passages: in 6:9:10 the slain who stand ὑποκάτω τοῦ θυσιαστηρίου call on him who is ὁ ἅγιος καὶ ἀληθινός to κρίνεις καὶ ἐκδικεῖς τὸ αἷμα ἡμῶν from the inhabitants of the earth; and in 16:5–7 the angel of the waters proclaims that God, ὁ ὅσιος, is δίκαιος because ἔκρινας, he has given those who have poured out the αἷμα of the saints and the prophets αἷμα to drink. Responding to this, the altar proclaims God to be ἀληθιναί and his κρίσεις to be δίκαιαι. For the significance of the altar in relationship to the martyrs' prayer, see 6:9–10; 8:3, 5; 16:7.

The Inclusion of "those who fear his name." But just as the prayer for just vindication was set in the broader context of the desire for the conversion of the nations, so the reward of vindication depicted here is qualified by this prior concern. God's reward is given to the prophets and the saints but also to τοῖς φοβουμένοις τὸ ὄνομά σου ("those who fear your name"), precisely those who respond to the church's witness in 11:13. Commentators disagree whether these signifiers refer to different groups or should be seen as one,[51] but perhaps more important than the precise identification of who they represent is how they function in the book.

Prior to this passage, προφήτης ("prophet") occurs in 10:7 where it refers to Israel's prophets and in 11:10 to the church in her role as witness. Although probably not excluding the emphasis of 11:10, it is probably Israel's prophets that are primarily in view here since 10:7 is tightly linked to 11:15-19, and since basically the same phrase is used in both passages to describe them.[52] As Israel's prophets, in whose tradition John and the ecclesial communities stand, proclaimed what the seventh trumpet is the fulfilment of, so they also reap the benefits of its fulfilment.

We have already observed that every time οἱ ἅγιοι ("the saints") has been used up to this point is in connection with the martyrs' prayer for vindication (6:8-10). By identifying them as part of the recipients of God's reward, John emphasizes that their vindication is part of the eschatological reward given to his people. But that this is not gloating vindictiveness is clear in the inclusion of "those who fear his name."

Who are these who fear God's name? Apart from the risen Christ's injunction to John and the church in Smyrna not to fear (1:17; 2:10), neither the noun φόβος ("fear") or the verb φοβέω ("to fear") occur before Revelation 11 depicts the church's martyrological role in history. In 11:11-13 we are told that a "great fear fell" (φόβος μέγας ἐπέπεσεν) on the inhabitants of the world, when the witnesses whose death they had gloated over were raised and taken to heaven. Those who are not killed in the subsequent earthquake were ἔμφοβοι ("terri-

---

51. One of the most debated questions in 11:18 is how the four dative clauses following καὶ δοῦναι τὸν μισθὸν are to be related to one another; see Beale, *Revelation*, 616-18; cf. Beckwith, *Apocalypse*, 610.

52. τοὺς ἑαυτοῦ δούλους τοὺς προφήτα (10:7) // τοῖς δούλοις σου τοῖς προφήταις (11:18).

fied") and "gave glory to God." That this is to be interpreted positively seems clear from the injunctions in 14:7 and 15:4 to do exactly what those in 11:13 do, fear God and give him glory.[53] Because of this, it is probably these who are most likely in view when "those who fear your name" are included among the recipients of God's reward in 11:18.[54] They have experienced God's just punishment but also responded to the church's witness in repentance. Precisely because of this, the expectation for vindication must be tempered by the desire for the redemption of the enemy. The saints and those who respond to their witness will together enjoy God's reward.

Considering how φοβέω ("to fear") is used in the rest of the book, the inclusion of those who fear God's name here anticipates the positive side of God's reward.[55] This is especially evident when we consider the relationship of 11:15–18 with 18:20—19:9, a series of heavenly songs which first focus on the just punishment of Babylon in which those who have suffered under the great prostitute are vindicated (18:20—19:4) and then focus on the reign of God that will replace her (19:5-8).[56] Note how 19:5-6 is structurally and lexically linked to 11:15–18:[57]

---

53. Against Beale, *Revelation*, 603–07, I follow Bauckham, *Climax of Prophecy*, 273–83, in seeing this as an anticipation of a real conversion of the nations.

54. Against Beckwith, *Apocalypse*, 610, I see the final καί not as an epexegetical but as a copulative καί.

55. That this is so seems to be confirmed by the way the verb φοβέω is used in the rest of the book. In 14:7 an angel who has the eternal Gospel to proclaim (14:6) exhorts the world to do exactly what the inhabitants of the world do in 11:13: φοβήθητε τὸν θεὸν καὶ δότε αὐτῷ δόξαν precisely because the final judgment of which those in 11:13 had only had a foretaste of is about to come. So also in 15:3–5 since 14:6–7 does not allow for a "negative" interpretation there.

56. Although 19:5–8 continues the heavenly praise commenced in 18:20, 19:4 signals a conclusion in the same manner as the heavenly worship ends in 5:13, suggesting that 19:5 begins something new, which is confirmed in a shift of focus from the city that has been judged to an anticipation of the reign of God in the new city (19:7–8 > 21:2, 9). Not many commentators note this break but see Caird, *Revelation*, 233.

57. NRSV, modified to reflect the parallels in the Greek better. Aune, *Revelation 1–5*, 642, notes how both 11:17 and 19:6 commence a response to a previous choir by affirming how The Lord God Almighty has commenced his reign. Caird, *Revelation*, 233, and Harrington, *Revelation*, 186, also note strong parallels to 11:15–19.

11:15–18	19:5	19:6
and there were loud voices in heaven, saying . . .	And a voice came from the throne saying,	
Then the twenty-four elders . . . saying, "We give you thanks, Lord God Almighty, . . . for you have . . . begun to reign.	"Praise our God,	Then I heard . . . a voice . . . saying, "Hallelujah! For the Lord God Almighty reigns.
. . . your servants, the prophets and saints and all who fear your name, both small and great,	all you his servants, and all who fear him, small and great."	

However, just as important as these strong links is the omission of the prophets and the saints in the call to worship in 19:5. These, though, play an important role in 18:20—19:4 where, with the apostles, "the saints" and "the prophets" are called to rejoice over the fall of Babylon (18:20) and are the two named groups of all those on earth that have been killed by Babylon (18:24).[58] Although not mentioned in 18:20—19:4, those "who fear him" are called to worship in 19:5. While those who suffered Babylon are called to rejoice over her destruction, those redeemed from its evil by the martyrological witness of the saints are called to praise God because his reign has commenced. This reign is here symbolized as the marriage supper of the lamb for which his bride has made herself ready, which in return anticipates the fuller depiction of the New Jerusalem in 21:1—22:5.[59] The regime change anticipated in 11:15 is in the songs of 18:20—19:9 seen first as the vindication of prophets and saints in the destruction of the city that persecuted them but, second, also as the establishment of God's kingdom on earth, where he will be the central ordering presence of all his servants, including those who fear his name. Thus, while "the prophets and the saints" in

---

58. Note, how οἱ ἅγιοι and οἱ προφῆται are consistently used of how they either suffer at the hands of their enemies or in the defeat of these enemies (13:7, 10; 16:6; 17:6; 18:20, 24; 20:9).

59. In 19:7 we are told that the bride has made herself ready and in 21:2 New Jerusalem is "prepared as a bride beautifully adorned for her husband" (21:2; cf. 21:9).

11:15 functions within the martyrs' expectation for vindication which dominates the trumpet sequence, "those who fear your name" anticipates how those who will enjoy life in the everlasting community ordered around the throne of God includes precisely those who have heeded the saints' prophetic witness and have come out of the evil city destined for doom (21:24, 26).[60]

THE FINAL RETURN OF GOD'S PRESENCE AMONG HIS PEOPLE (11:19)

Revelation 11:15–19 concludes with a theophany in which God's heavenly temple is opened, revealing the ark of the covenant in it. Accompanying the vision are "flashes of lightning, rumblings, peals of thunder, an earthquake and a great hailstorm." These two aspects of the theophany "correspond then with the two parts of v. 18," the expectation of God's final reward to his covenantal people (the ark) and the final judgment (the earthquake, etc.).[61]

In the seismic and atmospheric aspect of the theophany, consistent with the focus of the whole passage, we are reminded of God's coming in final judgment on the nations who oppose him.[62] The expectation of God's judgment is also seen in the opening of the temple which already has been associated with judgement in 8:1–5 and does so again in 15:5.

However, by mentioning the ark of the covenant John also picks up on the positive aspect of the expected eschatological theophany of

---

60. This possible conversion of the nations is also seen in how δόξα and τιμή are used in conjunction with each other in the book. The combination occurs six times in the book (4:9, 11; 5:12, 13; 7:12, 21:26), always in contexts of heavenly worship of God and/or the Lamb, except in 21:26, where it is the nations who bring their δόξα and τιμή into the city. Thus, in 21:26, the nations do exactly what the heavenly choirs do previously in the book, bring their honour and glory into the city whose radiance is the holiness of God. This is also precisely what those who fear God do in 11:13, and this stands in stark contrast to 16:9, where those who receive their just judgment because they refuse to heed the call to give God glory (14:7) blaspheme God. See Bauckham, *Climax of Prophecy*, 307–9; "Theology of the Book of Revelation," 98–104 on the two fates that are open to the nations, depending on how they respond to the church's witness.

61. Beckwith, *Apocalypse*, 611.

62. See Bauckham, *Climax of Prophecy*, 199–209 on how John alludes to the theophany in Exod 19 which was accompanied with similar phenomena, and how John combines this with the great earthquake in order to signal how God is coming in final judgment against the nations who oppose him.

Israel's God.[63] Within Jewish hope the reappearance of the ark often played a significant role in the expectation of the restoration of the covenantal community in the kingdom of God.[64] Before the exile, God's presence was enthroned on the ark and it played a central role in the cultic maintenance of the people's covenantal life with God. The ark was lost during the Babylonian captivity, accentuating the judgment for Israel's sin since it signalled the departure of God's presence. Although a literal return of the ark was not commonly expected, it nevertheless signalled what was hoped for, "God's gracious presence with his redeemed community and his provision of grace by atonement."[65] The brief appearance in 11:19 of the heavenly counterpart of the ark that had been lost on earth thus anticipates the day when the covenantal presence of God with his people will be restored. Considering that the ark and the throne of God are closely related since it was above the ark that God was enthroned in the temple, the appearance of the heavenly ark here anticipates 21:1—22:5, when instead of the ark, the throne of God and the Lamb descends on earth and becomes the ordering center of the everlasting kingdom on earth,[66] when the σκηνή ("dwelling") of God σκηνώσει ("dwells") with his people.[67] This eschatological appearance of God's covenantal presence goes far beyond his presence over the ark in the earthly temple—no longer veiled by a heavy curtain, humanity will "see his face" (22:4). This vision is the final answer to "the cry of the martyrs under the altar—how long, O Lord?" But the vision does not only resolve this question but also intensifies it "because the resolution

---

63. John's depiction of the ark departs from other early Jewish literature where the ark never features in the inventory of the heavenly temple (Aune, *Revelation 6–16*, 678, who also notes that the throne may be seen as its heavenly counterpart). See Beale, *Revelation*, 618 on how John may be employing the song of Moses (Exod 15:13–18) here to indicate the final reward to God's people.

64. Beale, *Revelation*, 619; Beasley-Murray, *Revelation*, 190-91; Harrington, *Revelation*, 126.

65. Beale, *Revelation*, 619; cf. Charles, *Revelation*, vol. 1, 298; Aune, *Revelation 6–16*, 678.

66. The "presence of God without a literal reappearance of the ark is the idea in Rev 11:19, which is expanded in 21:3, 22" (Beale, *Revelation*, 619).

67. Σκηνή is a common translation for "the Hebrew *mishkan* (tent), which was the symbol of God's abiding presence in the midst of Israel" (Caird, *Revelation*, 203) and is here used to indicate the fulfillment of Lev 26:11 and perhaps Ezek 37:27 (204; cf. Beale, *Revelation*, 1046-47; Beasley-Murray, *Revelation*, 311; Witherington, *Revelation*, 255; Harrington, *Revelation*, 207).

has been glimpsed in the foretaste of the new Jerusalem, but still not yet attained."[68]

Conclusion

11:15–19 depicts the fulfilment of God's eschatological purposes as a regime change (11:15) and anticipates how it will be accomplished (11:16–19). Negatively this is accomplished in God's final judgment on the powers that now hold the position of authority on earth, which spells their final and utter demise (11:18a, 18c, 19b). Positively, this means the arrival of God on the central throne of earthly authority; and in his arrival, he will reward his servants, those who have remained and become loyal to him (11:18c, 19a). The negative aspect is a dominant theme in this proleptic pericope since it, as the seventh trumpet, is the climax of the trumpet sequence that is closely linked to the martyrs' prayer for vindication. However, John not only augments the expectation for vindication by placing it in the context of a prior concern for the conversion of the nations, he also anticipates their positive response by including those who do heed the church's witness among those who will commune with God in the eternal kingdom.

In setting this expectation of a regime-change within the context of the martyrs' prayer for vindication, in structurally linking the third woe with both the seventh trumpet and the destruction of Babylon in ch. 18, and in anticipating the reward that awaits the servants of God, 11:15–19 both tersely describes the fulfilment of themes that have dominated the book so far, and also anticipates themes the following chapters focus on: Revelation 12–13 explain why the followers of the lamb should expect to be martyred by the powers to be; Revelation 14 proleptically anticipates the primary role Jesus and the slain saints will have in the eschatological judgment; Revelation 15–16 delineate the arrival of God's anger on the nations who exercised anger, a judgment further explained in Revelation 17–20; and Rev 21:1—22:5 contains the vision of the glorious regime that will replace the one that has been judged.

---

68. Gilbertson, *God and History*, 141.

A New View of History in the Light of an Expected Regime Change

In our introduction to Revelation, we noted the unbearable tension between what the book confesses, God's undisputed sovereignty over his creation, and the present state of affairs, the irresistible reign of God's enemies on earth. Revelation 11:15–19 resolves this tension by anticipating how the One Enthroned and Christ, whose sovereignty is established in heaven, will take over the βασιλεία that now is occupied by the powers of the world. Since βασιλεία in 11:15 does not simply refer to an activity but to the whole complex that is the concrete position of geopolitical authority, it cannot be seen as a utopic "rule" divested of its geopolitical connotations, but must be seen as actual political authority over a concrete realm that is exercised from a concrete center. Revelation 11:15–19 envisions a "regime change" in the earthly realm, and as such, is a gateway into the second half of the book.[69] In the following discussion we will therefore look at how Revelation 12–22 fleshes this out, how it portrays the order of the beast, how this order comes to its end, what the order of God and the lamb that replaces it is like, what the discontinuities and the continuities between the two are, and what understanding of history this produces. But first a note on terminology. While in the above exegesis we have focused on how βασιλεία and κόσμος are used in the book, in the following discussion "kingdom" and "world" will be used in a broad sense, the former of socio-political orders as a whole, and the latter of the human world, in distinction to the non-human creation.[70]

The Kingdom of the Dragon and His Beasts

In Revelation, the kingdom of the world has a defined power structure, particular ways in which this power structure is maintained, all of which lends a fundamental character to this kingdom.

---

69. If chs. 1–11 as a whole "introduce and imply" what is developed in greater detail in chs. 12–22 (Beale, *Revelation*, 622), the seventh trumpet seems to gather together the pivotal themes that will be explored in the rest of the vision.

70. So, e.g., in the following discussion, "kingdom of the world" and "kingdom of God" will refer to the human community organised as a political entity as it is defined by the rule of God's enemies and of God respectively.

The transcendental authority that stands behind it is the Dragon, identified in 12:9 as the arch enemy of God, the ancient serpent, Satan, the Devil, whose purpose is to lead the world astray (12:9),[71] who desires to destroy the people of God (12:13) and makes war with the saints of God (12:17). In order to accomplish his purposes the Dragon gains entrance to the earthly realm by establishing a beast in its own image as the geopolitical ruler on earth (13:2).[72] This beast establishes its own authority through another beast who deceives the world to submit to the beast (13:11–17) as well as through a network of vassal rulers.[73] In the way John describes this regime he makes it clear that he has Roman power primarily in mind, the first beast most likely referring to imperial power as centered in emperors, the second to Rome's political religion, the imperial cult as a pivotal institution of maintaining imperial cohesion. Babylon, first introduced in 14:8 (cf. 16:19) and more fully depicted in chs. 17–18, refers to Rome as the geopolitical center of the 'global'[74] empire which as such also represents the empire as a whole. However, precisely because John casts Rome in these mythological roles of God's primordial enemies, they should not be limited to Rome, but are transferable to every power that takes on the role that Rome played.[75]

This draconic order maintains its power primarily by a willing submission of its subjects to the allure of the apparent invincibility of its power (13:3–4, 13–14)[76] and by an unjust distribution of goods and

---

71. "The deceiver of the whole world appears to generalize the narrative of Genesis 3 and apply it to the race (cf. Wis. 2:24)" (Beasley-Murray, *Revelation*, 202).

72. Note how the first beast is cast in the image of the dragon (12:3; 13:1).

73. While the close connection between the city Babylon and vassal kings is made more explicit (17:2; 18:9), such associations are also made in relation to the beast (17:11–12, 15; 19:9).

74. The beast is "given authority over every tribe and people and language and nation" (13:7; cf. 13:12; 17:2).

75. "At the time when John was writing Rome had inspired his views, but because of the description of the city as Babylon the image can be of universal application, a symbol of military power, exile and, for those who witness to the ways of the Lamb, oppression" (Rowland, "Lamb and the Beast," 185).

76. See Bauckham, *Climax of Prophecy*, 431–50 on the distinct use of the *Nero Redivivus* myth in Revelation 13 and 17, the former of the consolidation of imperial power after chaos following the fall of Nero's and the latter to the belief that Nero had not really died but was gone into hiding and would return to take his vengeance on Rome. On the ironic way John employs the myth in Revelation 13, Bauckham says, *Climax of Prophecy*, 433: "Just as Jesus, crucified by Roman power, was vindicated by

privileges to its elites.⁷⁷ However, it tries to subject those who resist it by brute force and with the fear of death (13:9-10, 16).

"Deception" is a catchword Revelation uses to depict the basic character of this kingdom of the world.⁷⁸ First, this deception consists in a blasphemous claim to absolute power. Through the beasts, the Dragon tries to accomplish on earth what it failed to do in heaven, taking the dominion that properly belongs to God.⁷⁹ Through the dazzling might of the first beast and its cultic mystification by the second beast, all "the inhabitants of the earth" are deceived to participate in this blasphemy, perceiving the draconic power as irresistible rather than as a temporary aberration.⁸⁰ In this way, the whole world is deceived to pledge its allegiance to the political order that is moving toward its own destruction in the eschatological judgment of God.⁸¹ Second, this deception consists in the promise of wealth and luxury. For John, it is not the *pax Romana*

---

his resurrection, as Christians saw it, so the beast, struck down by divine judgment, was vindicated by his recovery, as the world in general saw it."

77. This is vividly depicted in ch. 17-18 where the ruling classes are able to live a life in unsurpassed luxury because of their intimate allegiance with the center of power (17:2; 18:2-3, 9-19). On the "unholy allegiance" of Rome's unjust economic structure to the imperial cult, see Kraybill, *Imperial Cult*; he argues that one of John's primary pastoral purposes is to call Christian who might be involved in this economic structure "to sever or to avoid economic and political ties with Rome" (17), and as such be "identified with the poor and marginalized because he believed Christians no longer could participate in an unjust commercial network thoroughly saturated with idolatrous patriotism" (23).

78. Of the 8 times πλανάω occurs in the book, it refers four times to Satan as the one who deceives the world, twice of the second beast as it deceives the world to worship the first beast (13:14; 19:20) with its draconic voice (13:11), once of Babylon as she deceives the world by her magic (18:23), and once of Jezebel (2:20) (this suggests Jezebel advocates compromise with Rome; cf. Witherington, *Revelation*, 65-66).

79. Having failed to destroy the messianic child (12:4-5), having consequently lost his place in the heavenlies (12:7-9), and having failed to conquer the woman who represents God's people on earth, the Dragon begins to make war against her children (12:13-17).

80. Within the spatial and temporal expansion of the book, this invincibility is but the last spasms of the dragon during the "short time" it is banished to earth (12:12), and this power is destined for doom, it will be cast out from the inhabitable creation with the dragon (18:21; 19:20; 20:10).

81. Participation in the draconic order, no matter what one's social status is, entails culpability in its blasphemy and injustice, and thus also entails the same judgment (14:9-10; cf. 6:15; 16:2) "If the existing structures are sinful, participation in them is necessarily complicity with sin" (Wengst, "Babylon," 198).

that characterizes the empire but Babylon the Great whore who with her abominable luxuries enriches those who fornicate with her.[82] This is her φαρμακεία ("magic spell") by which all nations are deceived (18:23; cf. 14:7). The kingdom of the world will be judged precisely for the dark underside of its dual deception, its draconic oppression of those who refuse to submit to its enticing power (13:9–10, 16–17; 15:4–7; 18:24) and its socio-economic injustice, the accumulation of wealth at the expense of "bodies and souls" (18:3, 7, 13).

In summary, the kingdom of the world is the socio-political reality which now holds the sway on earth. It is determined by the reign of God's enemies who maintain their rule through deception (idolatry, power, and economic privileging) and it is characterized by gross injustice and persecution of those who remain faithful to the ways of God as revealed in Christ.

The Fall of Babylon and the End of the Draconic Regime

The *lex talionis* judgment on this draconic regime anticipated in 11:18 is fleshed out in Revelation 14 and following. Here two double motifs dominate: first, those who judge are both God and the Lamb (accompanied with an army of martyrs),[83] and second, the judgment focuses both on Babylon, the geopolitical center of the draconic order, and on the beasts and all their allies.[84]

Let us begin by considering two pivotal aspect of the fall of Babylon. First, its quick and catastrophic demise[85] is God's judgment

---

82. See Bauckham, *Climax of Prophecy*, 338–83 on Revelation 18 and its critique of Roman economic structures.

83. Throughout the impending judgment is attributed to God, often depicted as the fulfillment of God's ὀργή (14:10; 16:19; 19:15). The role of Jesus as eschatological judge begins to emerge in ch. 14 where he is first introduced as the Lamb accompanied with his army of martyrs (14:1–5) and as the agent of the double harvest (14:14–20). His victorious role in the final battle of the beasts and those allied to them is anticipated in 16:15, explicitly stated in 17:12–14 and depicted in 19:11–21.

84. This double concern is evident in 14:8–11, where the angelic call to repentance in light of the impending judgment is followed first by an anticipation of the fall of Babylon (14:8) and second by the final judgment on the beast and its allies (14:9–11). While both of these concerns are evident in the bowl sequence, chs. 17–18 focus on the judgment of Babylon and 19:11–21 on the defeat of beast's regime.

85. The swiftness is repeatedly emphasised in Revelation 18. The chapter begins anticipating that her plagues will overtake her ἐν μιᾷ ἡμέρᾳ (18:8a), and in their three-

on the city for its blasphemous ways, its injustice, and its culpability in the death of the martyrs as well as its other victims.[86] However, second, although God is seen as the agent of the city's destruction, both as it is anticipated and after it has been accomplished, 17:15-18 suggests his actual involvement is indirect. Probably drawing on fears associated with the *Nero Redivivus* myth, John anticipates how precisely one of the emperors who have occupied the position of the beast, accompanied with an alliance of other kings, will turn on its former center of power and destroy it.[87] Babylon falls on the basis on which it is built. The Real Politik of brute force breeds the force that eventually will destroy it.

Now let us consider the final judgment of the draconic order of the beast. First, just as God was seen as the decisive origin of the fall of Babylon, so Jesus, as a great warrior king accompanied with his army of martyrs, is seen as the agent who defeats the beast and its accomplices.[88] Second, however, despite the strongly militaristic imagery of 19:11-21, this is not to be seen as a literal battle but as a legal judgment, where the draconic order of the beast is defeated by Him who is called "the Word of God" (18:13) and makes war with the sword of his mouth. Although this suggests that this battle is not won by conventional military means, this does nevertheless mean that it is a decisive and effective battle since the divine word accomplishes its purposes by merely uttering them.[89]

---

fold lament, the city's vassal kings and merchants cry that her judgment came μιᾷ ὥρᾳ (18:10, 17, 19).

86. Revelation 14:8; 16:19; 18:5, 8b, 20, 24; 19:2.

87. See especially Bauckham, *Climax of Prophecy*, 407-31, who also notes that "redivivus" may be a mistaken term since it implies the belief that Nero has died, which is not a common motif in the myth; rather, people thought he had fled, "in hiding somewhere in the east, and would return across the Euphrates" (421; cf. Witherington, *Revelation*, 177-79; Beale, *Revelation*, 17-18, 877-78).

88. The judgment of Christ as the warrior on the white horse accompanied with his army of martyrs in 19:11-21 is first anticipated in 14:1-5 where Christ, as the Lamb, is introduced as standing on Mt. Zion with his 144.000, then in depiction of the treading of the wine press in 14:20, and finally Christ's anticipation of his own coming as a thief is set in the middle of an anticipation of the final battle in 16:13-16. Against Collins, *Combat Myth*, 224; Swete, *Apocalypse*, 253, I follow Beale, *Revelation*, 960, and others in seeing τὰ στρατεύματα as the saints (Caird, *Revelation*, 244; Harrington, *Revelation*, 191; Witherington, *Revelation*, 243).

89. Just as it there symbolises the effectiveness of the kerygmatic witness (cf. 11:5), so here it represents the effectiveness of the word of judgment. Is this perhaps to be seen as a counterpart to the creative word in Genesis 1, the divine word that is effective simply in its utterance?

Third, this judgment may be depicted as a battle precisely to emphasize that before the kingdom of God can appear as the new geopolitical order on a transformed creation, the kingdom of the world, both its central elite and everything associated with it must be removed.[90] Fourth, precisely because the Messianic warrior is accompanied by the army of martyrs, this also suggests that just as the martyrs in history expose the fundamental weakness in the power of the beast, and thus demonstrate that it is God and not the Beast who has authority over the natural world, so in the eschaton their way is vindicated. In the final demise of all violent pretence of transitory human power, the way of the martyrs who follow the lamb will stand.[91] Finally, and perhaps most importantly, how this judgment actually takes place is never stated. Considering how the actual fall of Babylon is depicted, it is tempting to see the demise of the beasts within the same self-defeating logic of violence.[92] At minimum it must mean that the way of the warrior on the white horse in Revelation 19 cannot be inconsistent with how he as the Lamb won the decisive victory at Easter.[93] However, since the text is silent on the matter, it is perhaps better to be agnostic about the mode of this judgment.[94] This silence may indeed be important since it neither

---

90. Bauckham and Hart, *Hope*, 140–41.

91. See Collins, "Political Perspective," on traditions of resistance in first century Judaism, raging from active revolt to two types of non-violent resistance. Revelation stands within a synergistic tradition of non-violent resistance in which the suffering and death of the saints play an active role in the impending judgment of God on his enemies.

92. See Bredin, *Jesus, Revolutionary*, 200–214 for a non-violent reading of Revelation19. Regarding the rule of the Lamb revealed at Easter Bauckham, *Theology of the Book of Revelation*, 64 says, "When the slaughtered Lamb is seen 'in the midst of' the divine throne in heaven (5:6; cf. 7:17), the meaning is that Christ's sacrificial death *belongs to the way God rules the world*.... Christ's suffering witness and sacrificial death are, in fact ... the key event in *God*'s conquest of evil and establishment of his kingdom on earth." Similarly, Barr, "Apocalypse," 42, sees a reversal of militaristic imagery in ch. 19, in the same fashion as it is seen in 5:5–6. Ford, "Shalom," 67, in her unlikely reading of the rider of ch. 19 as the Memra, sees Revelation as "pacifist apocalyptic writing." See Collins, "Eschatology," 65–72, for counter arguments.

93. "All that is opposed to God's rule, we are to understand, has been defeated by the Lamb.... The continuing and ultimate victory of God over evil which the rest of Revelation describes is no more than the working-out of the decisive victory of the Lamb on the cross" (Bauckham, *Theology of the Book of Revelation*, 74–75).

94. See Bredin, *Jesus, Revolutionary*, 25–35 for a helpful overview of ways in which the violent language of Revelation has been interpreted.

provides an eschatological justification of the use of coercive force nor forecloses the possibility that the exercise of such force may at times be appropriate.[95]

While the focus may be on the judgment on Babylon and the Beasts, the regime change is not completed before the Dragon that has been banished from the earthly realm (20:1–2, 10) and humanity as a whole have been judged according to what citizen registry their deeds have landed them in (20:11–15). This ultimate legal action sounds the final death-knell to the kingdom of the world, both to the powers behind it and those who persist in allegiance to it, and it paves the way for the appearance of the kingdom of God as the divine throne descends from heaven to the earthly realm, in which not a trace of the old order will be found (21:8, 27; 22:15).

The Kingdom of God Centered in the New Jerusalem

When we turn our attention to the nature of the kingdom of God we see that the kingdom of the world is but a parody of what is true of God's rule.[96] In this way John highlights the stark contrast between the two.

First, the way the Dragon attempts to stave off its impending doom by establishing its own kingdom on earth through the astonishing power of the first beast and the religious dazzle of the second is but a poor imitation of how the one enthroned in heaven has won the decisive victory in the martyrological death and the glorious exaltation of the Lamb who now, in the Spirit, extends his victory through the world in the church's martyrological witness. Likewise, Babylon the Great, the earthly center of the Dragon's power, who claims sovereignty of the whole world is proven to be but an unjust Prostitute that will collapse under the very logic by which she hoarded wealth for herself in the light of the New Jerusalem that will descend on earth, brilliant in the

---

95. This is a good example of how while the book has "an implied intense suspicion of the values of the surrounding culture and institutions," it nevertheless does not "set down precise rules of how one should exemplify the divine wisdom" (Rowland, *Revelation* [NIB], 523).

96. If Bauckham's and Hart's suggestion is correct that Jesus avoids making God the subject of βασιλεύω in the Synoptic gospels to emphasise that God does not rule like earthly kings do, (*Hope*, 164) Revelation might be seen as spelling out what this difference lies in. In Revelation, βασιλεύω is always used either of God (11:15, 17; 19:6) or the saints (5:10; 20:4, 6; 22:5).

dazzling glory and holiness of God and the Lamb that occupy its central throne.[97]

Second, in contrast to the illegitimate rule of the Dragon and its earthly cartel, God exercises his sovereignty in a fundamentally different way and for a different purpose.[98] While the rule of the Dragon is characterized by the deceptive threat of its dazzling force, God's just punishment only plays a limited role in his kingdom. In history they are exercized in order to bring people to their senses so they will not perish in the eschatological judgement. And even in this, they can only be successful in tandem with the witness of the church. The purpose for their respective rules is also diametrically opposite to each other. Babylon is structured to enrich the few at the expense of the many while the New Jerusalem exalts all God's servants, so at the end all rule at no one's expense (22:5). And while Babylon's economy is centripetal, privileging the central elite at the expense of those who occupy the periphery,[99] the flow of goods in the New Jerusalem is centrifugal, the river of life flows from the throne, feeding the sap of trees that heal those battered by history (22:1–2).[100] It is from this overflow of divine glory and life that kings and nations respond by bringing their own honour and glory into the city (21:24–26).

Thus, the Kingdom of God is the socio-political reality that has the one and only true claim for the whole creation as its realm. It is

---

97. See Rossing, *Two Cities*, 143, for an overview of what are likely intentional contrasts between the two cities. Kraybill, *Imperial Cult*, 207–14, argues that John uses Ezekiel and Isaiah in his portrait of the New Jerusalem in order to portray her as infinitely better than Babylon; in her, the economic justice of God will replace the injustice and violence of Roman power and commerce.

98. Revelation strongly affirms that God, as creator (4:11) and redeemer (5:10), both rightfully can and does exercise his sovereign rule. Although he seeks to draw all to his way, he will eventually enforce it in eschatological judgment and redemption.

99. "Luxury goods here gravitate to the center to supply an insatiable need. This has the effect of making the rest of the world peripheral. Those on the periphery become merely means of supplying the needs of others" (Rowland, "Lamb and the Beast," 186; cf. Richard, *Apocalypse*, 137).

100. Compare the centripetal logic in the laments of 18:9–19 (cf. 18:3, 7, 24) with the centrifugal wealth and glory of the New Jerusalem in 21:22—22:5 (cf. 21:6-7; 22:17). The cycle of centripetal worship and centrifugal grace is seen particularly well in 22:3–5 where it is precisely οἱ δοῦλοι αὐτοῦ who λατρεύσουσιν αὐτῷ (22:3) who will βασιλεύσουσιν εἰς τοὺς αἰῶνας τῶν αἰώνων (22:5). For the background and appropriation of the idea of the saints participation in eschatological rule, see Roose, *Eschatologische Mitherrschaft*, and "Sharing in Christ's Rule."

determined by the reign of God and is maintained by his justice and his life-giving presence. It is characterized by a peaceful order in which all God's human subjects are exalted to the highest position of honour. This stands in stark contrast to the kingdom of the world, which is based on deception and brute force and maintains its order in order to enrich its central elite at the expense of its peripheral subjects.

What Fades Away and What Remains

In the above discussion of the regime change Revelation expects we discover some stark discontinuities but also some fundamental underlying continuities. The fundamental discontinuity between the future and the present is the agency which rules the earth and the implications this has for life on earth. This includes a replacement of the ruling elite, the political center from which this rule is exercized,[101] and the citizenship of the realm, as well as the eradication of everything associated with the kingdom of the world with the arrival of God's just and life-giving kingdom.[102]

However, intrinsic to the radical discontinuities are some underlying continuities. First, although the regime is replaced, the position of authority which structures the human community remains. The regime change is the correction of a temporal aberration on earth, in which God assumes the position on earth that he already occupies in heaven. Second, the socio-geographical realm which is ruled remains the same, the ordered human social cosmos within its earthly concrete geographical and material context.[103] It is not another realm that is expected but its transformation as God occupies its shaping center.[104] Since the king-

---

101. The throne of God and redeemed humanity gathered around it in the New Jerusalem replaces Babylon and the order of the Beast. Note how while Babylon is geographically limited, the walls of the New Jerusalem stand at the borders of the inhabitable cosmos (cf. 21:8, 27), perhaps indicating that in the eschatological order redeemed humanity as a whole enjoys the privileges limited to city elites in history.

102. The exclusion lists in 21:8, 27; 22:15 function not to identify particularly "bad" sinners but rather refer to those who persist in allegiance to the draconic order (cf. Beasley-Murray, *Revelation*, 314; Caird, *Revelation*, 267; Gundry, "New Jerusalem," 258; Richard *Apocalypse*, 166–68; Witherington, *Revelation*, 256–57).

103. Therefore, "Liberation theologians," rightfully "note that it is the *form* of this world which is passing away rather than this world itself" (Rowland and Corner, *Liberating Exegesis*, 135).

104. Moltmann points out that the eschatological moment is the universal fulfillment of God's radical identification with creation in the cross, "when the whole creation

dom of God will be populated by those who now live on earth and since entrance into the eternal kingdom is contingent upon allegiance to it in history, everyone is kept open to this future, the ecclesial communities must persevere in order to enter it and the rest of the world can enter it if they change their allegiance.[105]

Here we have considered continuities and discontinuities particularly in relation to the book's use of kingdom language but the same dynamic is seen in its expectation of the renewal of the earth as seen in the use of Eden imagery in 21:1—22:5.[106] However, this ecological transformation is contingent on God's dealings with humanity. It is only as God defeats and judges human rebellion and restores humanity to its covenantal relationship with him that the whole created order is transformed.

The Upside Down View from the End

> Revelation attempts to give meaning to the present suffering of the community not with reference to a divine plan of history, but with an understanding of the present from the horizon of the future, that is, from the coming kingdom.[107]

---

will become his dwelling, God's cosmic temple. In the enduring presence of the living God, heaven and earth and all things will become new, and from this new creation death and pain will be excluded. That is the cosmic vision of Revelation 21: the world will become the living-space and the dwelling of the eternal God" (*SW*, 123).

105. So while the churches are those whose future is in the kingdom, they will only enter it if they "hear" the messages the risen Christ gives to them by the Spirit in chs. 2–3, the peoples and nations that now stand under the judgment coming to the order of the dragon will enter the New Jerusalem (21:24–26) if they hear the Gospel and repent (11:13; 14:6–7; 15:3–4). Rowland, "Apocalypse," 137, rightly points out that although the "future triumph of righteousness is assured" in apocalyptic, human destiny is not for-ordained, but is left open.

106. Although 21:4 could be read as indicating a radical and absolute discontinuity between the present and the coming creation, a close reading of 21:1ff suggests not a replacement but a radical transformation of this creation. When God says, "I am making everything new" (21:5), this is best taken quite literally, he does not create new things but rather makes anew what already exists, transforms it, he "still works with the raw materials of the old cosmos. The new creation improves the old but does not substitute one cosmos for another" (Carroll, "Creation," 255; cf. Beale, *Revelation*, 1040; Caird, *Revelation*, 265; Harrington, *Revelation*, 208).

107. Schüssler Fiorenza, *Justice and Judgment*, 50.

John's visions contradict experienced reality. At the time of his writing Jerusalem lay in ruins, occupied at best by animals, while the metropolis of Rome radiated splendour and delighted in its pulsating vitality. In his visions precisely the reverse is the case.[108]

The view of history which emerges from how Revelation sees the future as a regime change does not rely on how things are or what one can hope to develop from the present state of affairs. Rather through an expansion of spatial and temporal categories what appears to be is revealed to be false. This expansion of reality encourages "readers to live faithfully and to avoid damaging compromise with the prevailing political, economic and religious climate of their times"[109] Apart from revelation, the kingdom of the world appears to be the indisputable power on earth, exploiting the earth for its own enrichment and oppressing the few subjects of the rival kingdom. However, within the spatial expansion of Revelation, God is revealed to be the rightful sovereign over both heaven and earth, who already has established his undisputed sovereignty in the heavenly realm and has already won the decisive victory for its establishment on earth. In the temporal expansion of the text, we are shown how God will establish his sovereignty on earth and be the life-giving center of the human community within the earthly realm. Thus, within this temporal and spatial expansion the view of the kingdom of the world is transformed from the one inescapable power whose global expansion it is futile to resist to a temporary and fleeting order that will vanish at the appearance of the kingdom of God.[110] In this vision, the followers of the lamb are transformed from a despised and marginalized sect on the Roman periphery to an army who through their martyrological suffering conquer the powers to be.[111]

Within a framework that expects the perpetual continuation of the present state of affairs, the only rational course of action is to submit to this order, prosper as well as one can by exploiting the possibilities it of-

---

108. Wengst, "Babylon," 197.

109. Gilbertson, *God and History*, 140–41; cf. Wengst, "Babylon," 197.

110. On how the book uses expressions indicating 3 1/2 years to signal the indefinite but short time of the last intensification of the power of evil in the eschaton, see Beale, *Revelation*, 565–68; Beckwith, *Apocalypse*, 252.

111. We will discuss this further in the next chapter.

fers.[112] However, this is turned upside down in the spatial and temporal expansion of reality in Revelation. How things are is the world "as it will not be" while the vision of the kingdom of God is the world "as it is not yet."[113] Therefore, those who seek their own welfare by conforming to the way of the beast will share in the beast's destruction while those who are now crushed by its "irresistible" power will in the end remain standing.[114] They are the victors because theirs is the future. This vision determines the true nature of historical reality as it reveals its end, how everything that opposes God will come to its end when his sovereign presence appears and transforms both creation and the human world that dwells in it.

In this upside-down view of reality, things as they are are revealed to be an illusion. However, this is not a denial of the concrete actuality of the present state of affairs. Beastly rule is as tangible as the slaying of each saint. The unreality of the kingdom of the world and the privileges it can confer to those who play by its rules are real enough. The illusion that is Beast and Babylon is first a relational one. The kingdom is false because it is based in a false claim to authority, separated from the only true sovereign, the One Enthroned in Heaven. And precisely because of this it is also a temporal illusion, an aberration in history, which from the divine perspective is a short-lived revolt.[115] What makes the kingdom of the world illusory is its end, its eventual destruction. *Roma Aeterna* has but a broken time, 3 1/2 short lived years.

---

112. Cf. Bauckham, *Theology of the Book of Revelation*, 36–38.

113. Similarly, Pannenberg notes how Ebeling understands the Word as "an ability to make what is hidden present, especially what is past and future. By making what is not there present, it frees us from bondage to what is there" (as quoted in Gilbertson, *God and History*, 151).

114. It is precisely for this reason that worship is such a key feature of Revelation. Not only does it call attention to whom one should rightly pay homage, but in worship believers acknowledge and give glory to who God is from his viewpoint of reality, and as such worship works "to shape a strategy of resistance" (Ruiz, "Politics of Praise," 393). And so, in the structure of the book, the manifestation of the kingdom in worship is prior to the actualisation of it in narrative (Barr, "Apocalypse," 47).

115. Prigent, *Apocalypse*, vi–vii sees Revelation providing "a complete conversion" of temporality, in which the actuality of the present situation "almost takes on the status of an appearance" by a greater reality where the future "has present undertones" and the present "is open toward eternity."

Therefore, those made rich by Babylon are the poor who cannot escape the city's destruction.[116] In contrast, the future of the kingdom of God is secure, although it now seems to suffer continuous defeat by the powers of the world. It is safe in the promise of God's coming sovereignty on earth. Precisely for this reason those who suffer now because of their allegiance to it are called to endure—theirs is the future.

This view of history then calls for a counter-intuitive praxis, an upside-down way of life, in which one does not conform to how things are but as they are purposed to become.[117] Instead of manipulating the present to fashion one's own desires, one seeks to anticipate this future within the possible. It is precisely "apocalyptic" contexts as reflected in Revelation where this is most starkly revealed. They show the only rational praxis when "the possible" prohibits living from the future: if life can only be maintained by evil means it is better to resist and die than conform and live.[118]

Interaction with Moltmann

Revelation's anticipation of a regime change and Moltmann's understanding of the kingdom as symbol of hope for humanity have some striking consonances but also a fundamental difference. Here, we will first look at how both articulate the expectation of the transformation of the world into the kingdom of God when God's unqualified presence arrives on the earth in similar ways, and how because of these similarities, Moltmann's messianic understanding of history may help us read Revelation theologically within our contemporary situation. Second, we will focus on a pivotal difference, how Revelation's portrayal of the problem the history of the kingdom responds to stands precisely within the traditional trajectory that Moltmann rejects as insufficient. We will then try to show that the traditional understanding may indeed be preferable and can meet Moltmann's criticisms of it. We will conclude by suggest-

---

116. So the exalted Christ proclaims as poor the Laodiceans who think themselves rich (3:17), and urges them to buy true wealth from him (3:18).

117. "Eschatological vision and paraenesis have in Revelation the same function. They provide the vision of an alternative world and kingdom in order to strengthen Christians in their consistent resistance to the oppressive powers and persecution of the Roman Empire" (Hellholm, *Apocalypticism*, 312).

118. Rowland notes (*Revelation* [NIB], 522) that for Revelation "the only acceptable stances are resistance and withdrawal (18:4)."

ing how Revelation's focus on rebellion as the fundamental problem may sharpen and focus Moltmann's understanding of the kingdom as a symbol of hope.

Kingdom Consonances

Hope for the Kingdom of God

> Hope is clearly what the Apocalypse shows us: the affirmation of a counter-reality, but a counter-reality (not at all idealist or future) hidden in the present and of which hope can discern the signs, which never derive from a simple observation of an observable reality . . . Therefore, hope, manifested in the Apocalypse, is always that which declares to the present: "No, it is not the Kingdom of God, nor the reign of Christ"; but it demands that the Christian be situated in the present in terms of this Kingdom. Thus hope is the positive act in face of the too evident absence, which hope measures and knows but also recognizes (in the passage from faith to hope). Therefore the relation between hope and apocalypse is fundamental, but in a totally different sense from the simplistic one which spontaneously comes to mind.[119]

Both Moltmann and Revelation see the future as the transformation of the world into the kingdom of God. At the heart of both is the expectation of a divine interruption of the present state of affairs which will transform everything. For both its arrival has been made possible in the paradoxical victory of Christ at Easter, and for both it is therefore the events of Easter that give a christological shape to the hope for the kingdom. For Moltmann it is because Christ has risen into the future of the kingdom he proclaimed, that his proclamation of the kingdom and the way it is related to his death and resurrection are the hermeneutic anchor for any theological exposition of the kingdom. In Revelation this christological foundation is based in Easter as the decisive victory in a cosmic battle. By his blood, Christ as the Messianic king reconciled a people from all the nations that now exist in rebellion and made them a "kingdom to God." It is in, from, and according to the lamb that people who now live in "occupied territory" can orient themselves toward the liberation of earth by its rightful divine ruler.

---

119. Ellul, *Apocalypse*, 60.

For both, then, kingdom language is not only eschatological but also irreducibly political. Just as Moltmann reminds us that the hope for the kingdom makes politics eschatological and eschatology political, so the use of βασιλεία and other political language in Revelation reminds us that although the kingdom of God is now not politically manifested, it has lost none of its political force but has as its horizon the coming manifestation of God's geopolitical rule in the realm of the whole earth.

For both, this transformation of the world at the arrival of the kingdom involves both discontinuities and underlying continuities. The kingdom as the telos of human history is so only as an interruption of things as they are. As such, the light the coming kingdom sheds on the present state of affairs prophetically uncovers their true nature. However, underlying this discontinuity that places the present in the prophetic light of the future, is an equally important continuity, that the kingdom hoped for is not an abstract utopia, an idea without a place, but is intrinsically related to the concrete and actual socio-political realities that are now the ordering principles of human communities. Since, as Bauckham notes of Moltmann in particular but which is true of Revelation as well, "it is hope for the future of this world, its effect is to show the present reality to be *not yet* what it can be and will be. The world is seen as transformable in the direction of the promised future. In this way believers are liberated from accommodation to the status quo and set critically against it. They suffer the contradiction between what is and what is promised."[120]

Thus, against an influential strand in New Testament studies, ἡ βασιλεία τοῦ θεοῦ ("the kingdom of God"), at least in Revelation, does not refer to God's rule abstracted from its geopolitical implications.[121] Rather, it points to the eschatological location of this manifestation, and then seeks to extrapolate what is the appropriate political stance during the time when this kingdom is awaited but not yet geopolitically manifested, an issue we will return to in the next chapter.

---

120. Bauckham, *Theology of Jürgen Moltmann*, 10.

121. See, e.g., France, "Church and the Kingdom" (who draws on Perrin, *Jesus and the Language of the Kingdom*); Beavis, "Kingdom of God."

History as Seen from the End

From this future, hope and the way in which they configure it, emerges for both a view of history in which the way things appear is turned upside down. For Moltmann it is precisely those who are the victims of the history of the world that are the main subjects of the history of the kingdom of God, and for Revelation it is precisely those who now suffer at the margins of Babylon for their allegiance to Christ who now, in their paradoxical victory, push history toward its transformation. Referring specifically to Revelation, Moltmann sees the importance of apocalyptic to lie precisely in unsettling the status quo of the powers to be by revealing their eschatological instability, that "they will perish in the sea of chaos out which they rose. 'But he who endures to the end shall be saved.' The eschatological message of the New Testament . . . is geared towards resistance, and against resignation."[122]

The hope for the kingdom depicts the world "as it is not yet," and the light this vision gives reveals the present state of affairs as "the world as it will not be." For both this results in a historical praxis that goes against the grain of the obvious; in light of the way the kingdom is revealed in Christ, one "is not brought into harmony and agreement with the given situation, but is drawn into the conflict between hope and experience."[123] In Revelation, reflecting a context of socio-political marginalisation, this means faithfulness to the prophetic kerygma that proclaims the crucified as Lord and exposes the deceptive nature of the order of the Beast. Central to this proclamation is a refusal to engage in the idolatry and injustice of the draconic order, even if this means suffering death at its hands. Reflecting a context where 'faith-full' socio-political engagement is possible, Moltmann emphasizes how this kerygmatic resistance involves a messianic mediation of history: Since Jesus brought the kingdom into history, the kingdom is the eschatological future that determines the present; therefore "we can already live in light of the 'new era' in the circumstances of the 'old' one."[124] In this light, "set free from the power of the facts of the present time, and from the laws

---

122. *CoG*, 137.
123. *TH*, 18.
124. *CPS*, 192.

and compulsions of history," Christians anticipate the kingdom within the world as it is, and in this way history becomes eschatological.[125]

While Moltmann and Revelation share this eschatological perspective on history, Revelation also sets present earthly reality within a larger spatial context. The future of the world comes from above, it is the earthly manifestation of what is already the case in the heavenly realm. Revelation's emphasis on how the sovereignty of God and the Lamb are already established as the *de facto* actuality of the heavenly realm, may suggest ways in which Moltmann can overcome the singularly temporal focus that characterized his early theology. Moltmann has more recently sought to complement this in paying increasing attention to spatial categories, especially in his doctrine of God and in his understanding of the relationship between God and creation. However, his discussion of "heaven" as the realm of God's presence is still overtly abstract. It literally has no 'room' for concrete created realities since heaven is the realm from which their potential grows but not where they are actualized.[126] Despite the difficulty "heaven" poses to a modern cosmology, Revelation's emphasis that it is not simply the realm of God's presence but the place where God's sovereignty is the ordering reality of the heavenly community, can provide Moltmann with "a wider, deeper reality within which present, earthly reality is to be seen."[127] If this is granted, then the hiddenness of God does not have to be seen in only temporal terms. Rather, the true nature of reality is then revealed in a spatial expansion of reality, and this spatial expansion is verified in the vision's temporal expansion.[128]

Reading Revelation through Moltmannian Lenses

The book of Revelation is written within a context where faithfulness to the gospel necessarily means social marginalisation. The positive ministry of the church to the world is seen solely in terms of its prophetic

---

125. *CrG*, 1; cf. *CPS*, 192.

126. Although Moltmann calls heaven as "the kingdom of God's creative potentialities" which have an ontological priority to "the kingdom of the world's reality," it nevertheless remains the realm of the potential, not the actual. It is the realm of "potentialities and potencies" that due to their proximity to God's presence "acquire almost no form of their own which could be defined" (*GiC*, 166).

127. Gilbertson, *God and History*, 178.

128. Ibid., 179.

testimony to the alternative of the Lamb, which includes both warning the world of how it moves toward a deadly end and calling people to a repentance that necessarily leads to marginalisation and possibly death. As such the book is always first the book of oppressed and persecuted Christians, empowering those rendered powerless, assuring them that the way of the kingdom will eventually defeat their oppressors.[129]

However, can the book also speak to Christians who occupy position of social and economic privilege, for whom political engagement is not only possible but often also a responsibility? It is precisely here Moltmann can give some insight. First, his messianic dialectic affirms what is central to Revelation, the church's kerygmatic proclamation. Whether one agrees or disagrees with how he develops this, Moltmann is a confessional theologian, one who seeks to articulate what it means to proclaim and live the apostolic kerygma within our contemporary setting.[130] And in doing so, he has continually emphasized what Bauckham sees as central to Revelation, to reject any allegiance to the status quo that benefits the powers to be and situate oneself with their victims. Bauckham says: "John's critique of Rome therefore did more than voice the protest of groups exploited, oppressed and persecuted by Rome. It also required those who could share in her profits to side with her victims and become victims themselves."[131]

Second, his understanding of a Christian anticipatory praxis can help bridge Revelation's kerygmatic resistance into a context of engagement. As an example, let us return to the contrast between Babylon the Great and the New Jerusalem, focusing on the place of economic wealth within them. A basic question Moltmann would want to ask of the immense wealth associated with both cities is for whose benefit it exists?[132]

---

129. Therefore, a crucial aspect of reading Revelation today is to consider how those who are located on social and geopolitical peripheries read it today; so Richard, *Apocalypse*, 2, intentionally writes his commentary for the base ecclesial communities in their struggle in Latin America.; see also *JSNT* 25:2, a volume on the use of apocalyptic in Liberation theology, collected in the hope it "will allow a broadening of the process of dialogue" (Nogueira, "Introduction," 126).

130. So, in *TH*, 195, he says "the Christian consciousness of history . . . is a missionary consciousness in the knowledge of a divine commission, and is therefore a consciousness of the contradiction inherent in this unredeemed world, and of the sign of the cross under which the Christian mission and the Christian hope stand."

131. Bauckham, *Climax of Prophecy*, 378.

132. On Moltmann's view of theology as a critical theory informed by the cross, see *CrG*, 68–75.

Babylon's wealth is centripetal. The city enriches itself at the expense of others. This is implied in the pronouncement of her *lex talionis* judgment in 18:4–8—she will be punished according to the measure she has unjustly enriched herself—and is most poignantly depicted in the cargo list of 18:12–13. Through the trading system she controls, Babylon is able to draw every conceivable luxury into herself, even "bodies and souls of people." For John the *pax Romana* did not exist for the peace of the realm, but for the sensuous and material lust of Rome.[133] The power structure of the city exists precisely to maintain this unjust distribution of wealth. Babylon is a Prostitute queen who fornicates with the kings she has political power over (17:2,18; 18:3, 7). This imagery of sexual promiscuity is closely linked with the city's unjust economics, the kings' fornication is their participation in her sensuous luxury.[134] The ruling class amasses this wealth through a merchant class which enriches itself by providing the luxurious goods the city desires.[135] This ruling elite of the powerful and rich maintain the centripetal economics of Babylon not only by force, but also by keeping the masses of the city happy, letting some of the 'glory' they see trickle down to them.[136] The victims of this centripetal economy are the periphery, both the actual geographical periphery that is stripped of its resources and the social periphery, the slaves and other victims that this system relies on.[137]

---

133. Babylon lives for ἐδόξασεν αὐτὴν καὶ ἐστρηνίασεν (18:7).

134. The association of wealth with her identity as a prostitute is first made in the way she is dressed in the wealth she amasses (18:4; note how all the things she is wearing in 18:4 is repeated in the cargo list of 18:12–13). 18:9 links the kings' fornication with their partaking in Babylon's wealth.

135. While the ruling elite is able to gratify its material lust by power (note the phrase τῆς δυνάμεως τοῦ στρήνους αὐτῆς in 18:3), the merchants grow wealthy by their ability to satisfy this craving (thus, they grow rich from Babylon's power for self-gratification; 18:3; cf. 18:11, 17b, 19b).

136. This is likely what John refers to when he uses various collective terms for the whole of humanity as intoxicated with Babylon's wine (13:14, 16–17; 14:8; 17:2, 8; 18:3, 23). Being enthralled by her might and dazzling wealth, even those exploited by her, "the ordinary people of the empire, welcome her rule" (Bauckham, *Climax of Prophecy*, 228–30).

137. The real cost of Rome's economy is poignantly emphasised in the last items of the cargo list, σωμάτων, καὶ ψυχὰς ἀνθρώπων (18:13). See Witherington, *Revelation*, 228–30 for a brief overview of the importance of slavery in Roman economy and society.

In contrast, the economics of the New Jerusalem is centrifugal. While Babylon seeks to glorify herself with the luxuries she draws into herself, the glory of God is the center of the New Jerusalem and the wealth associated with God's glory is its constituent fact—the New Jerusalem has no need to rob other of wealth for she is wealth.[138] Instead, her riches flow from the central throne of God and the Lamb to those who need it: her citizens can freely drink of the river of life that flows from the throne, and the trees that are nourished by this water bear leaves that are for the healing of the nations (21:6; 22:1-2; cf. 22:17). This centrifugal overflow of God's life-giving glory results in a centripetal response; when the glorious presence of God is the geopolitical light of the world, the nations and their kings bring in their own splendour, honour and glory into it (21:22-26). But this submission of the nations to the throne of God does not result in bondage but rather in exaltation. Those who submit unconditionally to the centripetal attraction of the rule of God are drawn into the centrifugal grace of God; those who serve God forever are precisely those who will rule forever (22:3-5). Thus, while the order of the beast deals in the bodies and souls of men and women in order to enrich its own elite, the servants of God and the lamb are exalted to a position of authority where all rule and no one is ruled.

Barbara Rossing has convincingly shown that one of the primary reasons why John contrast these two cities as the choice between two women, is precisely in order to urge his readers to abandon the deceptive way of the prostitute, to come out of her (18:4) and orient themselves toward the other, to be those whose righteousness the Bride is clothed with (19:8).[139] How may Moltmann help us heed this call today?

First, and not unlike the task John called his audience to do, it will consist in analyzing particular power structures in light of this vision of the liberating authority of God.[140] In the political sphere, this means

---

138. Note how the brilliance of the divine glory that shines from this city is likened to precisely the precious stones that Babylon dresses herself with (21:11: cf. 17:4; 18:12). Second, while Babylon amasses gold, precious stones and pearls that she clothes herself in by her power (17:4; 18:12, 16), these are the constituent material of the eternal city, her wall and foundation stones are various kinds of precious stones (21:19-20), the city and its streets are pure gold (21:18, 21b) and its gates are pearls (21:21a).

139. Rossing, *Two Cities*, 140-44.

140. In the next chapter we will consider in greater detail the actual differences between Moltmann's and Revelation's understanding of the liberating rule of God.

to unearth the often hidden motives within the structuration of society, uncover the reality beneath the rhetoric. For example, is our current economic and at times military export of Western democracy fuelled by a desire for others' freedom or an attempt to retain our own global privilege? Second, having done this, Christians need to seek a restructuring of economic life and the power mechanisms that maintain it, seek to turn centripetal tendencies into centrifugal possibilities. Christians, in their political praxis, must seek to establish a political system which exists to exalt its citizens, that is designed to struggle to create the context in which all flourish and everyone can enter the fullness of their personhood. This Moltmannian mediation of Revelation's vision into a context of political engagement is possible precisely because it accentuates what often has been denied or marginalized in both biblical study and theology, the concrete and this-worldly aspects of the language of the kingdom of God, that although the βασιλεία τοῦ θεοῦ is now manifested in hidden ways, its ultimate claim is the whole human community as it exists in the earthly realm.[141]

A Time for Rebellion and Sin?

> No form of Christian teaching has any future before it except such as can keep steadily in view the reality of the evil in the world, and go to meet the evil with a battle-song of triumph.[142]

Both Revelation and Moltmann want to meet "the evil in the world . . . with a battle-song of triumph" in their visions of the future kingdom that is the resolution to the apparent absence of God in history. However, they account for this evil and this absence in fundamentally different ways. For the former Evil has gained entrance on earth in human rebellion, while for the latter human evil is symptomatic of a fundamental contradiction in creation. Picking up the critique of Moltmann's position with which we concluded our analysis of his understanding of the kingdom as symbol of hope, I will try to respond to Moltmann's misgiv-

---

141. Likewise, in relation to creation generally, Moltmann notes that if the last vision in Revelation anticipates the final "cosmic indwelling" of God in creation, this now necessarily means that we now see the earth as God's temple "and keep all earth creatures holy" ("Progress and Abyss," 314).

142. Aulen, *Christus Victor*, 159.

ings about the tradition Revelation stands in and in return show how it can better account for the weaknesses in Moltmann's own proposal.[143]

Has Sin Had Its Time?

Although ἁμαρτία ("sin") occurs only three times in Revelation, its usage is significant: at the outset of the book we are told that Christ "freed us from our sins by his blood, and made us to be a kingdom" (1:5b–6a), and in the depiction of defeated Babylon, God's people are urged to flee the city in order not to participate in its sin and consequently share in the judgment for her sin (18:4–5). However, what Paul labels "sin" is more commonly depicted in Revelation as a rebellion of cosmic proportions.[144] The arch enemy of God, the Devil, has been able to gain entrance to the earthly realm through the earthly powers that have the authority over human societies and structure them. The rest of humanity is culpable in this rebellion as they submit to its deception.[145] This is the situation human beings need and can be redeemed from by shifting their allegiance to Christ who establishes them as "a kingdom to God" by his paradoxical and decisive victory on the cross. It is in the fulfilment of the history Easter is the center of that the whole created order will be transformed in the arrival of God's sovereign presence on earth.[146] In the following discussion we will return to our earlier discussion on why Moltmann finds such a view insufficient and consider how Revelation may respond to these critiques.

Sin as the Fundamental Human and Pivotal Cosmic Problem

Moltmann's first objection was the impossibility to trace death and suffering directly to sin in light of what we know today about ecological

---

143. When Moltmann speaks of sin and death in Revelation, he only notes how it distinguishes between the first (physical death) and the second death (separation from death), and how it personifies death (*CoG*, 82–83).

144. On ἁμαρτία in Paul, see Gaventa, "Cosmic Power," who suggest that he understands sin within an apocalyptic framework in which Death gains entrance into the world in human sin, and as such reflects a similar idea as found in Revelation.

145. Although Babylon is judged for deceiving the whole world (18:23), those deceived are culpable for their submission to the draconic order (14:9–10; cf. 18:4).

146. This does not preclude that God may have other concerns, as the references to "sea" and "curse," in 21:1–7 and 22:3 may indicate, only that the book focuses on the manifestation of the demonic rebellion in humanity and the radical implications this has for the whole cosmos.

history. However, although a strict causal relationship between sin and suffering is perhaps but certainly not necessarily implied in Revelation, the point accented is not the possible state of creation before the fall nor whether transience in an absolute sense is necessarily problematic. What is pivotal for Revelation, as well as for Paul in Romans 8, is the way in which human rebellion is *the fundamental problem* facing humanity, and how as such it is *the pivotal problem* for the rest of the created order.[147]

As the fundamental problem of humanity, sin is a fissure in the relationship between God and humanity which corrupts all the relationship humanity stands in. In Revelation this is depicted as a fundamental and universal rebellion that has gained entrance in the human cosmos in and through the reign of the beast. Redemption is made possible precisely in a divine irruption, in the lamb's purchase of a people who are to be a kingdom to God.

However, there is a close relationship between this history of redemption and the transformation of creation. The fundamental problem in human history is also the pivotal problem in the history of creation. This is obvious in Paul, where the liberation of creation from its own bondage is dependent upon "the freedom of the glory of the children of God" (Rom 8:21).[148] Although the consequences of the corruption of human authority are not spelled out as in Rom 8:19–22, certain texts in Revelation imply a similar relationship: the displacement of God's life-giving presence during the history in which the draconic beast has usurped God's rightful βασιλεία on earth results in the devastation of earth. But when God finally takes the βασιλεία that is rightfully his, not

---

147. See Gowan, "Fall and Redemption," on how apocalyptic consistently discusses creation as it is related to the fate of humanity. Also, even Paul may not see as a strict relationship between sin and transience as such as often assumed. Although the term he uses for "decay" in Rom 8:21, φθορά, refers commonly in Greek literature to the mutability and eventual decay of all material things, Jonathan Moo (personal correspondence, February 2005) suggests that Paul rather is appealing to Isaiah 24:1, emphasising the devastation of sin on the material order but without necessarily making a statement on the nature of transience as such. Paul's concern is not the metaphysical question of the origin of transience but the devastating effect human sin has had on creation and why God has allowed it (Moo, "Nature").

148. So, the fundamental problem in creation is not the same as that of humanity but is contingent upon it, just as its liberation is.

only is humanity reconciled but the whole created order is transformed in the life-giving glory of his presence.[149]

While this does not answer the origin of transience as such, it makes a sufficient account for the pathologies of human existence in its relations before God within the realm of creation. What is significant for humanity is not the final cause of creation's transience, but how their own condition impinges on creation, what happens to creation, for better or worse, because of the way humanity interacts with it.

Sin as Social Structuring and Personal Internalization

Moltmann's second objection was that "suffering as *punishment for sin*" is only of limited value[150] and particularly inappropriate when considering the victims who suffer the violence of others.[151] However, Revelation's picture of sin as rebellion can both uphold the universality of human sinfulness and a differentiated understanding of how people, whether individually or corporally, partake in and experience the consequences of sin.

First, since the center and source of the rebellion is in the demonic and idolatrous usurpation of God's position of sovereignty on earth, sin is logically a socio-political structural phenomenon before it is a personal and individual one. The blasphemous beast occupies the central structuring position in human society and as such corrupts the "social construction" of society.[152] As such, sin can be seen as the transpersonal power that is the systemic web that orders social practices, a web that "once ministered to life" but "now work for death."[153] It is through the socio-political web of the Beast that the Dragon can deceive the inhabitants of the world.[154] However, second, unlike Moltmann, Revelation

---

149. While the geopolitical manifestation of the dragon results in the destruction of the earth (11:18; cf. 18:2), the creation made new in the descent of God's presence (21:5) has a life-giving river and leaves that heal (22:1–2).

150. *TKG*, 49–50.

151. See *CrG*, 274–90, where Moltmann suggests panentheism as a response to Auschwitz.

152. It is the beast that blasphemes God that has received the authority of the dragon "over every tribe and people and language and nation" (13:7).

153. *WJC*, 184–85.

154. In 12:9 Satan is depicted as the Dragon that deceives the whole world (ὁ πλανῶν τὴν οἰκουμένην ὅλην; cf. 20:3, 8, 10), a deception which is accomplished through the earthly powers he works through (13:14; 18:23; 19:20).

unambiguously sees a universal and culpable submission to this corrupting order.[155] All "the inhabitants of the earth" have submitted to the beast and as such have become like it, are marked by it. Borrowing language from sociology, sin is both the objectified social order which the ruling elite have externalized but also the way in which everyone who lives under that order has internalized it and made it their own.[156] As we will consider in the next chapter, this complex understanding of sin may be reflected in the two parallel statements on what Jesus accomplishes in his death (1:5-6; 5:9:10), in redeeming a people God both liberates them from their bondage to the corrupting order of the Beast and forgives them for their own culpability in submitting to it.[157] Therefore, rather than "having a limited value," as Moltmann claims, the atonement of the Lamb for the sin of all human beings as the Lamb "laid down his life in sorrow and love" gives an "awareness of the depth of love involved in the atoning sacrifice" that even exceeds Jesus' identification with the sufferings of the victims in the world.[158]

Although this means all are sinners, it does not mean that this proclamation and call come in the same form to all. First, to those at the center of the draconic order of the beast the gospel comes as a warning: The order whose injustice they enjoy is a historical aberration, and in order to avoid perishing with its destined destruction,

---

155. While Moltmann is best ambiguous on the universality of sin as an individual phenomena (seen best in his reluctance in seeing the poor as sinners) and unclear about an individual's responsibility for their own sin, Revelation strongly affirms that humanity as a whole has been corrupted and is culpable for its corruption (14:9-10; cf. 13:3-4, 7-8, 14; 18:4).

156. See Berger, *Sacred Canopy*, ch. 1, on the dynamics of social construction as a process of externalisation, objectification and internalisation by which anomic chaos is held at bay by the construction of a social cosmos. However, in Revelation this logic is turned on its head. What is held at bay is the cosmos as intended in the creative purposes of God while the order that is internalised is the chaos of the beast.

157. In 1:5b the Lamb's act of liberation is depicted as λύσαντι ἡμᾶς ἐκ τῶν ἁμαρτιῶν ἡμῶν ἐν τῷ αἵματι αὐτοῦ, reflecting the cultic need for forgiveness for personal defilement by sin. However, in 5:9b Jesus ἠγόρασας τῷ θεῷ ἐν τῷ αἵματί σου a people, reflecting language used for ransom paid in order to free people that have been taken by an invading army (Schüssler Fiorenza, *Justice and Judgment*, 74). If this is case, then the constitution of the redeemed people as a kingdom to God is established both by liberating them from the transpersonal structure they are enslaved by and the defilement of their own sin.

158. Williams, "On Giving Hope," 16.

they must change their allegiance.[159] If they do, they can expect suffering but also an inheritance among the redeemed who will "reign forever and ever" (22:5).

Second, to those who occupy the peripheral location of the social realm of the beast, the gospel comes as the promise that the order whose injustice they suffer is coming to an end.[160] However, unlike Moltmann, Revelation unambiguously affirms that those who persist in the rebellion of the beast, no matter whether great or small, will share in its destiny (14:9–10; 18:4). Unlike Moltmann, therefore, the community of the poor do not by definition constitute one of Christ's two "congregations."[161] It assumes that even those who suffer under an unjust order are marked by its injustice, and that fundamental to their liberation is the repentance that reorders human thinking and praxis. This may, in the end, provide a better rationale to one of Moltmann's own concerns, that the 'counter-intuitive' way of the Lamb goes beyond both accommodation to the order as it exists and the rebellion that merely reverses the positions of privilege and oppression but leaves the fundamental structuration of the order intact.[162]

Third, although not an emphasis in Revelation, the promise that God "will wipe every tear from their eyes" (21:4) suggests also how such a view of sin as the universal problem redemption responds to can ac-

---

159. This is a warning directed as much to those inside the ecclesial communities as those outside as is evident in the addresses to the churches in chs. 2–3.

160. In this, Moltmann's pastoral concerns can accentuate what only exist in suggestive form in the text, how the promise of the gospel gives hope to all whose blood is found in Babylon (18:24).

161. Moltmann's discussion of the "congregation of the poor" is heavily dependent on identifying the τούτων τῶν ἀδελφῶν μου τῶν ἐλαχίστων // τούτων τῶν ἐλαχίστων in Matt 25:40, 45 as the poor in general. This of course is a debated issue, several commentators seeing it as referring to the disciples (so Gundry, *Matthew*, 514–15; Kingsbury, *Matthew*, 76; Luz, *Theology*, 129–30; but against them, Davies and Allison, *Matthew*, 428–29). Acknowledging that this is "the weight of exegetical opinion," Rowland, "Lamb and the Beast," 188–89, nevertheless opts against this "exclusive" understanding, since the letter of the text does not demand it and since crucial to the text is that "it does not allow the reader to be complacent in the face of judgment."

162. Here, Christ's command to the Laodicean community to buy wealth from him is suggestive: He calls them from their accommodation to the Roman way (3:17–18) by calling them to give place for the way of his messianic banquet (3:20), whose final fulfillment we find in the life of the New Jerusalem (note how 19:9 anticipates 21:1ff in the imagery of a wedding banquet), which is characterised by the free and gracious flow of resources (21:6–7, 22–26; 22:1–5; cf. 22:17).

count for suffering that cannot be reduced to perpetuating or suffering injustice. There is suffering, deep suffering, that cannot be traced to anything but the painful absence of God's life-giving presence on earth. While the ultimate cause of this absence is humanity's primordial rebellion, such suffering does not have its basis in any particular sin but rather the condition sin produced. Therefore, the church must resist tracing such suffering to individual or structural sin but simply walk with the sufferer, and in the darkness that suggests otherwise, hope for the eschatological verification of God's goodness.

Transformation: Restoration and Maturation

The last objection Moltmann has to the traditional understanding is that it leads to a conservative vision of a pristine primordial state corrupted by history. This, however, is not necessarily so; Revelation's vision of the future is both restorative and transformative: In its use of creation imagery, Revelation 21–22 expects a *restoration* of humanity to its intended role which results in a *transformation* of the whole cosmos.[163] Such a vision does not only counter the charge of conservatism but is also politically more open than Moltmann's view. Since it contains both restorative and transformative elements, it neither favours a return to an ideal past nor assumes that the new always bears the seeds of the preferable, which Moltmann tends to do since the old always inheres in creation's fundamental contradiction. If one is bound by the expectation of *the restoration* of humanity's relationship with God which will *transform* all things, one is radically free when seeking to discern what mixture of restoration, preservation and innovation a particular situation calls for.[164]

A Time for Rebellion?

Having shown how the understanding of sin depicted in Revelation can account for the criticism Moltmann levies against it, we now turn to how it avoids the weaknesses in Moltmann's own view.

---

163. In the final vision, humanity is not only restored in its covenantal relationship with God (21:3) but the return of God's presence as this relationship is restored effects a transformation of the created order that goes far beyond the original creation (21:1b, 4).

164. Similarly, Gilbertson, *God and History*, 199–201, argues that the vision of the New Jerusalem may transcend the difference between Moltmann and Pannenberg since it envisions both the transformation (Moltmann) and completion (Pannenberg) of the present.

The Goodness of Creation and the Cataclysm of the Fall

We have argued that Moltmann in the end cannot affirm the goodness of creation because he postulates a fundamental contradiction in its very structure that must be overcome if it is to be liberated. However, one way of understanding the relationship between *creatio orginalis* and *creatio nova* that allows for movement, where telos and origin are not identical, but nevertheless avoids postulating a fundamental contradiction in creation is the notion of maturation in which humanity plays a pivotal role as the *imago dei*.[165]

First, although *creatio orginalis* is intrinsically good, it is so in a similar way as a well-formed new born. It is good as it is but an essential part of its goodness is its potential for maturation, and therefore cannot be seen apart from its telos.[166]

Second, humanity was created to play a pivotal role in this history of the created order. They were to be God's rulers of the earth[167] through whom the earth flourishes and all who live in it find a meaningful place in the community of the living. As such, although humanity on its own is mortal and creation transient, they were purposed for immortality and intransience as humanity lived in life-giving communion with God and mediated his life-giving presence to creation.[168] However, both these were contingent on obedience, free will being a condition for human freedom.[169] Apart from humanity growing into its own maturity to freedom, creation cannot attain its own completion. Within this logic, the goodness of creation can be unambiguously affirmed because it, in

---

165. The idea of both the maturation of creation and humanity is primarily associated with Irenaeus.

166. Such a notion of movement may indeed by imbedded within the creation narratives themselves, both in the notion that humanity as those created in the *imago dei* are to be the stewards of the earth and are commanded to fill it, and in the image of Adam as the one who tills the temple garden of God.

167. See Wenham, *Genesis*, 27–32, for an insightful exegetical study on Gen 1:26.

168. Says Lossky of Maximus the Confessor: "It was the divinely appointed function of the first man, according to Maximus, to unite in himself the whole of created being; at the same time to reach his perfect union with God and thus grant the state of deification to the whole creation" (Lossky, *Mystical Theology*, 109) However, I would not follow Maximus' unitary notion of perfection (Lossky, *Mystical Theology*, 110).

169 Walsh, "Theology of Hope," 64, who suggest freedom gives creation a "structure . . . open to two directions, viz., obedience or disobedience."

its pre-fall condition, does not require an interruption in its basic constitution in order to mature into its own fulfilment.

Third, it is when we consider how humanity, as God's vice-regents, were purposed to order creation towards its telos within God's life-giving presence, that the cataclysmic effect of sin becomes explicable. In their rebellion, absolute death gains entrance on earth, and through humanity spreads throughout the earth as the final horizon which creation moves toward.[170] This does not mean that before the fall creation was intransient but that it has been cut off from the kind of intransience it was destined for through the mediating agency of humanity.[171] This is the cosmic fissure creation suffers in the fall of humanity, it has lost its orientation toward life and moves relentlessly toward barrenness and eventual disintegration. This leaves pre-lapsarian suffering unanswered, the "shocking [fact that] ... wherever a number of different animals live together, for example in a marshy lake or in the open sea, each kind of animal is the terror of the others!"[172] However, it does explain what is significant for humanity, its own relationship to creation in both creation and redemption. Perhaps this restoration of humanity's place in creation is what the visionary complex of Revelation ends with, humanity gathered around God's throne as his servants who rule a transformed creation that is bursting with life (22:1–5).[173]

Fourth, we can now more clearly understand both the restorative and the transformative elements in Christian hope: Humanity is *restored* to its proper place in the created order. But this does not constitute a return to a pristine primordial order. Rather, this restitution *transforms* humanity from being the destroyers of the earth (11:18) to those in whose guardianship creation not only attains its own fulfilment in the life-giving presence of God but also becomes the creation that can heal

---

170. For a suggestive exploration of how Paul may understand sin in precisely such a way, see Gaventa, "Cosmic Power."

171. This leaves the questions also open whether transience as such is necessary problematic and suggests it is perhaps only problematic relationally, i.e. transience is only problematic in regard to that which was purposed to be or become intransient. Within biblical faith, this seems at minimum to include humanity and the created order as a whole, leaving the question open what other creatures are destined for eternal life.

172. Heim as quoted in Gowan, "Fall and Redemption," 86.

173. Since themes from Genesis 1–3 are a dominant factor in Rev 21:5—22:5, how the final vision in Revelation concludes may well be John's anticipation of the fulfillment of Gen 1:28 (so Gundry, "New Jerusalem," 264).

humanity from the wounds of its sin-battered history (22:2). Against Moltmann, it is perhaps better to follow Paul who sees the groaning of creation "in terms of Adam's sin, not the inherent structure of creaturliness, and promises liberation for that same creation when redemption is manifest in the appearing of the 'children of God,' the 'redemption of our bodies.'"[174] Seeing redemption as the restoration of humanity's role in creation, then does not allow for escapist faith, but, as Moltmann rightly emphasizes, calls those who believe into a praxis for the transformation of the world and creation they inhabit.

An Anthropocentric Concern for Creation on Its Own

Our second criticism of Moltmann's adaptation of the logic of redemption was that, against his intentions, it anthropomorphized creation. But have we not done exactly the same in the view proposed here? It certainly is anthropocentric in its focus on human history and its assumption that human history plays a central role in the destiny of creation.[175] But it is not anthropomorphic precisely because creation is contingent on humanity's salvation. While humanity and the rest of creation are cast in parallel terms in Moltmann's understanding of the cross and resurrection, here it is only humanity that needs forgiveness and is redeemed in the cross. Creation's liberation is indirectly related to the cross; the cross makes its liberation possible because it reconciles humanity with God and in this way restores humanity to its proper role in creation. It is only as this communion is restored, as the kingdom of God descends on earth, that creation finds its own fulfilment in the life-giving presence of God's rule mediated through his priestly servants who will rule forever.

Since this central human role in creation and history is ultimately grounded in a theocentric vision, it ought to resist a utilitarian view of creation. A critique of just such a utilitarianism may be discerned in Rev 11:18b, where the enemies of God are not only punished because of their persecution of the saints but also because they have destroyed the earth. Humanity's stewardship of creation cannot simply be for its own

---

174. Walsh, "Theology of Hope," 64.

175. Although Revelation and apocalyptic literature generally has a higher view of creation than often is assumed (Carroll, "Creation," 259; Gowan, "Fall and Redemption," 101) its discussion of the state of creation is closely linked with its concern with the history of humanity (Gowan, "Fall and Redemption," 100).

benefit but must fundamentally involve nurturing the creation God deemed very good.

When viewing the central role of humanity in creation within a larger theocentric vision, we can develop an appropriate Christian response to the ecological crisis we face today:[176] a) negatively, the current devastation of the creation is the result of human sin and is intrinsically link with its abuse of its position of authority in creation;[177] b) as we now see the devastating effects of our ecological sin, we must resolve to reconsider what our appropriate place in the created order is; c) for Christians, a pivotal part of this reassessment is the conviction that when God reconciled humanity to himself in the cross, he did it not simply for their own sake, but also so that through them his purposes for creation may be fulfilled;[178] d) therefore, if Christians believe the cosmic implications of the cross and resurrection they proclaim, they must anticipate the coming healing of creation by tending to its wounds now.

In the end, then, such an anthropocentric view of creation does not come at the expense of creation but rather points realistically to the role in creation we cannot avoid having. The attempt to heal creation's wounds and help it to come into its own is no less anthropocentric than

176. The contemporary urgency to recognize creation's integrity on its own is ironically anthropologically grounded. While many of our ancestors also disregarded the natural order, or even despised it, their detrimental influence was local and limited. However, now our impact on the ecological order is universal and potentially irreversible and therefore a new "tradition-building" is paramount (Gowan, "Fall and Redemption," 102). For an example on the potential of neglected NT nature text for developing a responsible ecological theology, see Bauckham, "Wild Animals," a study on Mark 1:13, where Bauckham argues that the terse phrase ἦν μετὰ τῶν θηρίων depicts the messianic restoration of humanity's relationship with the wild animals in the person of Jesus.

177. Seen in this light, Paul's depiction of the relationship between sin and the plight of creation seems to be more relevant today than when he first penned Romans 8. If one questions how Paul relates sin and the plight of creation, as Moltmann does, the fact remains that today, more than ever, the ecological problems facing the earth are directly linked to how humanity relates to it.

178. As Douglas Moo ("Nature") says in an unpublished essay, "God is at work bringing blessing not only to his people but to the physical cosmos itself." When we are freed from our modernistic presuppositions, Bauckham, "Wild Animals," 4, argues, we can "read the New Testament differently. We can recognize that, in continuity with the OT tradition, it assumes that humans live in mutuality with the rest of God's creation, that salvation history and eschatology do not lift humans out of nature but heal precisely their distinctive relationship with the rest of nature." For a recent attempt to do precisely this, see Bouma-Prediger's *Beauty of the Earth*.

the exploitation and disregard for creation. As such, it is precisely a robust but differentiated understanding of how the cross responds to sin and its cosmic effects that can provide a theological foundation for precisely the kind of ecological responsibility Moltmann calls Christians to today. While it leaves questions that yearn for an answer unanswered, it gives a sufficient account of the ecological crisis as it relates to humanity's interaction with creation.

Hope without the Loss of Divine and Human Freedom

A traditional understanding also avoids the problem we saw in Moltmann's universalism. If the cross responds primarily to sin, the history of redemption is not the necessary overcoming of the double contradiction in God and creation. Rather, it is the history of His free love. Therefore, although God desires the salvation of all His children, they are free to embrace or spur the gracious invitation of the cross. God remains God in his love and freedom as he extends his grace, and humanity remains free to respond to this grace. Hope remains universal but the human embrace of the grace that hope is grounded in is left open.

Conclusion

Re-appropriating sin as the fundamental human problem God responds to in the history of redemption and as the pivotal concern in the liberation of creation provides an importance corrective to the often weak, diffused and marginal place sin has in Moltmann's thought. Revelation locates the problem both politically, as the demonic rebellion that has gained access to the earthly realm through its centers of power, and also personally, as the willing submission to the corrupt order these powers spin around the world. It sees this rebellion as the fundamental problem that explains why God's rightful rule and presence is not actualized on the earth now, and how the displacement of his presence and rule has devastating effects on the earthly realm, both for its human but also its non-human subjects.

Redrawing Moltmann's Hope around a Cosmic Rebellion

If we accept the logic of sin and redemption reflected in Revelation, we need to modify Moltmann's understanding of the kingdom as symbol of hope.

First, the "kingdom of God" can still be seen in one important sense as the mediating symbol of hope between the individual's hope of "eternal life" and the cosmic hope of "the new heaven and the new earth." The former must be seen within the expectation of the redemption of the human community and the latter refers to the context in which redeemed humanity will exist.

Second, however, against Moltmann, it is also the primary symbol of hope. Both personal and cosmic hope is contingent on the redemption of humanity in the kingdom of God. It is only as God descends to earth as king over his people that creation can exist from his life-giving presence.

When augmented in this way, Moltmann's vision of the kingdom can indeed help Christians live their faith in the challenges their own contemporary setting faces them with. With this focus, Moltmann's concept of a messianic mediation of history helps Christians to live Revelation's call to a kerygmatic resistance within the challenges their own contemporary setting faces them with, and thus more successfully enables Christians as they "go to meet the evil with a battle-song of triumph."

7

The Presence and Reign of God in History

> We suffer on account of God's patience. And yet, we need his patience. God, who became a lamb, tells us that the world is saved by the Crucified One, not by those who crucified him. The world is redeemed by the patience of God. It is destroyed by the impatience of man.[1]

Introduction

IN THE LAST CHAPTER WE CONSIDERED THE ESCHATOLOGICAL ASPECT of the kingdom of God in Revelation, which the book sees as a regime change, the time when God and Christ assume the position of geopolitical authority that is now occupied by the enemies of God. Now we turn to the relational aspect of the kingdom. In the first major section of the chapter we will consider how the book understands divine rule. Second, we will turn to how the church is constituted as a kingdom to God and how this kingdom now is manifested in ecclesial communities. Lastly, we will place this discussion in conversation with Moltmann.

The God of the Kingdom

As Rev 11:15–19 depicts how God will assume the position of authority on the earth *de facto*, it does so by describing him as the one who is already sovereign *de jure*.[2] Not only is he identified as κύριος ἡμῶν ("our Lord") but John, patterning vv.16–17 in strong thematic, structural, and lexical parallels to the doxology in ch. 4, emphasises that the fulfilment that the twenty-four elders proclaim here is precisely what God is

---

1. Pope Benedict XVI, Inaugural Sermon, 24 April 2005.
2. Caird, *Revelation*, 141.

worshiped as in the heavenly throne room in 4:8–11. The God who will assume the position of sovereignty on earth is the one who already is the rightful sovereign over creation; "the great power" he takes is the power that is already his. Thus, 11:15–19 both affirms the constancy of God as the true sovereign over heaven and earth but also sees the exercise of this sovereignty within a certain narrative framework. Our discussion on divine sovereignty will first focus on two titles for God that are used in 11:17 that reflect this dual focus, "the Lord God Almighty" and "the one who is, who was, and who is coming."[3] Next we will consider how Jesus is the divine agent through whom this sovereignty is exercised. We will conclude with a discussion on the role the Spirit plays in the rule of God.

The Constancy and Narrative of God's Undisputed Sovereignty

As is the case with most titles for God in Revelation, he is identified as both "the Lord God Almighty" and "the one who is, who was, and who is coming" in the prologue.[4] In 1:8 John binds these two titles together, placing the latter within the former, κύριος ὁ θεός, ὁ ὢν καὶ ὁ ἦν καὶ ὁ ἐρχόμενος, ὁ παντοκράτωρ ("the one who is, who was, and who is coming").[5] In the following discussion we will first show how "the Lord God Almighty" functions within the presentation of God as the only true and almighty king of creation who is present and worshipped as such in the heavenly realm,[6] and second how the tripartite title emphasises the narrative of God's sovereignty in relation to the earth, how he will establish *de facto* on earth what he is already *de jure*.

---

3. Below we will discuss why the last element, "he who is coming" is omitted here.

4. Titles mentioned or anticipated in the prologue are "the Alpha and the Omega "(1:8), "the One who sits on the throne" (anticipated in 1:4), and King (anticipated in 1:6). The only other title, ὁ δεσπότης (6:10), is a functional synonym for ὁ κύριος (ὁ δεσπότης is a common translation for the imperial titles *dominus* and *princes*, and might be used in 6:10 to contrast God with Caesar [Aune, *Revelation 6–16*, 407]).

5. The two titles are not only closely linked here but the tripartite title is always linked closely to ὁ κύριος ὁ θεὸς ὁ παντοκράτωρ (note that 1:4 forms an inclusio with 1:8); see Bauckham, *Theology of the Book of Revelation*, 30.

6. Although βασιλεύς is most commonly used of the rulers of earth in their enmity to God and allegiance to the Draconic order (6:15; 16:12, 14; 17:2, 9, 12 (x2), 18; 18:3, 9; 19:18, 19—but note the positive depiction in 21:24), this is contrasted with God's rightful rule when he is identified as βασιλεύς τῶν ἐθνῶν (or possibly αἰώνων).

The Lord God the Almighty: The Constancy of His Sovereignty

Of the seven occurrences ὁ κύριος ὁ θεός ὁ παντοκράτωρ[7] ("The Lord God the Almighty") in Revelation, all occur in doxologies set in heaven, except the first and the last one. The title is first used to identify who it is that says: "I am the Alpha and the Omega" (1:8). This merism emphasises the constancy of God as the eternal one.[8] By linking this self-designation to "The Lord God Almighty," Revelation emphasises who God is as the first and final word, namely the sovereign Lord who is the almighty. We meet the title for the last time in 21:22 where it depicts the eschatological establishment of God's eternal sovereignty on earth: "The Lord God Almighty" and the Lamb are the temple of the New Jerusalem, the socio-religious center of the eternal kingdom. What the first occurrence establishes as a fundamental part of who God is in his eternal constancy, the last occurrence describes as the defining fact of the eschatological reality.

Elsewhere, the title occurs in heavenly worship. God is constantly praised as "The Lord God Almighty" in the inner court of heaven (4:8),[9] and, the last time the title occurs in worship (19:6), a great multitude in heaven worships him as such because his rule has now extended from heaven to the earth (19:6). In the three intervening occurrences, the twenty-four elders proleptically praise God for having assumed the position of authority on earth that is rightly his (11:17), the slain martyrs anticipate how the nations will come and worship God when his just authority is revealed (15:3), and the heavenly altar praises God for having vindicated the saints in judging Babylon (16:7).

Taken together, the Lord God Almighty speaks of God's absolute sovereignty of the whole cosmos: he is the sovereign creator and sustainer of all things, and as such can and will bring about his rightful sovereignty on earth, a sovereignty revealed in His final acts of judg-

---

7. The full title occurs in Rev 1:8; 4:8; 11:17; 15:3; 16:7; 19:6; 21:22, and variations of it 4 times (ὁ θεὸς ὁ παντοκράτωρ in 16:14 and 19:15 and κύριος ὁ θεός in 18:8; 22:5; 22:6).

8. "These merisms express God's control of all history, especially by bringing it to an end in salvation and judgment" (Beale, *Revelation*, 199).

9. Note how the worship of the living beings and the elders in 4:8–11 is closely linked together structurally and lexically as an eternal round of praise.

ment[10] and redemption, in which people share the destiny with the power to whom they have pledged allegiance. The doxological depiction of "the Lord God Almighty" who is enthroned in heaven is an important counter image in Revelation to the way in which the imperial cult was used as a pivotal tool to organise space and time, centring space in Rome and organising time primarily around Augustus as well as the achievements of other emperors.[11] As space and time are expanded in vision and worship, Rome is displaced and the heavenly throne of God is seen as the true center of the cosmos, and the time of Rome is seen as an aberration between the Easter victory of the Lamb and the arrival of God's city on earth.

The Lord God Almighty, the creator and sustainer of all things, is the one eternal sovereign who both has the power and right to exercise his absolute sovereignty. However, the doxologies also assume a narrative of God's sovereignty, that which he is *de jure* awaits its *de facto* establishment on earth. It is precisely this dual emphasis on the eternal constancy of God's sovereignty and the narrative of how God exercises this sovereignty that John combines when he sandwiches ὁ ὢν καὶ ὁ ἦν καὶ ὁ ἐρχόμενος between κύριος ὁ θεός and ὁ παντοκράτωρ in 1:8. God's self-designation, "The Alpha and Omega," points us to the eternal constancy of the sovereignty of the creator, while the tripartite title reminds us of the dynamic narrative by which he establishes his sovereignty on earth.

---

10. Judgment is in view when παντοκράτωρ occurs on its own, first in the anticipation of the final battle in 16:14 and in the actual depiction of it in 19:15.

11. See Friesen, *Imperial Cults*, for a detailed analysis on how the imperial cult functioned to both order time around significant events in the lives of the Caesars and space around Rome. Whereas "The Lord God the Almighty" points to his sovereignty as such, ὁ καθήμενος ἐπὶ τοῦ θρόνου indicates the central location of God's sovereignty, how it functions as the ordering center of the heavenly realm (note how chs. 4–5 organises everything in relation to the throne), as the source of the divine activity that prepares the way for the establishment of the throne on earth (8:3; 14:3; 16:17) and as the central location of the eschatological presence of God on earth: when the throne of the Beast has been judged and its kingdom darkened (16:10; cf. 13:2), the throne of God and the Lamb will be the central reality of the New Jerusalem and the glorious light of the eternal kingdom (21:23; 22:2–3).

"... AND THE ONE WHO IS COMING: THE NARRATIVE OF GOD'S SOVEREIGNTY

Although not the most frequent title for God in the book, the tripartite title is the most prominent title used of God in the prologue[12] and plays a crucial function in the book's depiction of the narrative of God's sovereignty. The full title occurs three times (1:4, 8; 4:8[13]) while the last element, καὶ ὁ ἐρχόμενος, is omitted in 11:17 and 16:5. Most commentators agree that the tripartite title is an interpretation of the divine name[14] and that the last element is anomalous—instead of a future form of εἰμί we get καὶ ὁ ἐρχόμενος. Although the tripartite title may allude to the eternity of God, how he is both Lord over time and not contingent upon it,[15] this anomaly suggests that John's primary concern is with what God does in time. Therefore, many commentators rightly point out that the title is closely linked with the eschatological expectation of the book.[16] McDonough sees the incorporation of the expectation of God's coming salvation into a divine title, especially as it is closely linked with the book's christology, as "one of John's supreme theological achievements."[17] But what does it achieve?

---

12. It occurs twice, as the first title ascribed to God in the book (1:4), and as one of the titles by which God identifies himself in the book (1:8). For a comprehensive study on the Greco-Roman and Jewish background to the tripartite title and how it is used in Revelation, see McDonough, *YHWH at Patmos*.

13. The first two elements are reversed here, perhaps because the context emphasises God as creator (McDonough, *YHWH at Patmos*, 212).

14. McDonough, *YHWH at Patmos*, 201–2 has convincingly shown that the primary background for the tripartite title is Exod 3:14, which in later Jewish tradition was at times expanded in a three-fold temporal phrase; he also notes that it may also have a secondary polemic significance since such phrases were also used of Zeus (197–98). On how other titles in Revelation allude to the divine name, see Aune, *Revelation 1–5*, 57; Bauckham, *Theology of the Book of Revelation*, 27–28.

15. See McDonough, *YHWH at Patmos*, 208–9 for a helpful distinction between "hard line" understanding of timelessness, and the "soft line" reflected in Revelation, which simply affirms, without making any claim on what this means metaphysically, that as Creator God is Lord over time. If John has not simply what God does in time in view but also alludes to who he *is* by designating him as ὁ ὤν, it may be significant that in 17:8, 11 the beast is depicted as οὐκ ἔστιν, perhaps indicating its un- or anti-reality (McDonough, *YHWH at Patmos*, 206, 227, 229).

16. Beale, *Revelation*, 188; Beasley-Murray, *Revelation*, 54; Sweet, *Revelation*, 65; Schüssler Fiorenza, *Justice and Judgment*, 49; Caird, *Revelation*, 141; Swete, *Apocalypse*, 5; Charles, *Revelation*, vol. 1, 10.

17. McDonough, *YHWH at Patmos*, 214.

We have already noted that in the prologue (1:4, 8) the title is closely associated with the affirmation of God's sovereignty. This dominates also the context in the last occurrence of the full title in 4:8. John has patterned the worship of the four living beings after the doxology in Isa 6:1ff but with one significant alteration, in 4:8, after the affirmation "Holy, holy, holy, the Lord God the Almighty" we do not get Isaiah's "the whole earth is full of his glory" (Isa 6:3) but "the one who was, who is and who is coming."[18] We will return to the significance of this alteration but will first look at the two instances where καὶ ὁ ἐρχόμενος is elided (11:17; 16:16).

In the context of the proleptic depiction of the future in 11:15–19, the twenty-four elders respond to the heavenly voices' proclamation of the regime change: "We give thanks to you, Lord God Almighty, the one who is and who was," and now instead of "the one who is coming" they say "because you have taken your great power and have begun to reign." This suggests that what καὶ ὁ ἐρχόμενος anticipates is precisely the arrival of God's sovereignty within the earthly realm, the moment when what is true of God and which is established in heaven will also be established on earth.[19] This is depicted in 11:15–19 as God assumes the position of geopolitical authority that is now occupied by the powers of the world.[20]

It is the negative aspect of God's assumption of his reign that is at the fore when the title is used in 16:5. Here, the third bowl in which the rivers and springs of water are turned to blood is seen as the just answer to the martyrs' prayer for vindication in 6:10. Here God is called "you who are and who were, the holy one." Perhaps John replaces ὁ ἐρχόμενος with ὁ ὅσιος here in order to indicate the covenantal relationship between God and his people.[21] If this is the case, then 16:5

---

18. The order of the first two designation may have been reversed here because John now focuses on God as creator (so Sweet, *Revelation*, 120).

19. Bauckham, *Climax of Prophecy*, 32.

20. See previous chapter. As we noted there, the seventh trumpet emphasises how this means the vindication of the saints and judgment on God's enemies, precisely what the prophets anticipate at the coming of the Day of the Lord (McDonough, *YHWH at Patmos*, 215).

21. In the LXX ὅσιος is most often used as a translation of חסד, and most often refers to people, of their holiness as those who fulfil their duties in their covenant relationship with God. But it can also be used of God when describing his covenantal activity with Israel, as e.g. in Ps 99:3, where God is proclaimed holy in the context of establishing his justice in Zion (so also Ps 111:9; cf. Beckwith, *Apocalypse*, 675).

emphasises that when God comes in final judgment on his enemies, this is part of his covenantal faithfulness to his people.

The positive aspect of John's use of covenantal language reaches its apex in the depiction of God's dwelling with his people in 21:3–5. And it is in the vision of the New Jerusalem that precisely that element in Isaiah that the tripartite title replaces in 4:8 comes into full prominence. In 4:8 John omits "the whole earth is full of his glory" (Isa 6:3) because at the beginning of the vision the glorious presence of the sovereign Lord is only present in the heavenly realm but absent on earth.[22] In its place is a title for God that anticipates how what is already established in the heavenly realm is what God purposes to establish on earth as well. By describing God as "the one who is, who was and who is coming" the living beings anticipate the day when what is true in the heavenly realm, that it is full of the glorious presence of God, will be realised on earth.[23] And this is precisely what 21:1—22:5 depicts, the descent of the New Jerusalem which center is the throne that God and the Lamb occupy, whose glory is the light by which all its inhabitants walk (21:11, 23–24).[24]

When John describes God as "the one who is coming" instead of as "the one who will be" he has embedded into one of his major titles for God the anticipation that runs throughout his vision, namely the realization of God's proper rule on earth. The incongruence between the confession of God as Sovereign creator and how things appear on

22. McDonough, *YHWH at Patmos*, 225 rightly notes that John reads Isa 6:3 with other OT passages, such as Ps 72:18–19, that anticipate how "God's glory will fill the earth."

23. Moltmann, therefore, correctly observes that the basic eschatological question is "when will God show himself in his divinity to heaven and earth?" and the fundamental answer is found "in the promise of the coming God: 'the whole earth is full of his glory' (Isa. 6.3)" (*CoG*, xvi).

24. Moltmann then is right when he says this title for God in Revelation "already sets present and past in the light of his eschatological arrival, an arrival which means the establishment of his eternal kingdom, and his indwelling in the creation renewed for that indwelling" (*CoG*, 23). However, against Moltmann, the way the title is used in Revelation does not suggest that God comes to us from the future and the future therefore "must become the theological paradigm for transcendence" (*CoG*, 24; cf. *GiC*, 132–35). If anything, the opposite seems to be the case in Revelation: since God who comes, comes from the heavenly realm, transcendence is the paradigm for the future— but not transcendence as the eternal moment that can meet us at any moment, but as the realm where God's sovereignty is already established, and from which he will come to establish it on earth.

earth is resolved in the depiction of the constancy and narrative of the sovereignty of God within the vision's spatial and temporal expansion of reality. God has always been the true sovereign over heaven and earth, he has established this sovereignty in the heavenly realm, and he will come and establish it on earth. On the crucial role this title plays in the interplay between the temporal and spatial expansion of the text, Gilbertson says,

> God, the coming one, brings about a transformation of the earthly present (chs. 6–19) in order to achieve the consummation of chs. 21–2. The process does not grow out of earthly reality: it comes from the ultimate to transform the earthly present. Thus, spatially, the process consists of the extension of manifest divine rule downwards from heaven to embrace the rest of the cosmos. Temporally, the process consists of the transformation of the present, via the penultimate future, to bring it into line with the peace and justice of God's kingdom in the ultimate future.[25]

The Divine Mediator of the Kingdom of God

Although God is the sovereign creator from whose throne both judgment and redemption proceed, the book sees Jesus as the primary agent through whom his sovereignty is exercised. Although there is a whirlwind of angelic agents and activity in the book, Jesus is the fulcrum on which everything turns and is held together, and it is in his appearing in victory and salvation that God comes to the earth. Here we will consider how Jesus is depicted as such, and how this portrayal includes Jesus in the divine identity.

Jesus as Agent of God's Sovereignty

Easter and the Establishment of God's Sovereignty on Earth. Revelation 1:5b–6 and 5:9–10 establish Jesus as God's paradoxical Messiah,[26] as

---

25. Gilbertson, *God and History*, 174.

26. In Rev 5:5–6 we find perhaps the most astonishing transformation of imagery in the New Testament where Jesus as Israel's Messiah (5:5) is depicted as a slain lamb (5:6). "A more complete reversal of value would be hard to imagine" (Barr, "Apocalypse," 41). Here John juxtaposes what his readers would expect and what is the case in a hear-see formula, where what is seen reinterprets what is heard (see also 1:10–12; 7:4–10; 21:9–10; and 12:6–12 where the order is reversed).

the Lamb through whom God's purposes are accomplished. These two passages are structurally, lexically and semantically closely tied together[27] and depict Easter as the possibility-making event in which Jesus accomplishes the fundamental victory which paves the way for God's assumption of the position of sovereignty on earth. Intertwining messianic expectation with the image of the slain lamb John establishes Jesus' death as the pivotal victory through which God's purposes will be accomplished. The book sees this as the defining moment of Jesus' messianic role. It is on basis of his death and what it accomplished that Jesus is exalted to the highest position of authority, as he is given a place on the divine throne in heaven.[28] As such, the death of Jesus is the defining center, and so, not surprisingly, the Lamb is the most common designator for him in Revelation.[29]

But what does the death of Jesus accomplish that makes it the pivotal messianic event? In a movement of separation it liberates people from the condition they are in and in a movement of incorporation it constitutes the liberated as a new community.[30] This is a people, as we

---

27. Both are set in context where Jesus is presented (1:5a) or depicted (5:5–6) in his paradoxical messianic role, are structured in closely parallel ways, share semantically pivotal terminology (ἐν τῷ αἵματι αὐτοῦ, ποιέω, βασιλεία, ἱερεῖς, τῷ θεῷ) and both depict what Jesus accomplishes in his death in two parallel movements.

28. 7:17; cf. 7:9; 22:1, 3.

29. In 28 of the 29 occurrences of ἀρνίον in the book it refers to Jesus, and in the one exception, the second beast is seen as a parody of the Lamb (13:11). This is also a title that is fairly unique to Revelation (elsewhere, it is only used of Jesus in John 21:15). In this way the reader is constantly reminded of how it is in his paradoxical paschal role (the allusion to Exod 19:5–6 makes clear that ἐν τῷ αἵματί σου has paschal overtones) that Jesus establishes the purposes of God on earth. Against Malina who interpreters ἀρνίον as a symbol of power (see Malina, *Genre*, 101–04), I follow Johns (*Lamb Christology*, 204) and most commentators in seeing the lamb as a symbol of vulnerability. Although there may be tradition of a warrior ram that John could have alluded to (cf. Slater, *Christ and Community*, 64; cf. de Moor and Staalduine-Sulman, "Aramaic Song," on the possibility of a Jewish messianic ram tradition), Johns shows that ἀρνίον was most commonly used to indicate vulnerability not only in Jewish tradition but also generally in the Ancient Near East, including in the first century Greco-Roman world. That Revelation has the latter in mind is indicated by the fact that the Lamb is slain and in the juxtaposition of images of power and vulnerability in 5:5–6. "Such vulnerability is no weakness; instead, it proves triumphant over the powers of evil and exposes the weakness of violence" (Johns, *Lamb Christology*, 204).

30. In both 1:5b and 5:9b the καί (following ἀγαπῶντι ἡμᾶς and ἐσφάγης respectively) is epexegetical while those preceding ἐποίησεν and ἐποίησας respectively are copulas.

will see in our discussion on the church below, that are delivered from their culpable bondage to the draconic deception of the order of the Beast to become a priestly kingdom to God who are destined to rule the earth.

As this complex event, Easter is the possibility-making event of the kingdom of God. By establishing a people as a kingdom to God in the territory now occupied by the forces of the dragon, Jesus' death is the beginning of the accomplishment of God's purposes on earth. Easter reveals Jesus as the possibility-making agent of God's sovereignty. Now we turn to how he is also the pivotal agent in the history of God's sovereignty between Easter and the parousia.

Jesus and the Exercise of God's Sovereignty in the World. In the first extended description of Jesus in the book he is called "Jesus Christ, the faithful witness,[31] the firstborn from the dead, and the ruler[32] of the kings of the earth." If the first title here identifies Jesus as the Messiah of God,[33] if the second presents him in his paradigmatic martyrological role, and if the third focuses on the central event of his messianic victory, then the fourth title anticipates who he will be manifested as when his messianic purposes are fulfilled. As the one who will rule with God forever, Jesus is also, as we saw in the previous chapter, the agent of the final events that usher in the ultimate future. As the king of kings he is both the warrior that defeats his opponents and their final judge in history.

While Easter points to how Jesus has exercised God's sovereignty on earth[34] and the image of the warrior king and judge anticipates how he will again exercise it on earth,[35] the book sees Jesus as absent from

31. NA 27 reads ὁ μάρτυς, ὁ πιστός. However, it seems better to omit the minor stop since in 3:14, which recalls 1:5 they are obviously seen as one title (so Beckwith, *Apocalypse*, 427).

32. On the messianic overtones of ἄρχων, see ibid., 428.

33. John identifies Jesus as χριστός from the outset of the book (1:1-2, 5) and at other significant points in the book (he is identified as the Lord's Christ in passages that speak of the arrival of God's kingdom (11:15) and God's Christ (12:15) and in 20:4, 6 in the context of the martyr's reign with Christ). There are also several other messianic allusions in the book, not the least 5:5 where he who will be revealed to be a slain lamb is said to be ὁ λέων ὁ ἐκ τῆς φυλῆς Ἰούδα, ἡ ῥίζα Δαυίδ.

34. 1:5b; 5:9-10; 12:4-5 refer to Easter.

35. Note how both 14:14-20 and 19:11-20 depict an action of Jesus that is initiated

the earth between these two points. Revelation 12:10–12 makes clear that while the initial victory of Jesus entails the expulsion of Satan from heaven and entails the arrival of "the salvation and the power and the kingdom of our God" in heaven (12:10), the realization of this victory does not extend to the earth yet, but rather results in an intensification of Satan's presence and fury (12:12). In this draconic time when Jesus is absent from the earthly realm, in this Holy Saturday of the world, he is present pneumatologically as Lord in the ecclesial communities, especially seen in 1:9—3:22.[36] The introduction to the addresses in Revelation 2–3 constantly emphasise that this exalted Christ of 1:12–20 is he who speaks to the churches. In the heavenly realm Jesus is the center of the lampstands that represent the churches on earth, and on earth he is present to them by the Spirit.[37] As this one, he directs the churches, comforts them, challenges them, warns them of impending judgment and promises them eschatological reward. As such, he orders the churches so they become and persevere in being proleptic anticipations of the kingdom, and in doing so, enables them to be the communities through whom his Lordship spreads to the world.[38]

Jesus then is the agent through whom the eschatological fulfilment of the kingdom is made possible at Easter, who extends the divine rule in the earthly territory occupied by the Dragon in his Lordship over the church, and who as warrior and judge will lead the final assault on

---

in heaven and is effected on earth, although the actual movement of Jesus to the earth is more prominent in the latter.

36. Many commentators naturally make a break between 1:12–20 and chs. 2–3 because the discussion moves from the exalted Christ to the churches he addresses. However, although they definitely are two distinct segments, these belong together as one visionary complex that first introduces Christ as the Lord who is the center of seven lampstands that represent the churches in the heavenly realm, and second consist in his addresses to the churches conveyed on earth by the Spirit (cf. Beckwith, *Apocalypse*, 433; Richard, *Apocalypse*, 48). The disadvantage of separating these two sections is seen well in how Gilbertson (*God and History*, 87–92) discusses them separately when considering the spatial dynamics of the text. If Gilbertson had discussed these together he could have brought out more clearly the important spatial dynamics between its two segments.

37. See discussion on the Spirit below.

38. Thus, it is not surprising that the book so extensively deals with the ecclesial health of the seven churches which the book is addressed to before the vision proper begins. It is not grounded simply in a concern for the churches but for the world since the health of the churches has crucial significance for the fate of the world.

God's enemies on earth that precedes the arrival of God sovereign presence on earth. This narrative of Jesus' exercise of the divine sovereignty is not only anticipated in the titles attributed to him in 1:5a but seems also to be implied in the doxologies of the heavenly throne-room scene that heads the main visionary complex (4:1—22:5). In Revelation 4, "the One who sits on the throne" is only worshipped at the heart of the heavenly court (4:8, 11). But after the confession of why the lamb can open the scroll (5:5–7), this worship begins to spread out. The central 'court's' song to the Lamb as redeemer (5:8–9) spreads to the angels who surround the heavenly throne (5:11–12)[39] and to every living creature in the cosmos who worship both God and the Lamb (5:13).[40] In the beginning what is true about God and his rule is confessed in heaven because it is only known there, but as the knowledge of the paradoxical victory of the Lamb extends to the farthest reaches of creation, the worship of both God and the lamb resounds through creation. The new song of the lamb is the desire of the cosmos.[41]

The Lamb and the Divine Identity

How then does the book see the relationship between God the Father who is sovereign and his Son as the agent of sovereignty?[42] Most commentators agree that Revelation reflects a high christology.[43] Here we will only consider how this christology emerges from the book's depiction of Jesus as the agent of sovereignty.

---

39. The lamb receives all the accolades the One Enthroned receives (δόξα, τιμή, δύναμις) as well as πλοῦτος, σοφία, ἰσχύς and εὐλογια.

40. They now receive together what has been attributed to them separately in the previous doxologies, δόξα, and τιμή, as well as a "power" word not used so far, κράτος.

41. As an aside, we note it is precisely as the central character of the book, the one through whom God will establish his sovereignty over the earthly realm, that Jesus is the primary revelatory agent of the whole vision (1:2; 5:1–7; 22:16). Jesus has the authority to reveal the secrets of God because he is the agent through whom they are made possible and are accomplished. He is bound to the message he bears: As the main actor of the vision he reveals, he is the protagonist of the message he gives.

42. Πατήρ occurs five times, always referring to God as the Father of Jesus (1:6; 2:28, 3:5; 3:21; 14:1).

43. For a recent and brief discussion on the book's high christology, see Witherington, *Revelation*, 27–32. See Carrell, *Jesus and the Angels*, on the christology of Revelation and first century Jewish angelology.

The inclusion of Jesus in the divine identity in Revelation is intrinsically bound up with the exaltation of Jesus to the throne of God. Jesus' exaltation to God's throne is based on his Easter victory (3:21; 12:2, 4b–6, 10; cf. 2:26–28),[44] and it is as the one who shares the throne of God that he is recognized as sharing the divine identity[45]—both as agent of divine activity[46] and as recipient of worship.[47] However, although the book's high christology develops from its depiction of how Jesus is exalted to the divine throne, it is not an adoptionist christology. The Jesus who is revealed to share the divine identity with God in his role in the narrative of God's sovereignty is also confessed to be as God, "the Alpha and the Omega," the one through whom everything is created and will be brought to conclusion.[48]

What then is the fundamental relationship between God and Jesus as they together are the plural unity that will establish their rightful sovereignty on earth?[49] The conclusion our discussion so far leads us

---

44. Note how John carefully distinguishes between the exaltation of Jesus and the victorious saints in 3:21–22.

45. It was "because Christians owed salvation to Jesus Christ that he was worshipped" (Bauckham, *Theology of the Book of Revelation*, 62).

46. This is seen in how titles that emphasise divine sovereignty are used of both God and the Lamb, e.g. κύριος—both God and Jesus are in parallel ways and in close proximity called the Lord of the saints (11:8, 15; cf. 4:11; 14:13; 22:20) and βασιλεύς (of God in 15:3, of Jesus in 17:14 and 19:16).

47. So, at the forefront of the worship of Jesus is precisely his paradoxical victory as the slain Lamb (5:9–10, 12, 13). In Revelation the worship of God and the Lamb on the throne is then set in contrast to the false worship of the beast; see Bauckham, "Millennium," and Hannah, "Throne," who, although they differ slightly on the tradition of the theme, both show how unique Revelation's depiction of Christ sharing God's throne is in early Jewish thought, the only other instance being *1 Enoch* 45:3.

48. This is seen in how the three parallel designations attributed to Jesus in 22:13 (τὸ ἄλφα καὶ τὸ ὦ, ὁ πρῶτος καὶ ὁ ἔσχατος, ἡ ἀρχὴ καὶ τὸ τέλος) are a combination of titles attributed to Jesus and God elsewhere in the book (1:8, 17; 2:8 21:6). We then see in Revelation a similar movement as in Phil 2, in which the exaltation of Jesus from his sacrificial death points to a prior exalted state. In 3:14 Jesus is called ἡ ἀρχὴ τῆς κτίσεως τοῦ θεοῦ, ἀρχὴ likely referring to Jesus as the origin of creation, since this is the usage in the only other occurrences (21:6 and 22:13) (Bauckham, *Theology of the Book of Revelation*, 56).

49. This plural unity may be indicated in 11:17 if both ὁ κύριος ἡμῶν and ὁ χριστὸς αὐτοῦ are to be seen as the implied subjects of the singular βασιλεύσει. Although Aune suggests (*Revelation 1–5*, 639; cf. Ford, *Revelation*, 181) the inconsistency might be due to an interpolation of τοῦ χριστοῦ αὐτοῦ, Bauckham notes (*Climax of Prophecy*, 139–40) how a singular form is also used of both in 6:17 (pre-

to is Jesus as the divine agent through whom the sovereignty of God is exercised.⁵⁰ So, while the book emphasises that the fulfilment of God's purposes is to be seen in how he will come and establish on earth what he is and always has been, what the book expects and prays for is the coming of Jesus:⁵¹ It is in the coming of Jesus that God comes to the world.⁵² This seems also to be the operating logic in the imagery of 21:22–24. Here we are told that the New Jerusalem needs no light ἡ γὰρ δόξα τοῦ θεοῦ ἐφώτισεν αὐτήν, καὶ ὁ λύχνος αὐτῆς τὸ ἀρνίον (for the glory of God lights, and the lamb is its lamp"). Here we see what is true of the relationship between God and Jesus throughout the book: Jesus is the agent in whom God becomes present, and thus through whom the activity of God is accomplished.

---

ferring αὐτοῦ over αὐτῶν since it is the harder reading) and in 22:3–4. Beckwith notes (*Apocalypse*, 609) that if "τοῦ χριστοῦ αὐτοῦ were an editorial insertion,... the interpolator would hardly have failed to change the vb. to the pl." (cf. Beasley-Murray, *Revelation*, 189; Carrell, *Jesus and the Angels*, 115; Charles, *Revelation, vol. 1.*, 294–95; Harrington, *Revelation*, 125–26; Swete, *Apocalypse*, 142).

50. Garrow, *Revelation*, 39. Beale, "Origins," 618–19 notes that Rev 17:14 may intentionally allude to Dan 4:37 (LXX) in order to express "the absolute deity and kingship of the messianic Lamb" that defeats eschatological Babylon (cf. Slater, "King of Kings," 159–60; cf. also Stott, "Note," 70, who argues that this anti-Roman polemic in the depiction of Christ may already start with the reference to κυριακῇ in 1:10).

51. Considering the number of times ἔρχομαι is found in the mouth of Jesus as a promise of his coming (16:15; 22:7, 20a; cf. 2:5, 16; 3:3, 11) as well as in two instances as an expectation of his coming (1:7; 22:20b), it is surely not incidental that God is called ὁ ἐρχόμενος (1:4, 8; 4:8). Commenting on this close relationship, McDonough says (*YHWH at Patmos*, 233): "John cannot utter the name of God without at the same time invoking the person of Christ." Roloff argues (*Revelation*, 24) that the title "interprets the coming of Jesus as the event in which God's power over history is visibly achieved." Such a relation is also suggested in the close link between the tripartite title and the self-depiction of Jesus in 1:18, καὶ ὁ ζῶν, καὶ ἐγενόμην νεκρὸς καὶ ἰδοὺ ζῶν εἰμι εἰς τοὺς αἰῶνας τῶν αἰώνων; note also how the similar depiction of the Beast in 17:8, 11 forms a parody on this (Bauckham, *Climax of Prophecy*, 431–41; Beasley-Murray, *Revelation*, 254; Caird, *Revelation*, 215–16).

52. "The sovereignty of God and the authority of his Christ are strictly equivalent, although the theology of both Old and New Testaments would suggest that the former is exercised through the latter" (Beasley-Murray, *Revelation*, 202).

The Spirit: Agent of Divine Presence

INTRODUCTION

Although Revelation's pneumatology is not as extensively developed as its christology, references to the Spirit play a pivotal role in the book:[53] 1) as "the Seven Spirits," the Spirit is included in the epistolary greeting at the head of the book (1:4) and is closely linked to God (1:4; 4:5) and to Jesus (3:1; 5:6); 2) the whole visionary complex is experienced ἐν πνεύματι ("in the Spirit") (1:9; 4:2; 17:3; 19:10); and 3) the Spirit is seen as the agent in whom Jesus addresses the churches in Revelation 2–3,[54] a concern also reflected in the two times the Spirit speaks in the book (14:13; 22:17). In our discussion on the role of the Spirit in the book's understanding of the kingdom of God, we will look at how the book uses τὰ ἑπτὰ πνεύματα ("the Seven Spirits") and τὸ πνεῦμα ("the Spirit") to articulate two aspects of the Spirit's crucial role "in the divine activity of establishing God's kingdom in the world."[55]

"THE SEVEN SPIRITS" AS THE POWER OF GOD IN THE WORLD

In Rev 1:4 and 3:1 τὰ ἑπτὰ πνεύματα are first closely associated to God and Jesus respectively, and in 4:5 and 5:6 the significance of this designation for the Spirit is developed in clear allusions to Zechariah 4 in Rev 4:5 and 5:6, first to Zech 4:2 describing τὰ ἑπτὰ πνεύματα as

---

53. Bauckham, *Theology of the Book of Revelation*, 109. While John's pneumatology is not as developed as that of Paul (see, e.g., Fee, *God's Empowering Presence*) it suggests precisely two pivotal aspects of the development of a "high" pneumatology, the Spirit's close relationship to both God and Jesus without equating his agency to either one of them. How τὰ ἑπτὰ πνεύματα are to be understood is debated. Aune notes (*Revelation 1–5*, 33–35) three main views, they are 1) the Holy Spirit, 2) the seven archangels who stand before God (cf. Rev 8:2), or 3) seven astral deities. Aune dismisses the third one and claims that the first one is an unlikely anachronism of later trinitarian thought. He opts for the second view because of the way angels are depicted in a similar way in the Qumran literature (cf. Giblin, *Revelation*, 71–72; Witherington, *Revelation*, 75). However, considering how reference to the seven spirits functions in a similar way as other epistolary greetings in the NT and how it is related to Zechariah 4, I follow the majority of commentators and see it as a reference to the Spirit (Bauckham, *Climax of Prophecy*, 162–63; *Theology of the Book of Revelation*, 25, 110–15; Beale, *Revelation*, 189; Beckwith, *Apocalypse*, 424–27; Caird, *Revelation*, 15; Sweet, *Revelation*, 65).

54. Revelation 2:7, 11, 17, 29; 3:6, 13, 22.

55. Bauckham, *Theology of the Book of Revelation*, 109. The following discussion is largely drawn from Bauckham, *Climax of the Covenant*, 150–73; and *Theology of the Book of Revelation*, 109–25.

"seven lamps burning before the throne" and then to Zech 4:10 describing them as the seven eyes on the horns of the Lamb. Between these two references in Zech 4 a word is given to Zerubbabel—the completion of the temple will "not be [done] by might, nor by power, but by my Spirit," a power strong enough to make the mountain before Zerubbabel a plain (4:6–7). In placing the seven eyes on the seven horns of the Lamb, John seems to read these three elements in Zechariah together—τὰ ἑπτὰ πνεύματα represent the Spirit as the power through whom God establishes his purposes on earth.[56] Τὰ ἑπτὰ πνεύματα represent the Spirit as the effectual power in which the divine purposes which originate from God are accomplished through the slain Lamb, a stark contrast to precisely the draconic forces that one day will be decisively defeated by the power of the Lamb.

Revelation focuses on the pivotal role the churches play in how τὰ ἑπτὰ πνεύματα spread the victory of the Lamb. Not only are τὰ ἑπτὰ πνεύματα closely linked to Jesus' relationship to the churches (3:1) but the depiction of the church's prophetic ministry in Revelation 11 recalls 4:5 and 5:6 since it too is heavily dependent on Zech 4.[57] The seminal victory of the Easter Lamb is now marching through the world in the prophetic witness of the churches by the same power that was at work in the Lamb, τὰ ἑπτὰ πνεύματα of God sent into the world. However, this does not mean that God is not present in the world apart from the churches, as is evident in but should not be confined to the depiction of God's judgments on the earth.[58] But it does seem to suggest that the way we discern the presence of the Spirit in the world is by the way it is active through the church.

In summary, the Spirit as τὰ ἑπτὰ πνεύματα is the divine presence on earth, the power in which God's purposes are accomplished in the world. Since Jesus is the agent of the sovereignty of God, the Spirit is

---

56. Bauckham notes that 2 Chr 16:7–9 also reflects such an idea (*Climax of Prophecy*, 164).

57. Although Revelation 11 does not mention "the Seven Spirits," perhaps because it would conflict with the image of the two lampstands there (so Bauckham, *Theology of the Book of Revelation*, 113; cf. Beale, *Revelation*, 577–78), the ministry of the two witnesses depicts how the church extends the victory of the Lamb in the world, "not by might nor by power" but by the Spirit.

58. Before the book starts its relentless depiction of the judgments that proceed from above, it confesses God as the one who has created and sustains all things (4:11).

the power in which Jesus accomplishes his paradoxical victory and the power in which the effect of this victory is extended into the world.

"The Spirit" and the Seven Churches

If τὰ ἑπτὰ πνεύματα refers to the work of the Spirit in the world, τὸ πνεῦμα focuses on the Spirit's presence in the church. At the end of each of the seven addresses to the churches in chs. 2–3, the formula ὁ ἔχων οὖς ἀκουσάτω τί τὸ πνεῦμα λέγει ταῖς ἐκκλησίαις ("the one who has an ear, hear what the Spirit says to the churches") identifies the words of Jesus to the churches as an admonishment from the Spirit to hear and abide by.[59] The Spirit is the agent of Jesus' Lordship in his churches. By the Spirit, Jesus, now exalted in heaven, is present to the churches, whose Lord he is and whom he corrects and consoles, warns and promises.[60] Considering how the Spirit functions in the addresses to the churches as the agency through which the messages of the exalted Jesus are mediated to the churches, this would suggest that ἐν πνεύματι in 1:10; 4:2; 17:3 and 21:10 does not simply signal the ecstatic state in which John receives the vision, but rather to the Spirit as the agent in whom John receives the vision.[61] As such, τὸ πνεῦμα is consistently used of the Spirit in Revelation to signify the Spirit's role *vis-à-vis* the churches, as the Spirit opens the church to the greater reality of God which is otherwise hidden. The Spirit is the agency in which reality is expanded both spatially and temporally, so that the churches, in their particular temporal and local nexus can live in light of how God and the

---

59. Beale argues (*Revelation*, 236–39) John's use of the Isaianic hearing formula (Isa 6:9–10) at the end of each address may suggest that "like Israel, the church has become compromising and spiritually lethargic and has entered idolatrous allegiances." This is suggestive but should perhaps not be pushed to far as it is not only used of the compromising communities but also in the address to those churches in whom the risen Christ finds no fault.

60. So, in the two places the Spirit speaks in the book, the Spirit promises rest to faithful saints who die (14:13) and in 22:17, it calls with the Bride, for the coming of Jesus, the coming which signals the establishment of the kingdom on earth.

61. So Jeske, "Spirit and Community," 452–66. In 1:10 and 4:2, in strongly parallel statements, the vision as a whole, and its major parts (1:10—3:22; 4:1—22:5) are introduced as occurring ἐν πνεύματι, and so are the visions of the two contrasted cities, Babylon and the New Jerusalem (17:3; 21:10).

Lamb are revealed to be sovereign over all creation and how they will establish their sovereignty on earth.⁶²

As such, the distinct way the Spirit is at work in the churches as τὸ πνεῦμα and τὰ ἑπτὰ πνεύματα are closely interrelated. The messages to the churches, which are what τὸ πνεῦμα says to the churches are also the words of the exalted Jesus who holds τὰ ἑπτὰ πνεύματα in his hands. As this one, Jesus addresses the churches in the Spirit and prepares them to be those through whom τὰ ἑπτὰ πνεύματα spread the victory of the Lamb to the world.

Conclusion

In the previous chapter we showed how the Kingdom of God as a symbol of hope is developed in the book of Revelation primarily as a regime change: the establishment of God's kingdom on earth signals when the βασιλεία, the position of geopolitical authority that now is occupied by the forces of the dragon will be transferred to God and his Christ. So far in this chapter we have moved from this eschatological axis of our concern to the relational axis, to who holds the divine sovereignty over both heaven and earth and how this now is present on earth: 1) God is enthroned in heaven and worshiped as creator and rightful sovereign of the whole cosmos and his purpose is to establish *de facto* on earth what is revealed to be his *de jure* in heaven, the fulfilment of which is seen as he and his heavenly order descends upon the earth in chs. 21–22. 2) Jesus is seen as the primary agent through whom God's purpose to establish his kingdom on earth are accomplished, his death and resurrection make it possible by redeeming a people to be a kingdom to God, and his eschatological coming as the king who is both warrior and judge obliterates the presence of the draconic order that now covers the earth and in this way makes room for the heavenly divine order to replace it. 3) As the book depicts Jesus as the agent through whom the sovereignty of God is accomplished, Jesus is included in the divine identity that possesses this sovereignty, and therefore the ordering center of the eschatological kingdom of God is the throne which is occupied by both God and the Lamb. 4) The Spirit is the presence in

---

62. The parallel visions of these two cities are pivotal in the admonishment to the churches since they starkly contrast the fate of those who pledge their allegiance to the beast, and of those who persevere in their faithfulness to the lamb. See Rossing, *Two Cities*.

and through which this is accomplished. As the book depicts the Spirit, it distinguishes between how it is the agent through whom Jesus is present as the sovereign Lord who orders the life of the churches, and how, primarily through the churches, the Easter victory of the Lamb is now spread through the world.

Throughout this discussion we have seen how in Revelation this divine rule is intimately connected to the churches. As we now proceed to move from the divine rule to the question of where this rule is present, what its "realm" is, the role of the churches becomes the central focus.

The Church as an Anticipatory Presence of the Kingdom

In our discussion on the relationship between the church and the kingdom, we will first look at how the church is constituted as a kingdom to God at Easter and how it exists as such in paradoxical and ambiguous ways in ecclesial communities. Second, focusing on Revelation 12, we will show that although the church has this exclusive relationship to the kingdom, between Easter and the Parousia it does by definition not exist in the geopolitical form of a kingdom.

The Claim of the Church: An Anticipatory Presence of the Kingdom

THE EASTER FOUNDATION OF THE CHURCH AS A KINGDOM

We now return to how 1:5-6 and 5:9-10 to establish the followers of the Lamb as the covenant people of God's kingdom, now existing as an international people; as such they are fundamentally a political entity destined to rule the whole earth.[63]

Easter is the church's foundational event because Christ in a dual act establishes it as people to be βασιλείαν ... τῷ θεῷ ("a kingdom ... to God) (1:6; cf. 5:10).[64] The first aspect of this dual event is the deliver-

---

63. Schüssler Fiorenza's magisterial study (*Priester*) is still the most extensive analyses of these texts.

64. That this is the church, understood as those who have pledged their allegiance to Christ who are now ordered by his Lordship and who persevere in this allegiance is evident by how John includes himself and his audience as this people in 1:5-6

ance of the people from the state they are in, which in 1:5-6 is seen as a cultic redemption from sin[65] and in 5:9-10 as a political redemption from slavery.[66] Considering our earlier discussion on the complex understanding of sin in Revelation, John might have the structural aspect in view in 5:9-10 and the personal in 1:5-6:[67] the people purchased to God are those who have been freed from their enslavement to the corrupting order of the Beast and have been forgiven of their own culpability in submitting themselves to this order in the first place.[68]

Having been liberated and forgiven, this people are constituted anew, as a kingdom and priests to God. In understanding what this means, the Old Testament background is crucial. Both structurally and lexically it is clear that John here has Exod 19:6 in view:[69] following the logic of God's redemption of Israel from Egypt, John sees this people to be constituted[70] as Israel was then, as a priestly kingdom to God. The

---

(where ἡμᾶς occurs 4 times) and in 5:9 broadens this to people ἐκ πάσης φυλῆς καὶ γλώσσης καὶ λαοῦ καὶ ἔθνους.

65. Schüssler Fiorenza, *Justice and Judgment*, 72.

66. Ibid., 74, argues that ἀγορίζω probably is a "reference ... to the ransom of prisoners of war, who were deported to the countries of the victors and who could be ransomed by a 'purchasing agent' of their country."

67. Since 1:5-6 and 5:9-10 are part of parallel passages, since these verses in particular display a strong parallel structure, and since the 1:6 and 5:10 clearly refer to the same "act," it is reasonable to see the first elements as different expressions or perhaps better different aspects of one act:

a) Τῷ ... λύσαντι	ἡμᾶς		a) ἠγόρασας []	τῷ θεῷ	
	ἐκ	τῶν ἁμαρτιῶν ἡμῶν		ἐν	τῷ αἵματί σου
	ἐν	τῷ αἵματι αὐτοῦ,		ἐκ	πάσης φυλῆς καὶ γλώσσης καὶ λαοῦ καὶ ἔθνους
b) καὶ			b) καὶ		
ἐποίησεν	ἡμᾶς ...		ἐποίησας .	αὐτοὺς ..	

68. Schüssler Fiorenza, *Justice and Judgment*, 68-76 rightly notes the distinct personal/anthropological and theological/political emphasis of the two passages. However, in light of how John elsewhere in the book emphasises both the structural evil of Beasts and Babylon and the personal culpability of those who submit to it, I do not follow her in seeing the latter as a reinterpretation of the former. Rather, the two mutually interpret one another.

69. Although there are slight differences between 1:5b-6 and 5:9-10, the vast majority of commentators agree that Exod 19:6 is alluded to in both cases. For the possible traditions John draws on here, see Aune, *Revelation 1-5*, 47-48.

70. Schüssler Fiorenza, *Justice and Judgment*, 72, notes that in the LXX ποιέω is commonly used for the installation of kings and priests, and therefore in 1:6 most

people bought and cleansed by the Lamb in Revelation are created to play the same role as Israel was intended to do, to be God's kingdom among all the nations on earth. "The new kingdom for God created by Christ through redemption is the realm and community where God is already on earth acknowledged as king. As the kingdom for God, the Christian community is understood in political terms as the alternative community to the Roman empire . . . They are the anti-kingdom to the Roman empire."[71]

Considering how John then in the rest of the book contrasts this people to the draconic order of the Beast, the implication is clear: In view of the universal domination of the Dragon, this people is to be the divine alternative to the kingdom of the world. Although the Beast now holds the position of geopolitical authority bequeathed to it by the Dragon, it is this redeemed people that are destined to occupy it,[72] a fulfilment depicted in 20:4–6 and in 22:3–5 ultimately as the elevation of redeemed humanity as a whole to positions of authority in the divine 'court' gathered around the throne of God and Lamb.[73] However, now this kingdom is not a particular nation in a limited geographical realm but is constituted from all peoples of the earth.[74]

However, although there is a basic redefinition of who constitutes the people, Schüssler Fiorenza has shown that this does not mean a spiritualising of the political function of the people,[75] a fact emphasised

---

likely is to be seen as referring to the dignity persons receive when Christ installs the redeemed to be a kingdom and priests to God.

71. Ibid., 75, 76.

72. "Als das königliche Volk Gottes stehen die Christen dem Römischen Reich als Alternative und Kontrast gegenüber" (Giesen, *Johannesapokalypse*, 72).

73. As in 11:15, I take βασιλεία in 1:6 and 5:10 not simply as rule (Beckwith, *Apocalypse*, 429) but as a position of political authority, the exercise of which is indicated by βασιλεύω.

74. See Bauckham, *Climax of Prophecy*, 326–37, on how fourfold phrases as found in 5:9 are used to express humanity in its most universal sense. The expansion of the people is also depicted in a hear-see construction in 7:4–10: John first hears an angel speak about the 144,000 that will be sealed from all the tribes of Israel (7:3–8) but then sees an enumerable crowd gathered from all peoples standing before the throne (7:9–10) (cf. Gundry, "New Jerusalem," 260). For a review on the debate on the relationship between 7:3–8 and 7:9–10, see Aune, *Revelation 6–16*, 440–47; cf. Smith, "Portrayal of the Church," 116–17.

75. Schüssler Fiorenza, *Justice and Judgment*, 73–76; see Schüssler Fiorenza, *Priester*, for the full development of her thesis that in 5:9–10 John modifies the baptismal

in how 5:10 concludes, καὶ βασιλεύουσιν ἐπὶ τῆς γῆς.[76] Although as we shall see, John sees the saints as already exercising this rule, the full geopolitical implication of this language is evident in the vision of chs. 21–22: within the eschatological expansion of reality in the book, it is clear that what John envisions is a real geopolitical reality which realm is the transformed earth, its subjects the priestly servants who also are royal co-rulers gathered around the throne of God and the Lamb, the divine throne being its ordering center.

An aspect of the people that space does not allow us to develop fully here, is that they are a *priestly* kingdom, as the strong allusion to Exod 19:4 in 1:5–6 and 5:9–10 makes clear.[77] While this should not be limited to a political function in general, it seems that it is the religio-political aspect of priesthood that is at the fore for John. Just as God and the Lamb are the religio-political center of the kingdom of God that is now established in heaven (chs. 4–5; 12:5, 10) and will come to earth (chs. 21–22), so the people constituted by the Lamb are a religio-political people.[78] The visionary complex ends with the fulfilment of this their identity. Redeemed humanity is those who give priestly service to God and the Lamb in the eternal kingdom, and who as such will rule forever.[79]

---

formula he has cited in 1:5–6 in order to draw out the theological and socio-political aspects of the installation of the people as a kingdom to God, something they are already now but which earthly geopolitical manifestation awaits the descent of the throne of God and the Lamb to the earth.

76. Against NA27 (cf. Schüssler Fiorenza, *Justice and Judgment*, 70, 77), I follow Beale, *Revelation*, 362–63, in seeing the verb as present rather than future. While neither reading can be favoured on the basis of the textual evidence alone, the present is the harder reading. However, with Schüssler Fiorenza and Roose, *Eschatologische Mitherrschaft*, 207, and against Giesen, *Johannesapokalypse*, 71–72, I see it as referring to the actual co-reign of the saints in the kingdom, both in the coming kingdom but also in the way they now partake in Christ's paradoxical rule on earth (cf. Bovon, "Self-Presentation," 699).

77. For John's interpretation of these passages, see especially Schüssler Fiorenza, *Priester* (cf. Gelston, "Royal Priesthood").

78. Not only does 1:5–6 and 5:9–10 state that they are constituted as a priestly kingdom, but the reference to the stars, sun and moon that the woman is clothed with in Revelation 12 may pick up an interpretive tradition where the priestly vestments of Exod 28 and 39 were depicted as the heavenly luminaries (Beale, *Revelation*, 626).

79. Although λατρεύω is not the technical term usually employed in the LXX for priestly service, the liturgical setting of 22:3 is confirmed by the obvious "temple" setting when this scene is anticipated in 7:15. Both Swete (*Apocalypse*, 103–04) and

If the Church, understood as those who have been redeemed from their sinful bondage to the order of the Beast, is the way the priestly kingdom of God exists now and who, as such, is destined to be God's kingdom on earth, how is this kingdom manifested in history? In a context where the present manifestation of the draconic order has ransacked and destroyed the last vestiges of Israel's geopolitical authority, where is the kingdom located, where is its realm?

CHURCHES AS PARADOXICAL AND AMBIGUOUS PRESENCES OF THE KINGDOM

The church that is the kingdom is now present on earth in churches.[80] So, in 1:12—3:22 Jesus is depicted as the exalted Lord of the seven ecclesial communities, who is present to them in the Spirit, and who rules them. However, that said, this presence of the Church that is the Kingdom within the churches must be carefully qualified since it is both paradoxical and ambiguous.

First, we note how the book portrays the manifestation of the kingdom in churches paradoxically: the communities that are commended for their faithfulness to Jesus are precisely those who now are economically poor and socio-politically marginalised (2:9; 3:8), while those churches who are economically successful and enjoy a relatively privileged social position are seen to be so compromising that their status as one of the communities gathered around Jesus is in danger (3:1b–2, 15–16). If the kingdom is to be seen in political terms in history, it is in a paradoxical way.

Second, the presence of this kingdom in the churches is ambiguous. Although John sees himself and his audience as being the people who are created to be a kingdom to God, only two of the seven churches, Smyrna and Philadelphia, are seen to accord with the kingdom (2:9–10a; 3:8, 10), and even their ecclesial status as those who will in-

---

Harrington (*Revelation*, 101) note that John may have used λατρεύω instead of the technical λειτουργέω in order to emphasise that it is the mass of redeemed humanity that gives priestly service to God and not an exclusive priesthood. Note also the close relationship between how the worship of redeemed humanity is depicted here and the worship of the elders in 4:9–11 and 5:8–10. It is precisely these priestly servants who will rule forever (22:5).

80. Although Revelation sees those bought by the Lamb as one people (1:5b–6; 5:9–10), they exist on earth in a multiplicity of communities (chs. 2–3) (cf. Swete, *Apocalypse*, 101–2).

herit the kingdom is contingent upon their perseverance in faithfulness (2:10b; 3:11).[81] Two of the churches, Sardis and Laodicea, exist in such a compromised situation that they are about to lose their ecclesial status (3:1b-3, 15-16), while the other three churches exhibit characteristics that are both consonant with their identity as communities of the alternative kingdom (2:2-3, 6, 13, 19) and indicate abdication to the way of the Beast (2:4-5, 14-16, 20-23).

To the extent churches live their allegiance to their Lord, they are places where the kingdom of God is present in the world. Inclusion among the people who constitute the kingdom of God is determined by allegiance. Thus, although ideally the ecclesial communities are actual manifestations of the kingdom as the communities of those who have been bought by the Lamb to be the priestly kingdom to God, their actual existence as such is always contingent on their faithfulness to Christ and their prophetic resistance against the all-pervasive social, religious and political force of the Beast. The churches, as the "realm" in which those who are a kingdom to God now exist, are the earthly "sphere" in which the rule of God can be experienced in history, and through whom the kingdom spreads to the world.

The Form of the Church: The Kingdom in Exile

> I have frequently been threatened with death. I ought to say that, as a Christian, I do not believe in death without resurrection. If they kill me I will rise again, the people of El Salvador. I am not boasting, I say it with the greatest humility. I am bound, as a pastor, by a divine command to give my life for those whom I love, and that is all Salvadoreans, even those who are going to kill me. If they manage to carry out their threats, from this moment I offer my blood for the redemption and resurrection of El Salvador. Martyrdom is a grace from God which I do not believe I deserve. But if God accepts the sacrifice of my life, then may my blood be the seed of liberty, and a sign of hope that will soon become a reality. May my death, if it is accepted by God, be for the liberation of my people, and as a witness of hope in what is to come. Can you tell them, if they succeed in killing me, that I pardon and bless those who do it? But I wish that they could

---

81. This is of course the case for each of the churches, as seen in the repetition of a final admonition to hear the Spirit and the promise to the victors.

realize that they are wasting their time. A bishop may die, but the church of God, which is the people, will never die.[82]

Considering the woman in Revelation 12, we will now try to show how although the churches have a claim to the kingdom, they do not exist in the geopolitical form of a kingdom. However, this does not make them apolitical. As Israel lived toward the Promised Land in the desert, so the churches live toward and according to their own fulfilment in the eschatological kingdom.

The Collective Identity of the Woman in Revelation 12

Revelation 12:1–17 is a pivotal vision in the book[83] whose main characters are a heavenly woman and a Dragon. The vision is held together by the Dragon's failing attempts to foil God's purposes: first it is thwarted in destroying the woman's son who is destined to rule the earth (vv. 1–6), and then, as a consequence of that failure it loses its place in heaven and is flung down on the earth (vv. 7–12), where, after having failed to destroy the woman, it starts to pursue her offspring (vv. 13–17).

Most of the characters are clearly identified in the vision, the Dragon is identified as the primordial enemy of Israel's God, the primordial accuser whose purpose is to deceive the whole inhabitable world (12:9),[84] the male child the woman bears is identified as the Messiah in an allusion to Ps 2:9 in 12:5,[85] and the woman's other offspring are clearly the saints, those "who obey God's commandments and hold to the testimony of Jesus" (12:17). The interpretive crux of the vision is

---

82. Archbishop Oscar Romero of El Salvador, two weeks before he was assassinated, as quoted in Rowland, *Revelation* (Epworth), 101.

83. Most commentators note the interpretive importance of ch. 12, Collins, *Combat Myth*, 231–34, calling it the "paradigm of the book of Revelation." Revelation 12 depicts the messianic victory that dethrones the Dragon/ Satan from his place within the heavenly realm, Revelation 13 then goes on to describe the temporally limited battle between the Dragon and the messianic community on earth, before Revelation 14 anticipates the final messianic battle against the Draconic forces and the final messianic judgment.

84. For the development of Satan as the arch demonic figure, see Beckwith, *Apocalypse*, 617–18; Aune, *Revelation 6–16*, 696–98, 700–01.

85. While the reference to the raging nations in 11:18 alludes to the eschatological fulfilment of Ps 2, the snatching up of the male child who will ποιμαίνειν πάντα τὰ ἔθνη ἐν ῥάβδῳ σιδηρᾷ to the throne of God refers to how this eschatological reign is already fulfilled in heaven (cf. Sweet, *Revelation*, 192–93, 197).

vv. 7–12.[86] Here, the snatching of the messianic child to the throne of God (12:5b) is first seen as resulting in a battle in heaven in which the Devil and his army lose their place in heaven and are thrown down on the earth (12:7–9). Then, in an auditory section, Satan's loss of his accusatory role in heaven is interpreted as both the establishment of God's salvation and undisputed sovereignty in heaven (12:10, 12a) but also as the intensification of his draconic force during the short time he is consigned to earth (12:12b).[87] In this way John shows that although Easter is the pivotal victory which makes certain the establishment of God's kingdom on earth, it for a brief while means an intensification of the demonic opposition to God's people on earth. However, this escalation of evil signals not the dragon's victory but its defeat, that it "has been decisively overthrown."[88]

If this is the case, how are we to interpret the woman in the sky who is the mother of both the Messiah and the saints now persecuted by the Dragon? Although the description of the woman may partly allude to an individual woman, Eve and perhaps Mary,[89] most modern scholars see her collectively, as representing the messianic community, both as faithful Israel among whom the Messiah arose and now as those who are gathered around the Messiah.[90] But what is the significance of this? We will try to show that she is Zion-Jerusalem as she represents

---

86. Questions on the unity of ch. 12 focus on these verses. Although this is likely an insertion, John has incorporated it as a pivotal interpretive of the whole vision. For discussions on the unity of the chapter, see Beckwith, *Apocalypse*, 620. For the vision's possible redaction history, see Aune, *Revelation 6–16*, 663–66.

87. As we noted in the previous chapter, 3 1/2 as a measurement of time (for John, years) was an apocalyptic image of the final escalation of evil. Here John interprets this escalation not as a sign of an actual accumulation of evil power but rather as an implication of its temporary restriction.

88. Beale, *Revelation*, 623. "The sovereignty of Satan has been terminated at source, even if externally it has achieved its summit" (Sweet, *Revelation*, 192).

89. If, as Sweet considers likely (*Revelation*, 196), the woman recalls Eve (cf. Beale, *Revelation*, 625), this may suggest why the imagery is elastic enough to be broadened from referring only to Israel to include all those constituted by the Lamb as a people to God. See Bruns, "Contrasted Women," for an argument for a partially mariological understanding of the woman on basis of how a likely reference to Eve suggests the woman is to be read both corporately and individually. For a more negative assessment of mariological readings of the woman, see Brown, et al, *Mary*.

90. Beale, *Revelation*, 627; Beasley-Murray, *Revelation*, 197–98; Beckwith, *Apocalypse*, 621; Sweet, *Revelation*, 203.

the church as she journeys through a geopolitical "desert" toward the coming kingdom. We will do so by comparing her to how other collective women function in the book and by looking at the mythological and Jewish themes uses to describe her.

THE SOCIO-POLITICAL CHARACTER OF COLLECTIVE WOMEN IN REVELATION

In addition to the woman in ch. 12, there are two other collective women in the book, the Great Prostitute in Revelation 17 and the Bride in Revelation 21 (cf. 19:7–8).[91] They symbolise two socio-political centers that represent their respective political orders; Babylon the Great Prostitute represents the actual order that now holds political authority on earth and the New Jerusalem the Bride of the Lamb represents the eschatological order that will replace it.[92] As the actual cities in which the ruling elites can and do enforce their way over their respective realms, and as the cities who therefore characterise the fundamental nature of their particular political orders, they do not only represent themselves but also the whole political orders of which they are the center. For John, Babylon is Rome as the geopolitical center that represents the whole empire,[93] and the New Jerusalem represents the coming

---

91. The only other woman mentioned in the book is Jezebel in 2:20, where it refers to an individual person and is not used collectively. Feminist critiques of Revelation focus particularly on the depiction of the two women in chs. 17–18 and 21–22 (see e.g. Kim, "Uncovering"; Pippin, *Death and Desire*, "Eros"; Selvidge, "Powerful and Powerless"; Stichele, "Apocalypse"). Barbara Rossing (*Two Cities*, 13), however, questions Pippin's and others' singular focus on the modern reader and the reduction of "desire" to sex and violence, neglecting economic, political, and spiritual desires. Rossing argues that John clothes his critique of empire and his own alternative to it in the imagery of two women because he employs an ancient tradition of representing an ethical choice as a choice between either a lascivious or a virtuous woman. By linking this topos to the two cities, John transforms this topos to a political choice. However, when we have sought to read the gendered language of the book within its own concern, Schüssler Fiorenza (*Justice and Judgment*, 199) rightfully points out what I have perhaps not sufficiently done in this thesis, that we need to translate the androcentric language of the book into forms appropriate for our contemporary "rhetorical situation."

92. The Bride of the Lamb is first introduced in 19:7–8, but it is not before 21:2, 9 that we are told that she is to be identified with the New Jerusalem.

93. Although John links the Beast and Babylon closely together (17:3, 7–8), there is also an important distinction between them: while the former represents Rome's political-military power that dominates by force, the latter corrupts by the deception of economic affluence.

kingdom of God, the eschatological geopolitical order gathered around the throne of God and the Lamb.[94]

Considering the role of these two collective women in Revelation, it ought to at least raise the question whether the woman in ch. 12 functions in an analogous way. Is she too, in some pivotal sense, a city that represents the kingdom it is the center of?

The Journey of the City of God in the Wilderness

That John sees the woman here in similar political terms as the women in Revelation 17–18 and 21–22 is evident in how Revelation 12 is patterned after the Leto-Apollo-Python myth, and the way in which John uses his Jewish heritage to identify her as Zion-Jerusalem.

In Revelation 12 John employs a mythical topos that has deep roots in the Ancient Near East and bears striking resemblance to a popular version of this myth in the Roman world where the goddess Leto is pregnant with Apollo who is destined to slay the Great Dragon Python.[95] Python pursues Leto in order to kill her unborn son before he has to time to slay him. However, Poseidon keeps Leto out of Python's reach by protecting her on an island that he sinks into the sea. There Apollo is born as an adult, and after four days seeks Python and kills him. John probably patterns his own vision intentionally after this myth because of the way Rome was cast as the goddess mother of Apollo, who in return was identified with the emperor.[96] As such, she was the city of the divine emperor who held anomic chaos at bay.

---

94. In contrast to Babylon, the New Jerusalem is depicted as covering the whole realm (although the city has a wall, it seems to be 'located' at the borders of the inhabitable cosmos since those who are excluded from it in 21:27 are precisely those who have no place in the new creation [cf. 20:15; 21:8]), perhaps to accentuate how here privileges are not limited to a central elite but extended to all.

95. See especially Collins, *Combat Myth*, 57–65 (cf. Aune, *Revelation 6–16*, 667–74) Most scholars note the likely allusion to this myth; however, note the objections of Prigent, *Apocalypse*, 16, 64–68, who thinks the parallels are too broad and that it is unlikely that John would employ a pagan myth. In reply we can note that the parallel structure is remarkable and the political reason for employing it is all but insignificant. It seems perfectly reasonable for a writer steeped in Jewish tradition to pick up the stories of his opponent and turn them on their head.

96. Witherington, *Revelation*, 165–66. This may also be one of the reason why John clothes the woman with sun, moon and stars as a contrast to how the emperors at times saw themselves as sons of a mother goddess, reflected in sun-moon emblems for Rome (Beale, *Revelation*, 628; cf. Caird, *Revelation*, 148).

John turns this on its head, Rome is now the earthly manifestation of the villain, while the Messiah of the woman in the sky is he who both conquers the dragon and its earthly manifestations.[97] Employing one of its own cherished myth, John portrays Rome as the villain bound for destruction.[98] If John has employed the Leto-Apollo-Python myth intentionally to contrast the woman in the sky with the false claim of the goddess Roma, this would suggest hers is also a fundamentally geopolitical identity. She is a contrast city to Rome, the center of a political alternative to the Roman empire.

Although the overall structure of Revelation 12 draws on the Leto-Apollo-Python myth, the details are steeped in Jewish tradition, not least the depiction of the woman.[99] First, most commentator agree that John recalls Zion-Jerusalem as he depicts the woman.[100] In its symbolic significance Jerusalem had by the time of Jeremiah and Ezekiel become a synecdoche for Israel,[101] "the great hopes associated with the chosen people seem now to be linked with the fate of a city, the very name of which is in the way of becoming a symbol."[102] Considering this and how John sets this woman in intentional contrast with the way Rome saw herself, this woman probably represents the city of God, Jerusalem, as she symbolises the whole kingdom of which she is the political center. Thus, before John has depicted the order of the Dragon, its beasts and its city, he has closely identified the followers of the Lamb with the central city that is the light of the whole world.

Second, G. K. Beale and others have shown that in the way John alludes to Zion-Jerusalem, he emphasizes in particular how she represents the faithful remnant of Israel as she suffers from oppression and

---

97. John's employment of this myth is one example of how John "used pagan imagery and practices as part of a broad apologetic assault on Graeco-Roman culture itself" (Aune, "Apocalypse," 481).

98. Cf. Richard, *Apocalypse*, 101–2.

99. For extensive discussions on the Jewish background of this vision, see Beale, *Revelation*, 625ff.

100. See Isa 66:7–11 (cf. 54:1–3; 61:9–10; 65:9, 23; 4 Ezra 10) for how Israel is represented as Zion, as a mother with seed (Beale, *Revelation*, 631). Elsewhere in the NT, this tradition is picked up in Gal 4:26–27.

101. Humphrey, *Ladies*, 21; cf. Beale, *Revelation*, 676–78, who notes that female Zion always represents the many people of Israel (Isa 49:14–25; 50:1; 51:1–3, 16–20; Ezek 16; Hos 4:4–5).

102. Porteous, "Jerusalem-Zion," 97.

anticipates God's redemption.[103] This, the centrality of the Messianic child, and the likely reference to Eve and her seed provides John the elasticity he needs to identify the people the woman represents:[104] she is the faithful messianic community, first as the faithful Jewish community that expected the one seed of Eve, the Messiah, and among whom he emerged (12:2, 5) and then the international community of the Lamb who also are her seed (12:17).[105]

Third, if the woman in Revelation 12 is clothed in the language of Jerusalem-Zion as she represents the faithful people of God, what is the significance of her journey in the "desert" (12:6, 14)? The "desert" is an ambiguous biblical symbol, sometimes used to indicate the desolation of sin and judgment[106] but also as a place of protection from evil forces.[107]

---

103. "The woman's birth pangs represent the persecution of the covenant community and the messianic line during OT times and the intertestamental period leading up to Christ's birth" (Beale, *Revelation*, 629; cf. Aus, "Relevance," 268). He notes that although the image of a woman in birth pain is often used of punishment (Isa 13:8; 21:3; Jer 13:21; 22:23), here it picks up another tradition, "of the suffering of the ideal city of God resulting from oppression" (Beale, *Revelation*, 637; cf. Isa 26:17–18; Mic 4:9–10; 5:3; Hos 13:13). Ford notes (*Revelation*, 189) how basani/zw and its cognate noun are used sixty times in 4 Maccabees of the suffering of the martyrs; cf. Matt 8:6, 29; 14:24; Mark 5:7; 6:48; Luke 8:28; 2 Pet 2:8.

104. Aune notes (*Revelation 6–16*, 708–9) that σπέρμα here is highly unusual since it normally is used of a male progenitor, and suggests the reason for this might be because it is an allusion to Gen 3, to the woman's seed that will make war with the seed of the Serpent (cf. Farrer, *Revelation*, 142–43). This would make good sense both of the seed of the woman in the singular being the messianic figure that signals the defeat of the serpent, and the ensuing war between the siblings of the messianic figure and the beastly order of the Dragon in ch. 13. If this is the case, then the city of God is represented as an Eve figure from whom both the messianic victor and his fellow warriors come, while the beasts who the Dragon conjures up out of the chaotic sea are associated with the city that deceives the world represented as a Prostitute. Beale, *Revelation*, 677, notes how "the equation of singular "male" with plural "children" and collective "seed," all alluding to the same offspring from Zion" in Isa 66:7–10 "is virtually identical to the phenomenon in Revelation 12 of the Jerusalemite woman bearing a male and also having plural seed" (cf. Fekkes, *Isaiah*, 185).

105. John does similar movements in 1:5–6 and 5:9–10 where he uses the language of Exod 19:6 to describe the people constituted at Easter; similarly in 7:4–10 he uses a hear-see formula to identify those gathered around the Lamb with Israel; cf. Beckwith, *Apocalypse*, 628.

106. Of judgment on Israel: Jer 9:10–15; 12:10–12; Ezek 6:14; Joel 2:3; of Jerusalem in particular: Jer 6:7–8; 7:34; of judgment on Israel's enemies: Isa 13:20–22; 34:10–15; Jer 50:39–40; Ezek 29:5; Joel 3:19; Mal 1:3.

107. Beale notes (*Revelation*, 646) how Deut 8:14–16 brings this dual emphasis of the wilderness together. See Williams, *Wilderness*, for an insightful study on the motif

This positive role of the desert has of course deep roots in Israel's story as the place of the people's journey from the bondage in Egypt to their establishment in the promised land.[108] Therefore, although the desert imagery is used for God's judgment on Israel, it is also used to depict the protection of Israel in exile[109] and the expectation of Israel's return from exile.[110] This is the rich tradition John alludes to here when he depicts how the woman is protected from the onslaught of the Dragon by being taken on the wings of an Eagle into the desert where she is nourished by God.[111] This is where she will reside during the time the Dragon has on earth.[112]

What picture can we draw from this? Although this woman, like the women in chs. 17–18 and 21–22, represents a city that is the defining center of a kingdom, unlike them, she is not manifested geopolitically. Between Easter and the Parousia, in the limited time the Dragon is confined to rage on earth, God's earthly Jerusalem is protected in the

---

of the wilderness in biblical literature. As the uninhabitable "unsown" land it was often associated with chaos and judgment (Jer 25:38). However, for Israel it was also an important motif in her covenantal life with God (as the place where God provided for her as well as "the place of testing and tutelage" [15] and as a place of refuge). See Williams, *Wilderness*, 22–27 on how the NT writers use wilderness as an exodus imagery.

108. Exodus 16:32; Deut 2:7; 8:2–3, 12–16; 29:5–6; 32:10; Josh 24:7; Neh 9:19–21; Ps 105:37–42; 136:16; Hos 13:5–6.

109. Beale notes (*Revelation*, 625–26) how later Jewish literature used passages as Cant. 6:10 to "emphasize Israel's faithfulness to God either in the wilderness wandering or in exile." For a similar notion of the desert as place of protection in the NT, see Matt 24:15–26; Mark 13:14–22; Luke 21:20–24.

110. A common motif in the expectation of the return from exile is not simply the journey through the desert but also the transformation of the desert into fruitful inhabitable land where the human community flourishes (Isa 32:14–15; 35:1; 40:1–5; 41:18; 43:19–20; 51:3; Jer 31:2; Ezek 34:25; Hos 2:14–20). On the transformation of the desert, see Williams, *Wilderness*, 14. Beale, *Revelation*, 643 notes that the desert community of Qumran saw itself as the first stages of the fulfilment of this last exodus.

111. If John alludes to Isa 40:31 (cf. Exod 19:4; Deut 32:11–12) here, (so Ford, *Revelation*, 191–92; Harrington, *Revelation*, 136; Swete, *Apocalypse*, 158) this is another example of how he uses end-time exodus motifs to portray the woman's time in the wilderness (cf. Beale, *Revelation*, 669; Beasley-Murray, *Revelation*, 205).

112. The 3 1/2 years that designate the short period in which the Devil manifests its draconic power on earth through the order of the Beast also designate the period that the woman is protected in the desert, a time period 12:6, 14 suggests lasts between Easter and the Parousia (see Sweet, *Revelation*, 46 on how references to 3 1/2 bind chs. 11–13 together; cf. Beale, *Revelation*, 647 who notes that the reference to 42 months echoes the forty two years Israel spent in the desert according to Num 33:5–49).

desert.¹¹³ This is a time that God's people suffer under the political rule of their oppressors, just as they did in Egypt and Babylon. However, this does not mean that they have lost their political identity. Although their city, their *polis*, has now been robbed of its rightful place, it has not disappeared. It is protected, kept alive by God outside the political structures, in the "desert." So, for John, the loss of Jerusalem as the political center of the kingdom of God is not a sign that God's promises have been defeated but that their fulfilment is near at hand.¹¹⁴ At Easter, the end-time Exodus has commenced as the Dragon and all its demonic forces have lost their place in the heavenly realm, and now the city of God is on its journey through the desert, protected from the ragings of the Dragon, waiting for its homecoming. This is the exodus now "experienced not in Egypt but in the heart of the Roman empire."¹¹⁵ The kingdom of God is not defeated, but the church, as it exists as an anticipation of the kingdom in ecclesial communities, "advances toward the heavenly Jerusalem and consequently she lives in hope."¹¹⁶ Thus, just as the New Jerusalem is the heavenly-eschatological counterpart to Babylon, so this woman-city in the desert is its earthly counterpart.

113. See Humphrey, *Ladies*, 107, on how the desert topos is employed to connect and contrast the woman in ch. 12 and Babylon.

114. One wonders if this is John's response to the destruction of Jerusalem and the dissolution of Israel as a geographical entity in AD 70. Although Jerusalem may be judged for rejecting its Messiah, this is not the end of the kingdom of God. Rather the death of the Messiah has cemented the victory of God's eschatological purposes and the present community of the Messiah is now God's kingdom that lives for and toward the re-establishment of the kingdom as a geopolitical reality which will cover the whole earth. As such the destruction of Jerusalem and the dissolution of the nation is not the end but the decisive beginning of the fulfilment of God's hope. It is a sign that the end of Satan and his powers is drawing near. The disappearance of a visible manifestation of God's kingdom on earth during the broken time of the Dragon is merely a 'brief' phase of the final battle before its undisputed establishment on earth. The time of this woman in the desert is the time between what Schüssler Fiorenza, *Justice and Judgment*, 56, has labelled the first and second step of the establishment of Christ's reign over the cosmos. In the first, at Christ's enthronement, Satan loses his place in heaven and is consigned to the earth; in the second, at the parousia, Satan is banished from the earth; and in the third and final establishment of the kingdom, Satan is destroyed.

115. Richard, *Apocalypse*, 77. Similarly Williams, *Wilderness*, 25, sets the woman, as "the new Jewish Christian Israel," within the conflict with Rome.

116. Ellul, *Apocalypse*, 55. Noting the prevalence of exodus imagery in the book, McDonough not unjustifiably claims "John's book may be fairly described as a 'New Exodus,' as God delivers his people from their oppressors" (McDonough, *YHWH at Patmos*, 200).

She, who is all light, waits for her true manifestation when the kingdom of the Beast has been darkened; she who is now protected in the desert waits for her own rightful place when the woman who occupies the center in history will be deserted, made desolate (17:16).

Bringing these various strands together, we conclude that the woman in Revelation 12 is likely to be seen as the collective identity of the messianic community that exists as the alternative to the draconic order of the Beast that now holds the position of geopolitical authority in the world. As such, the woman is depicted as Jerusalem-Zion as she represents the kingdom of God that now exists in a kind of 'exile', i.e. without an actual geopolitical manifestation.[117] The messianic community are the citizens, the children of the city which has been taken outside the geopolitical structures of the world into the desert to be protected by God during the time the Dragon rages on earth.[118] Because the city is hidden away during its time of protection while her children are being persecuted, many commentators see her as the "spiritual" identity of the church, the heavenly perspective on the church during history.[119] This is correct if one simply refers to the hidden-ness of this aspect of God's people in history that is only revealed in the vision's spatial expansion of reality—that the churches that are now constantly threatened by internal conflict and external pressure are also the manifestation of the Kingdom, which future is certain since its central reality,

---

117. Whether Jews at the time of Jesus saw themselves as existing in exile is of course a hotly debated issue. See Bryan, "Exile," 72, for a measured exploration of how exile functioned metaphorically for some Jews "to interpret the contemporary experience of the authors and to express their hopes. If John's depiction of the woman appeals to such imagery, his point is not what N. T. Wright argues in relation to Jesus in *Jesus and the Victory of God*, that the return from exile is happening in the kingdom ministry of Jesus. Rather, for him, Easter both intensifies exilic experience, but precisely this intensification is a sign that the final redemption of God has begun; although in a hidden way, the people of God already find themselves in the desert, on their way out of exile, their eyes firmly set on the promised city.

118. Commentators disagree on how the plural offspring of the woman in 12:17 is to be related to the woman. Against Beale, *Revelation*, 676, Beckwith, *Apocalypse*, 619–20 and Sweet, *Revelation*, 204–05, I do not want to see it as a distinction between the church as seen ideally or spiritually from the heavenly perspective and the suffering of the people on earth. Rather, the former is a depiction of the kingdom of God in exile, and thus refers to the collective identity of the people, while the latter refers to the people themselves as the citizens of this city and focuses on their plight in history, during the time of their "exile."

119. So Beale, *Revelation*, 648–50; cf. 676.

its city, is being protected by God, out of reach of the Dragon who rages against her (12:14–16). But if this is what we mean by the "spiritual" identity of the woman, then she has lost none of her political identity. Revelation's "utopia is political and unfolds in history," not "beyond history, but beyond oppression and death in a new world, where God's glory becomes visible over all the earth;" it is "a reconstruction of the Exodus at the heart of the Roman empire."[120] What has been taken away by the forces of evil (11:1–2) is kept safe by God until the day these forces themselves are defeated, and then the city that now sojourns through her end-time exodus will find her fulfilment in the New Jerusalem that descends from heaven.

The Homecoming of the Kingdom in the New Jerusalem

This naturally leads us to the question about the woman in Revelation 12 and the Bride of the Lamb.[121] Most commentators agree that there is a close relationship between the two, they are in some way "to be seen synoptically."[122] Edith Humphrey argues the glorious woman in Revelation 21 is a transformation of the woman in Revelation 12 whose glory is hidden during her time of persecution.[123] As such "both figures" represent "God's faithful people (18:4)."[124] While Humphrey rightly rejects Yarbro Collins strong distinction between the two,[125] it may be

---

120. Richard *Apocalypse*, 3–5.

121. Noting the prominence of the two women at the beginning and end of chs. 12–22, Barr ("Apocalypse," 44) argues that they "dominate the last half of the book." See Humphrey, *Ladies*, 103–4 on how in virtually every proposed structure of the book these two women play a pivotal role.

122. Humphrey, *Ladies*, 104; cf. Sweet, *Revelation*, 302.

123. "The Apocalypse describes the persecuted mother in the wilderness who is really Queen of Heaven, and who becomes the Bride, the New Jerusalem" (Humphrey, *Ladies*, 21).

124. Humphrey, *Ladies*, 109.

125. See Collins, *Combat Myth*, 132. The weightiest of her objections is that there are no internal textual cues for a close connection between the two. However, Humphrey (*Ladies*, 108) points out that elsewhere Collins, *Combat Myth*, 28, argues for certain such links as the open-ended nature of 12:17 anticipates a later fulfilment, how the New Exodus motif in ch. 12 anticipates the new conquest in 19:11–21, and the new fulfilment in chs. 21–22. See Humphrey, *Ladies*, 109–10, for other inner-textual relationships between the two. For a response to Collins' other objections, see Humphrey, *Ladies*, 105–9.

better, considering the earthly location of the former[126] and the heavenly origin of the latter, to see them as two distinct but closely related images that both refer primarily to the collective identity of God's people as his kingdom.[127] Revelation 12 focuses on the existence of this community in the history between Easter and the Parousia. As such, this woman depicts how the kingdom now exists in exile. The woman in Revelation 21 refers to the New Jerusalem that is the heavenly counterpart of the earthly people, in which the earthly people finds its fulfilment when it descends to the earth.[128] As the true political order whose center is God, the woman in Revelation 12 is clothed in every source of cosmic light (12:3), but in the time before the rule of the Dragon has been darkened on earth (16:10) she does not exist in the form of a kingdom. Nevertheless, in her exile her central religious and political identity is protected by God (11:1–2) while she awaits her fulfilment in the city

---

126. Some commentators place the woman in heaven, as the church's heavenly counterpart, since the vision occurs in the heavenly realm (12:1) (e.g. Beasley-Murray, *Revelation*, 197–98). However, although she is seen in heaven, the vision locates her firmly on earth (12:5, 6, 13, 14, 15), a fact made evident in her absence in precisely that part of the vision that takes place in heaven (12:7–12). This vision is not about the church's heavenly identity but her earthly political identity as symbolised in Jerusalem.

127. Farrer, *Revelation*, 215, seems to suggest such a distinction when he says: "For though the mother of Messiah is not, as such, the bride of Christ, both figures are allegories of the same reality, the 'daughter of Zion,' the congregation of God."

128. Humphrey, then, is right in seeing a transformation of the earthly woman since she finds her fulfilment in the arrival of the heavenly one (cf. Harrington, *Revelation*, 128). But this identity is the eschatological unification of the heavenly and earthly city. In history the woman in ch. 12 represents the earthly counterpart of the heavenly city. Perhaps John uses γυνή in 19:7 instead of νύμφη (cf. 21:9) precisely in order to recall the woman in ch. 12, thus making a close connection between the two. If this is the case the identification of the woman's βύσσινον with the righteous deeds of the saint (19:8) may point to how the subjects of the "Jerusalem" the woman represents only find their fulfilment in the New Jerusalem as they persevere in faithfulness to the God and the Lamb. (Rossing, *Two Cities*, 140 notes that the linen in 19:7 is not to be identified with the woman but rather signals "that the bride embraces and validates their righteous deeds [of the saints].") It is precisely in the political image of the city that the dicothemy between the city as people and place reflected in Gundry's study, "New Jerusalem," on the New Jerusalem as people can be overcome.

whose source of light is God's glory (21:11, 23)[129] and whose borders extend to the whole earth.[130]

There are three important implications of our discussion of Revelation 12 on how the people made a kingdom to God in the events of Easter exist as such. First, the church, understood as the communities of believers gathered around the Messiah, stands in an exclusive relationship to the kingdom, it is the only people that have a future in the kingdom. This assertion, though, does not mean that the Kingdom can be identified with particular ecclesial communities without qualification. The ecclesial communities are the manifestations of the kingdoms since they are where God's rule is exercised by Jesus in the Spirit.[131] However, they can only be such manifestations of the kingdom if their life is ordered according to and in communion with their Lord.[132] The church is the kingdom of God in anticipation of its fulfilment, and the churches are presences of the kingdom in the realm in which the rule of the kingdom is not yet established;[133] to the extent they are faithful

---

129. Humphrey, *Ladies*, 110 notes the relationship between how the woman in Revelation 12 is clothed in light and how the glory of God is the light of the New Jerusalem. This stands in contrast to the Beast and its kingdom that will be darkened when the fifth bowl is poured on its throne (16:10). This may be an intentional contrast since Isa 60:1–3, a passage that lies behind Rev 21:23–26, contrasts the darkness that covers the earth and its peoples with the light of God's glory that will dawn on God's people and which will attract the kings of the nations.

130. In history it is only the central religio-political identity of the kingdom that is marked for protection (11:1–2) and is protected in the desert, while "the horizon" of its geopolitical realm is now occupied by the forces of the Dragon (12:6, 14–16); in contrast, the angelically marked borders of the New Jerusalem extend throughout the whole inhabitable cosmos (21:15–17) and the glory and honour of the nations and their kings will stream into it (21:24–26) (cf. Humphrey, *Ladies*, 110).

131. Thus, Jesus who addresses the churches in chs. 2–3 is depicted in 1:12–20 as the exalted Lord at the center of the lampstands that represent them.

132. Note how a common theme in the warnings to the churches in chs. 2–3 is the risk of losing their ecclesial status (2:5, 16; 3:3, 16; cf. 18:4).

133. The relationship between the church as the one people and its pluriform manifestation is perhaps best seen in the image of the woman in Revelation 12. The woman refers to the one corporate identity of the church that awaits its earthly manifestation, while the children, who gather in ecclesial communities, are the individuals this people exist in. If the woman is the church as the city of God, her seed are the "exiled" citizens of the city that now gather in expatriate communities.

to their Lord and his mission they are the children of Jerusalem, and to the extent they do not, they partake in Babylon.[134]

Second, although the church has an exclusive *claim* to be the kingdom of God, she per definition does not exist in the *form* of a kingdom,[135] she is not manifested now as a geopolitical entity, has no earthly center of political power which orders an actual socio-political human community within a geographical realm. As such, the woman in Revelation 12 is both linked to the "old" and the New Jerusalem, the city that once was the actual geopolitical center of God's rule on earth and the city that one day will be the center of the whole inhabitable cosmos. What distinguishes her from her origin and her telos is not that she is apolitical but that she is in a political exile. Because of this, although the church, as this woman-city, does not exist in a geopolitical form, she nevertheless has lost none of her political identity.

Third, because of this exilic existence of the kingdom, the church's political praxis is radically transformed and yet nevertheless remains fundamentally political.[136] The ecclesial manifestations of the church do not rival the draconic order by establishing their own center of power in the world but in their prophetic existence in the world.[137] In Revelation, reflecting a context of marginalisation, this exists in resisting the way in which the Beast forces people to pledge their allegiance to the draconic

---

134. Note how the call "to come out of her" (18:4) suggests that the earthly people have some of the character of Babylon, the very city they are contrasted to, in themselves (so Humphrey, *Ladies*, 115).

135. Similarly Roose says, "Johannes differenziert damit zwischen einem gengenwärtigen Zustand, der darin besteht, dass die Christen zu einem Königreich und Priestern eingesetzt sind (Status), und der Verheißung, dass sie im neuen Äeon herrschen werden (Funktion)" (Roose, *Eschatologische Mitherrschaft*, 207).

136. "The church is a social and political reality that does things differently from other institutions, because it is eschatologically different, which means that the basis of its being and authority are also radically different" (Gunton, "Until He Comes").

137. In Revelation, it is not only the New Jerusalem and Babylon the Great that are set in contrast with each other, but also the activity of the powers of the Dragon and the followers of the Lamb. Note e.g., the way the depiction of either the activity or destiny of the Draconic forces is consistently followed by an exhortation to the saints: a) 13:1–8 > 13:9–10 (1. beast's temporary authority over saints > perseverance), b) 13:11–17 > 13:18 (2. beast's deception and persecution > calculate number; cf. 17:9), c) 14:6–11 > 14:12 (the 3 angelic pronouncements, incl. Babylon's fall, and judgment > call for patient endurance); cf. 18:1–3 > 18:4–8 (announcement of the fall of Babylon > call to leave and judge her); 18:9–24 > 19:1–4 (lament over and depiction of the fall of Babylon > call to rejoice at her destruction).

forces, unearthing the fundamentally idolatrous and unjust ways of the draconic order, and proclaiming the messianic way to the alternative kingdom, to the New Jerusalem that will descend from above when Babylon and all who are like her are but smouldering ashes. This is the way in which the saints "rule" in history. Those who in the eschaton will occupy the central court of the eternal kingdom and as such rule forever,[138] rule now in their prophetic witness. The prophetic witness, most vividly depicted in Revelation 11, is the exercise of actual and effective 'political' power, it accomplishes radical changes in the world which either are seen as punishment on the world as it resists the way of the kingdom of God or as an actual ordering of the world toward the future kingdom. And Rev 12:11 points to how the eventual demise of the kingdom of the world is unavoidable as the churches continue the campaign of their king and extend his paradoxical victory in their own martyrological existence. As such, in following his way, the church shares both the fate and the victory of Christ: risking death, they uncover the false logic of unjust power. Its martyrs are the undertow of God's kingdom: as they are swept from the earth, they join the heavenly army that one day will rush back to the earthly realm; then, the unassailable power of the forces of evil will be but sand castles that leave no trace of their existence as the evening tide washes them away.[139]

---

138. Roose sees Exod 19:6 LXX, Ps 2, Dan 7 and Matt 19:28/Luke 22:28–30 as the primary background from which John develops his understanding of eschatological co-rule (*Eschatologische Mitherrschaft*, 207).

139. Note first how when slain in the realm in which the Dragon attempts to cut them off from their allegiance to the Lamb, the martyrs are caught up to the heavenly realm where the kingdom is now established (compare 7:15–17 with 21:1ff). In this their own journey is patterned after Jesus' (3:22; 12:5; 14:4). Second, note how it is precisely their defeat at the hands of the draconic forces that constitutes their victory (12:11; cf. Bauckham, *Theology of the Book of Revelation*, 70–71, 88–94). Third, note that it is precisely these martyrs who make up the Lamb's army that inflicts the last defeat on the forces of evil in history (14:1–5; 19:14). As such, the victory of the Beast over them is their defeat over it and the Dragon behind it, since in their death they both enter the heavenly counterpart of the eternal kingdom and populate the army at which hand all draconic forces on earth will meet their end. In this way the martyrs are the paradigm for the whole church: "One conquers through persevering fidelity to God, and in John's world that means active, though non-violent, resistance to the Roman system even to the point of surrendering life itself. Conquest, that is, comes not by wielding coercive power, not by submitting to its claims to authority, but by resisting out of undying allegiance to God who—despite all appearances—is sovereign" (Carroll, "Creation," 254).

Interaction with Moltmann

Consonances

The above discussion of the reign of God and how churches are the places in which the kingdom now exists in exile is consonant with significant aspects of how Moltmann sees the dialectic between the future of the kingdom and its presence in history, the dialectic between the kingdom as the horizon and Christ as the center, and how he places the church between Christ and the Kingdom.

The Dialectics of the Kingdom

We noted earlier that as Moltmann turns to his relational understanding of the kingdom, he can account for the critiques placed against the singular focus on eschatology in *Theology of Hope* but in such a way that the earlier eschatological force is not lost. As such, the hope for the kingdom as the goal of history is "the rule of God in the kingdom of God as a future transcending the system," while its presence is the redemptive force of God within history that turns creation toward this future, "the kingdom of God in the liberating rule of God as a transforming power immanent in that system." Both are needed because "without the counterpart of the future of the kingdom, which transcends the present system, the transforming power immanent in the system loses its orientation. Without the transformation immanent in the system the future transcending the system would become a powerless dream."[140] Hope produces a form of praxis that is consistent with the way the rule of God hoped for is present in the world in anticipation—since the hope for and presence of the kingdom belong together, "in actual practice the obedience to the will of God which transforms the world is inseparable form prayer for the coming of the kingdom. The doxological anticipation of the beauty of the kingdom and active resistance to godless and inhuman relationships in history are related to one another and reinforce one another mutually."[141] While Moltmann develops this logic in fairly abstract terms at times, there is an important strand in his theology that

---

140. *CPS*, 190. Moltmann grounds this distinction in this discussion by noting that in the New Testament βασιλεία can refer either to the present and actual rule of God in the world (which is disputed and manifests itself in hidden ways) or to the universal goal of divine rule (which is eschatological, universal and undisputed). Cf. *JCTW*, 19.

141. *CPS*, 190.

can provide it with positive and concrete content, namely the dialectic between Jesus as the center and the Kingdom as the horizon. This, as we noted is already evident early in his theology but is perhaps developed most fully in *The Way of Jesus Christ*.[142]

The understanding of the kingdom in Revelation reflects a very similar dual logic. The eschatological kingdom is not a future that replaces the present but is rather the transformation of both the human community and the earth when God will assume the central political sovereignty on earth that is now in the hand of his enemies. As such, the eschatological kingdom is "the future transcending the system" that gives the present its "orientation:" the depiction of the future of both Babylon and the New Jerusalem calls the readers to abandon any allegiance with the former and throw their lot in with the latter.[143] As the city that awakens the aspirations for the kingdom of God, the New Jerusalem suggests fundamental aspects that should inform the social imagination of those who do pledge their allegiance to its Lord. This calls for a this-worldly praxis—the call to move out of Babylon is not a call to abandon this world for the coming but a call to engage in a messianic war for the future of this world in the New Jerusalem.[144] This praxis, as in Moltmann, is christologically informed. Although the vision of the New Jerusalem orients believers toward the coming kingdom, how they actually live toward it is shaped by how their risen Lord has gone ahead of them and shown them the way of participating in the messianic victory for the kingdom of God.[145]

142. So also Rasmusson (*Church as Polis*, 376), who thinks *WJC* is the apex of Moltmann's development of the church as a contrast society that "witnesses to an alternative social and political practice."

143. "John builds on hundreds of years of tradition to present Jerusalem and Babylon as opposing figures in the most thorough economic, political, religious, and ethical appeal of his time, calling believers to come out of the whorish city and to take part in the glory of a bridal vision" (Rossing, *Two Cities*, 1).

144. Not surprisingly, Revelation with its this-worldly hope and unmasking of the veil the powerful cast over reality is a crucial biblical text in various liberation theologies (Rowland and Corner, *Liberating Exegesis*, 133).

145. "The pivotal role which the history of Jesus plays in the Apocalypse does not detract from but rather reinforces, the eschatological outlook of the book. The corollary of eschatological hope in the Apocalypse is certainly not the meaninglessness of present existence. The present takes its meaning from the redemption already accomplished (1:5; 5:9) which guarantees the future hope, defines its content (the coming Lord is Jesus who was crucified, who was dead and is alive for ever: cf. 1:18) and also

While Revelation, depicting a context where every other venue is foreclosed, shows us how prophetic resistance is fundamental to the posture of Christians in society, Moltmann can help us to read the book in context where other modes of social engagement are possible without compromising one's faithfulness to God. To see this better, let us turn to a second similarity between the two.

The Church in the Mission of the Kingdom of God

> All inherent interests of the Church itself—maintaining the status quo, extending influence—must be subordinated to the interests of the Kingdom of God, otherwise they are unjustified. If the spirit and the institutions of the Church correspond to the Kingdom of God, then it is the Church of Christ. If they contradict the Kingdom of God, then the Church loses its right to existence and will become a superfluous religious community. The Kingdom of God orientation of the Church today consists of proclaiming the gospel of the Kingdom of God to all people and first to the poor in this world in order to awaken faith which lifts up and makes certain.[146]

This programmatic statement in *The Church in the Power of the Spirit* would not be an inappropriate summary for the basic thrust of Revelation 2–3. For example, in the address to the church in Laodicea, their capitulation to the social and political pressures of Rome is contrasted with their potential exaltation in the kingdom of God. Laodicea is in danger of losing its ecclesial status (3:16; cf. 2:5) because it has contradicted the kingdom of God in the way it has amassed the wealth of Rome.[147] The church had elevated its own self-preservation above the interests of the kingdom and was losing its right to existence. In contrast to this, Christ as the community's foundation and Lord, calls them to repentance. If they do so, the congregation will share his destiny and be elevated to his throne in the Kingdom of God (3:21–22).

Revelation, within its context of social isolation and impending persecution constantly draws us back to what Moltmann also sees as

---

provides the model for positively living towards the *parousia* meantime" (Bauckham, *Climax of Prophecy*, 171).

146. Moltmann, "Jesus and the Kingdom of God," 16.

147. Similarly Sardis has a reputation to be alive but from the vantage point of the exalted Christ is dead (3:1–2).

fundamental to the church, namely the kerygmatic nature of how the church is to be faithful to Christ in its existence toward the eschatological kingdom. Its faithfulness to and proclamation of the way of Christ to the coming kingdom is its fundamental service to the world. This is basic in Moltmann's theology[148] and Revelation depicts this as the way in which the church exists and participates in the battle of God against the forces of evil, and as such is intrinsically political. Because of the radical context Revelation is set in, the book very clearly sets out the contrast between capitulation to the forces of evil and perseverance in the kerygmatic faithfulness to Christ. As such, Revelation is pivotal for Christians who live on the underside of today's global society, it gives them the hope that the justice of God will not leave things as they are, no matter how set in stone they seem.[149] However, precisely because divine justice is at the heart of the book, it is a book for all Christians, and Moltmann can help Christians who occupy positions of privilege to read it in at least two important ways.

First, Moltmann's emphasis on the church's interested engagement with the world as it exists for the whole, gives the reader an appropriate context from which to read the book. Whatever one makes of Moltmann's proposed solution for the contemporary context of global economic injustice, he forcefully reminds Christians today that they cannot occupy a neutral position and that they have an obligation to seek the welfare of the poor in the globalisation of Western market economics. So, when Western Christians read how Rome was the Babylon of its day partially because of the unjust flow of material goods (18:3, 9–19), Moltmann reminds us that today we must read such text in light of the way the Western world is getting drunk on the intoxicating wine of the luxuries it drains from the rest of the world. Christians who participate in these processes without a concern for the justice for the poor are shifting their allegiance from Christ to the Dragon and its contemporary beasts. Faithfulness to the Gospel does not only mean rejecting every form of

---

148. Noting that God's kingdom "does not simply lie in readiness in the future" but must be sought if it is to be found, Moltmann adds, "[One] must seek this future, strive for it, and already here be in correspondence to it in the active renewal of life and of the conditions of life and therefore realize it already here according to the measure of possibilities" (*RRF*, 218).

149. While this is a concern throughout Moltmann's theology, he develops it specifically in relation to his ecclesiology in *CPS*, 168–76.

idolatry but also an orientation toward the rule of God in which those who suffer injustice now are exalted to the throne-room of God.[150] The call "to *come out* of her" for them is to *enter more consciously into* these processes in order to change the flow of goods.[151] As we do so, we must not only attend to how the book comes to us from the periphery but must also learn to read it with those who occupy the periphery.[152]

Second, while Moltmann's political iconoclasm is perhaps what is closest to Revelation's portrait of its own socio-political climate, his emphasis on the potentialities for the kingdom in the human social processes may also help us to highlight a less accentuated emphasis in Revelation, the possibility of the nations hearing the kerygmatic proclamation of the church and giving glory to God. It is understandable that the book itself, considering the social context it portrays and its dominant battle motif, does not spend much space on what this would look like in the here and now. However, Richard Bauckham has convincingly shown that it holds out the hope that although the order of the beast that now deceives the whole world will come to a final and decisive end, there is the possibility that the nations will repent.[153] Crucial for Christian people who can engage in the cultural, political and economic processes of society without compromising their faith is to know how one can appropriately form a society that is informed by the justice of the coming. Revelation leaves the door open for such engagement in its vision of the New Jerusalem as the alternative city to Babylon, and Moltmann can in many ways point us in the direction of how we can enter through this door. While we will shortly question how Moltmann relates present political and social structures other than the church to

---

150. This has been a constant emphasis in Moltmann's authorship, seen most recently in the extensive interaction with various forms of contextual theology in *EiT*, 183–299.

151. Fernandez, in his insightful study, "Judgment of God," interprets the religio-political economic dynamics of Revelation 18 against the backdrop of contemporary economic injustices. He rightly points out that the call to come out of the city is the refusal to take advantage of an unjust system that oppresses the poor; as such, even an actual separation if that is necessary is not an act of sectarian escape but of active resistance.

152. See e.g. Richard, *Apocalypse*. Although I am more confident than Steve Moyise, "Lion," 181–94, that Revelation holds its own correctives against oppressive readings of it, his observations on how Revelation can and has been read as such is to be heeded.

153. Bauckham, *Climax of Prophecy*, 238–337.

the coming kingdom, his constant attempt to discern the present situation, its pathologies and its possibilities, in light of what Christians hope for the whole world, is laudable. Since the church exists on the foundation of Christ and for his kingdom it must always be drawn beyond itself; because its Lord is the creator of the whole cosmos, it cannot exist in communities that live for themselves, and because the purposes of its Lord are *for* his creation, its children must never escape life on this earth in hope for another but must always "enquire about still closer political correspondences to the lordship of Christ, to the messianic mission and to the church's existence in a world-wide context ... The politically responsible concept of the church ... leads to the church that suffers and fights within the people and with peoples, and to an interpretation of this people's church in the framework of the divine history of liberation, whose goal is the new creation in peace and righteousness."[154]

In this, Revelation unflinchingly reminds us of the indisputable place that Christ has as the Lord of the church and that the church can never involve itself in the world in such a way that it compromises his Lordship, but Moltmann can help us to see how the nations that now get drunk with the deception of Babylon may become the nations that enter the New Jerusalem.

Differences

However, this discussion on the consonances between Moltmann and Revelation also brings us to two fairly important differences between the two, one that circles around how they understand the rule of God, and the other in how they see the relationship between the church and the kingdom.

THE SOVEREIGNTY OF GOD AND THE EGALITARIAN COMMUNITY

The Sovereignty of God and the Human Community. In a previous chapter we discussed how Moltmann has grown increasingly weary of theological language of divine rule and human obedience because of the hierarchical notions of power distribution it connotates, a concern at the heart of his critique of monotheism and the way he understands the God-world relation.[155] For him, emphases on God's absolute sover-

---

154. *CPS*, 18.
155. "If the concept of community, mutuality, *Perichoresis*, comes to the foreground in the understanding of God, and takes up, relativizes and limits the concept of one-

eignty become the tool of the powerful to substantiate their own unjust rule. Thus, in his later work, although the Kingdom of God remains a pivotal symbol in his thought, talk about God's sovereignty and human obedience have all but disappeared in favour of an emphasis on the reciprocal relationship between God and creation which forms the basis for a human society of the equal and free.

However, we also noted that Moltmann's own position had some fundamental problems, a notable one being that the biblical visions of the egalitarian community Moltmann appeals to precisely ground their ideal in the kind of divine sovereignty Moltmann rejects. This raises the question whether the categorical dichotomy Moltmann sets up is valid. According to Moltmann's logic, the vision of God's sovereignty in Revelation should produce a vision of a highly hierarchical political society; however, precisely the opposite is the case, the vision of the eschatological community in Revelation is radically egalitarian precisely because it anticipates the arrival of God's undisputed sovereignty on earth.[156] Considering this and how we also questioned Moltmann's necessary correlation between God's inner communion and his economic relations, his one-sided use of biblical tradition and his inability to account for the proper exercise of power in history, we will now first briefly consider a different way of constructing the God-world relation, second, hone in on how the rule of God as well as human freedom can be understood within it, and third consider what advantages this view may have over Moltmann's, how it both can maintain the ideal of the egalitarian community without compromising God's sovereignty, and how it can provide the positive content for the provisional but necessary structures of human power in history.

Christological Perichoresis. In a master's thesis that deserves wider publication, David Höhne has convincingly shown that the way pericho-

---

sided rule, then understanding of the determination of human beings among each other and their relationship also changes" (*HTG*, 181).

156. In 22:3–5, after the enemy is finally defeated and every vestige of its social, political, economical and cultural vestiges have been eradicated, redeemed humanity is first depicted as those who serve God (22:3) and who as such constitute those who rule forever. Here, humanity as a whole are exalted to the highest social position possible. When, Moltmann, in fact, does discuss this passage, he completely ignores the clear distinction made between God and his servants, and interprets the language of service and rule as "rule through the mutual give and take of power" (*CoG*, 319).

resis is used in the Cappadocian and Byzantine Fathers often diverges significantly from the way it is used among contemporary theologians who claim to revive them.[157] Höhne argues both the Cappadocians and the Byzantines who followed them used the term first and primarily to express how the two natures in Christ are hypostatically united and possess co-inherence (περιχώρεσιν) but without confusion or dissolution.[158] They achieved this by seeing the relationship between the two natures in a fundamentally asymmetric and dynamic way. In this asymmetric dynamism the movement is always from the divine through the human and "the human nature only penetrates the divine in so far as the divine nature penetrates itself with the human."[159]

Although later the Byzantines used the term in a different way for the inner-trinitarian communion[160] and although John of Damascus saw the perichoresis of Christ's two natures as based in the inner trinitarian communion,[161] when the Fathers related perichoresis to the

---

157. Although Höhne, "Perichoresis," focuses on how Colin Gunton appropriates the concept of perichoresis, many of his observations are as relevant to Moltmann's use of the term. For Moltmann's appropriation of John of Damascus' notion of perichoresis, see *TKG*, 174–76.

158. Höhne, "Perichoresis," 72. Although sometimes accused of Monophysitism in their use of Perichoresis in the incarnation, Höhne points out that "What the Byzantine Fathers described was theosis not Monophysitism. They wrote of the gracious restoration of the nature of humanity to its true participation in the nature of God brought about in the incarnation through the Perichoresis of the two natures and the hypostatic union" (Höhne, "Perichoresis," 78–79).

159. Höhne, "Perichoresis," 54; cf. 56–57. Pseudo-Cyril says: "The penetration (περιχώρεσις) was not of the flesh but of the deity. For it is impossible for the flesh to penetrate through the divine: but the divine nature was able having once penetrated (περιχωρήσασα) through the flesh to give ineffable penetration toward itself to the flesh" (*De Sancta Trinitate* xxiv, PG 77.1165 C, as quoted in Höhne, "Perichoresis," 54). This contrasts to how Moltmann sees the divine as the center of the human nature and therefore experiences and is affected by everything the human nature experiences (see *CrG*, 227–35). The asymmetric notion of the Byzantines seems to be able to account for the divine's nature's intimate involvement with the human nature but without having to resort to the mutual effecting Moltmann thinks necessary.

160. When the Byzantine understood the communion within God as perichoresis, they retained the idea of mutual containment and interpenetration but whereas the perichoresis between the two natures of Christ is both asymmetric and dynamic, the perichoresis in the Trinity is seen as symmetric, complete and is described in static terms (Höhne, "Perichoresis," 62, 79).

161. However, for John of Damascus, this does not mean they are to be seen in strict parallel terms, the inner communion remains symmetric and static while the relation-

redemption of humanity it was as it is patterned in the relationship between Christ's two natures. "The Greek Fathers wrote of perichoresis as the result of the hypostatic union and the dynamic that underlies the doctrine of theosis."[162] God's purposes for humanity are being brought into fulfilment as men and women are deified in Christ. Adopted into Christ, Christ by the Spirit enters into them, transforms them, and in this makes them able to penetrate into the divine. As such, perichoresis is indeed useful for considering how we are to see the relationship of God with creation and most immediately with humanity. But its usefulness lies not primarily in how creation's life with God is patterned after the inner trinitarian relationships but in how the incarnation shows God's purpose as entering into communion with his creatures.[163]

Perichoresis and the Rule of God. Although it is outside the remit of this thesis to work out how this way of seeing the relationship between God and creation may respond to all the problems we noted in how Moltmann accounts for this relationship, we will focus on the one question that is central to it, namely how it affects an understanding of God's sovereign rule in his kingdom.[164]

---

ship between Christ's two natures is asymmetric and dynamic (Höhne, "Perichoresis," 79, 127, noting *Contra Jacobitas* 52.35–37).

162. Höhne, "Perichoresis," 84.

163. Höhne concludes that when we interpret the "in" language of John perichoretically, "we conclude that perichoresis is what God *does* for us to empower us to *be* like him" (ibid., 123).

164. A response to the other problems we saw in Moltmann's understanding could be developed along the following lines: 1) In this model, both God's intimate involvement with creation and his self-sufficient freedom from creation can be maintained since in the asymmetric perichoresis the movement is always from the divine nature and only from the human to the divine as the human is enabled by the divine, the human is radically transformed but without the divine being changed. 2) This can respond to Moltmann's critique of the apathic God since although God in no way is shaped by creation, he nevertheless is intimately involved with and knows the human predicament. If the divine nature does not abrogate but completes Christ's human nature, one could argue this is possible only because God as creator most fully knows what it means to be human, including the capacity for love, anger, joy, suffering and so on. 3) Precisely because the redemption of humanity does not have a counter "need" in the being of God, the universalism that seems necessary within Moltmann's framework loses its force. Although God desires the redemptive transformation of his people, he himself is not dependent on it. Because of this, the human possibility to either embrace or rebel against communion with God is a real possibility. Hope remains universal but the rejection of what is hoped for remains a real possibility.

First, negatively, since it not only grounds our perception of God's rule in the economy but also understands it within the economy, this view avoids the analogies Moltmann too readily makes between what may be the case for the immanent Trinity and what therefore should be true of God's relationship to the world.[165] Basing God's rule in the asymmetry of the incarnation takes seriously that God's resolve always precedes any correlation there may between God and humanity. Communion with the triune God is grounded in God's resolve as revealed in the incarnated Son.

Second, positively, this model may suggest how we may resolve the perceived tension between how the center of the divine rule as revealed in the Passion radically turns notion of power and rule on their head, and how the horizon of that rule as seen in God's *acts* of judgment and redemption unambiguously affirms that God asserts the right of a sovereign—the creator who gives himself for his creatures does nevertheless not relinquish his undisputed authority over creation. Both of these strands are unambiguously affirmed in Revelation. The God who exercises his sovereignty through the slain Lamb is nevertheless also he who in the eschaton will not only judge those who persist in rebellion against him but also excludes them from the eternal kingdom. And so, the sacrificial victory of the cross and the final messianic judgment and battle form a part of the same cloth in the book. This dual affirmation is clearly seen in how the Christ who liberated a people to be a kingdom to God is also presented as the undisputed sovereign who has the right to order the life of communities of this kingdom in history. Moltmann, because he sees a fundamental incompatibility between the two, tends to either neglect the authoritative horizon or so reread it that it all but disappears. But if we consider the service of the passion and the rule in God's mighty acts within a model drawn from the perichoresis of the two natures of Christ, this perceived tension dissipates.

The descent of the divine into the human is a radical "service" to humanity in which humanity is enabled to become what it was created

---

165. Although Moltmann construes his understanding of the perichoretic union within God from the economy, he nevertheless uses this construal as a transcendent that governs his understanding of the God-world relation. Since this understanding is deduced from the economy but not intrinsically bound to it, it easily looses its moorings in the economy and is easily carried far beyond what the "economic facts" can bear.

to be, but it is also a process that is initiated and determined throughout from the divine, the formative movement is still from God and is oriented back toward God. As the first among many, the perichoresis of the Son reveals God's purpose for all humanity. As such the Son's servanthood is an exercise of God's sovereignty and God's sovereignty is the Son's servanthood in praxis. Within this framework God's sovereignty and human freedom are not mutually exclusive but the latter is dependent upon the former. It is only as people submit themselves unconditionally to the divine rule that they can be truly free, can enter that wide space where they can truly be themselves, where every relation, action and thought are truth because they drink from the deep wells of the divine wisdom that rules them.[166] If people submit to God's rule, they will be oriented toward redemption but if they reject it, they will incur for themselves the deadly consequences of being cut off from him. A creature's freedom is entering that mode of existence for which it was created, and therefore cannot be seen apart from the shaping force of the creator, from both God's rule and the way he makes conformity to His rule possible.

Although it is the Gospel of John and perhaps the Johannine epistles that most evidently lead us toward a perichoretic notion of the relationship between God and Jesus,[167] the exaltation language in Revelation can also be seen through this lens. The one who is the origin of God's creation (3:14; cf. 1:18; 2:8)[168] is the one who as he took on the condition of humanity and most radically gave himself for humanity in his death is exalted to the divine throne (3:21; cf. 12:5). As the one who has gone through this movement, Jesus is the one who promises a similar "theosis" to his followers, just as he was exalted to the Father's throne, so they will be exalted to His throne (3:21). This is to be seen as already fulfilled both in heaven and also paradoxically in history,[169] and

166. Although Moltmann emphasises how we arrive at our true freedom, to our true selves in communion with the coming God, he avoids the language of unconditional submission to God since it stands in conflict with the importance of self-determination in his understanding of freedom. See Rasmusson, *Church as Polis*, 89ff.

167. Höhne, "Perichoresis," 120.

168. Against Beale, *Revelation*, 298, I follow Witherington, *Revelation*, 107, in seeing ἡ ἀρχὴ τῆς κτίσεως as "an explicit reference to Christ's preexistence" (cf. Beasley-Murray, *Revelation*, 104; Beckwith, *Apocalypse*, 488 Caird, *Revelation*, 57; Harrington, *Revelation*, 73; Sweet, *Revelation*, 107; Swete, *Apocalypse*, 59).

169. The Kingdom is established unambiguously in heaven (12:10) and is present paradoxically on earth in the kerygmatic witness of the church (12:11).

the whole vision ends with the eschatological fulfilment of this promise as humanity is ordered as the servants of God around his throne and rule forever.

If God's rule is seen in this way, certain aspects of Moltmann's understanding of freedom must be corrected. "The individual's right to self-determination" which is central to Moltmann's notion of freedom,[170] plays only a limited role. In Revelation, freedom is not ultimately the possibility to form society in dialogue and without coercion[171] but rather most fundamentally the liberation from the deception of the dragon as well as its corruption, and entering that community in which people are shaped by the reign of God. People are not free to "determine" themselves but they have the possibility, by the grace of God in Christ, to choose whom they will be "determined" by, whether by the order of the dragon that is going toward its destruction or by the rule of God in Christ, in which they will move into the fullness of life around the throne of God.

If this is the case, Moltmann's three-layered stratification of freedom must be re-ordered. Here freedom is not a movement from servanthood toward friendship, but exists as servanthood and friendship, each mutually enforcing the other. The more one is the friend of God, the more radically one is his slave. The more one is God's slave, i.e. yielding to the perichoretic penetration of the divine Spirit, the more one is God's friend since one is brought more fully into communion with the divine. And while for Moltmann the freedom of the child of God is a mediating stratum between the freedom of the servant and of the friend, here it is the fundamental condition that one can be both God's servant and God's friend. It is only as one is adopted as a child of God in the Son, that one in the first place can become the servant that yields to the transformative power of the Spirit, and in the same Spirit enters communion with God.

The Absolute Rule of God and Provisional Human Authority. There are at least two great advantages in understanding the divine rule in this way. First, when we consider God's rule and human freedom within an asymmetric dynamic perichoresis, the fulfilment of humanity in the community of equals is inseparable from the confession of God's

---

170. *GSS*, 35.

171. The importance of the dialogue of the free to form true communities is seen throughout Moltmann's corpus (see e.g. in *TKG*, xiii).

unquestioned sovereignty. Christians cannot rightly justify any kind of absolutism precisely because it is only God, as creator and redeemer, who has the claim and ability to move into the human and transform it toward its created potential. Every human vision of ordering society, every religious or ideological utopia, is rendered provisional in the expectation of the arrival of the New Jerusalem from above. Since it is only in the coming city that the throne of God is found, every legitimate form of human power structures in history is rendered provisional.

However, second, in the absence of the divine throne on earth in history, forms of structuring the human community must be found. While Moltmann eloquently discusses the provisionality and the freedom orientation of every kind of position of human authority, this is precisely what his understanding cannot give an adequate account of. However, a robust understanding of God's sovereignty not only relativises all human authority and renders it provisional but also points to the parameters of how this humbled authority is to be exercised. Positively, it gives it orientation—it is to be oriented toward the mutual communion of all in the kingdom—and it informs its praxis—although those entrusted with "the sword" may at times have to use it, the exercise of their authority must be first and always a radical service in which the good of the whole is sought. Negatively, precisely because its authority is rendered provisional and the good to be sought is not necessarily self-evident, such authority ought always to be exercise among the people and seek ways to inculcate it against any deification of its own power. While Moltmann would agree, a robust understanding of God's sovereignty provides a firmer theological rational for such a stance.

The Provisional Relationship of Church and State to the Kingdom

Although there are some significant and mutually informative correspondences between Moltmann's and Revelation's understanding of the relationship between the church and the kingdom, there is also a pivotal difference: for Moltmann the church is a people of the kingdom that anticipates the future kingdom, but for Revelation the church is the kingdom in an anticipatory and paradoxical form. In this, Revelation makes a close and an exclusive relationship between the church and the coming kingdom which Moltmann would reject. While for Moltmann the various religious, cultural and political institution and processes in the world have their own unique future in the kingdom, for Revelation the whole world exists in a disjunctive between its present reality and its future in the kingdom, and the church is the community of conversion in which this disjunctive is overcome. Here, we will first look at how the claim/form distinction we developed in relation to Revelation's depiction of the church as the kingdom in exile may be a safeguard against precisely the triumphalist danger Moltmann sees as inherent in placing the church in an exclusive relationship to the kingdom. Then, second, we will try to show how this may overcome basic tensions in Moltmann's own understanding of the kingdom in the world, tensions between his pneumatology and Christology, and in his missiology.

The Kingdom without Triumphalism. The church cannot assume political authority because although it is the only people who can make a claim to be the kingdom, it does not exist in the form of a kingdom. Intrinsic to the church's political identity is her exile: before the throne of God arrives on earth, during the time the Dragon is confined to the earth, the kingdom is in the desert.[172] Therefore, the church's political praxis must be consonant with her political exile. Her life is political, it is the anticipatory presence of the kingdom in history; as such, ecclesial communities are now ordered by the rule of God and exist to draw the world into the community that one day will be the geopolitical reality that covers the earth. But since the throne that determines its identity and praxis has not yet arrived on earth, its political praxis is not exercised through geopolitical means but as a prophetic proclamation that uncovers the deception in any power, be it political, economic, cultural or religious that tries to place itself in the position that only belongs to God. The only true Christian 'triumphalism' is the one manifested "not through fighting but through martyrdom."[173] This means that for Revelation, the church's politics is its prophetic existence as the alternative community of the coming kingdom, rather than Moltmann's mediation of

---

172. As Moltmann rightfully points out, the problem of the early church, and especially in the post-Constantinian grasping of political power, was not the delay of the parousia but an over-realised eschatology, an assumption that the reign of Christ had arrived before either he or the throne of God had arrived on earth (*CoG*, 153–54, 161–62).

173. Bauckham, *Climax of Prophecy*, 228.

the church's particular relation to the kingdom to the common relationship of all to the coming kingdom.[174] That said, Moltmann's concern to seek "certain trends and lines of Christian action" in society without ecclesiasticizing it in order "to resist the power of death as well as the deadly powers"[175] and his notion of the Exodus church that exists for and moves toward the kingdom[176] has much to contribute as churches seek to find ways to live as this alternative society in their own social contexts at this point in history.[177] As they do this, Moltmann reminds the churches that they have to do so avoiding the triumphalism that has beset churches throughout history, and Revelation's image of the kingdom in exile will always stand at a critical distance to any Christian attempt to enforce the way of the church in the political sphere.[178]

The church as the kingdom in exile has not only no place for ecclesial triumphalism but neither can it legitimise any other political power as the present instance of God's rule on earth,[179] because no state, however much it conforms to a Christian vision of a just society,

---

174. See Rasmusson, *Church as Polis*, who proposes the theological politics of Hauerwas as a more adequate account of the church's political existence than Moltmann's. He says: "While Moltmann constantly wavers between claiming the public nature of the Christian convictions and practices and accepting the primacy of the political reason of modernity . . . , Hauerwas consistently claims the public nature of Christian practice and theology" (378).

175. *CPS*, 168.

176. *TH*, 325–38.

177. A corrective to the "revolutionary" emphasis in Moltmann may be found in Yoder's exposition of how Christians can live as a contrast society according to the freedom of God's coming kingdom within the social structures in which they find themselves; he notes that in Rev 13:10 "the key to the obedience of God's people is not their effectiveness but their patience" (*Politics of Jesus*, 238; cf. 189–92).

178. Our reading of Revelation 12 would suggest that whenever the church has seized and seizes political power for its own end, it places itself in danger, of having its lampstand removed (2:5), be spewn out of the mouth of its Lord (3:16). To the extent the church assumes the right to exercise the authority of the kingdom of God in the political sphere it ceases to be the kingdom and becomes the Beast that usurps the position of authority that only belongs to God and his Messiah. Commenting on how Revelation suggest that some Jews have placed themselves outside the community of the kingdom by rejecting Jewish Christians (2:8; 3:9), Bauckham, *Theology of the Book of Revelation*, 125, adds, "using Revelation's own conceptuality, it would have to be said of later Christians who played the beast's role against Jews, that they say they are Christians but are not."

179. Chiliastic triumphalism, in both ecclesial and national guise, is one of the fundamental problems Moltmann sees in the history of the church (*CoG*, 3–6, 159–84).

can make a claim to be the kingdom although it exists in the form of a kingdom. Therefore, since the telos of any political entity is not its fulfilment in the kingdom of God but its replacement by the throne of God and the lamb, there can be no kind of messianic triumphalism in the secular realm.[180] Rome filled the shoes of Babylon in John's day not only because of its idolatry and injustice but also because it claimed to be the eternal kingdom, and thus usurped a position only belonging to God. Because of this, churches, although they certainly should call the state to act justly, can never place their stamp of approval on a particular state or political philosophy[181] but must always stand at a prophetic distance to political power, always a reminder that no state is an end in itself or the mean to the end but can only seek to shape itself in light of the end.[182]

180. Although this means that there is no direct continuity between the nations as they now exist as geopolitical entities and the kingdom of God, it does not mean that there is no relation between their present and the future kingdom. Those who wield political power in the nations can have a future, are not necessarily destroyed in the destruction of Babylon, but they only have a future as they relinquish the position of authority they held in history to God and the Lamb. When the kings of the nations enter the New Jerusalem, they bring their own glory and splendour into this city that will order the whole earthly realm (21:24–26).

181. Although Christians can applaud modern democracy for, among other things, its inbuilt checks and balances on power and its protection of the freedom of conscience, Western Christians, perhaps especially in the United States, must be careful not to legitimise the present export of our particular forms of democracy, usually wed with market economics, as the way in which the world will be free. Not only is it questionable whether such forms of government are appropriate for all contexts, but precisely by making such an absolute claim, the West has become oppressive as it seeks by both military and political means to impose its own political structure on the majority world. One suspects that part of the present drive to "democratise" the world is the maintenance of the West's global economic interests.

182. Cornelison notes ("Reality of Hope," 112) how this is a fundamental aim in the political theology of both Moltmann and Baptist Metz. In addition to its fundamentally provisional "ontology," the state is also rendered epistemologically provisional. Precisely because the global manifestation of the kingdom as a geopolitical reality is future, when form and claim are united in one political reality, neither the church as the institution that can lay a claim to be the kingdom or the state that exists in the form of a kingdom, can fully know what the kingdom will look like. While Israel as a concrete but geographically and ethnically limited manifestation of the kingdom and the church as it exists in voluntary communities ordered by the Lordship of Christ may be lights that suggests how to order a just society, every image is always necessarily a provisional anticipation, it always contains an "it will be otherwise" because it is always an image formed within the "not yet."

The Church and the Mission of the Kingdom. Having shown how Revelation's depiction of the exclusive relationship between the church and the kingdom has no room for the triumphalism Moltmann rightly rejects, we now turn to how it may resolve the tensions we saw in Moltmann's own view.

Earlier we noted that there is a fundamental tension between how Moltmann accounts for the kingdom christologically and pneumatologically. On the one hand he links not only the presence of the kingdom closely to Jesus but also entrance into the kingdom to an embrace of his person and history. On the other hand he sees the kingdom as present in everything that ministers to life since the Spirit that sustains all creation is ordering it toward the eschatological kingdom.[183] However, if the kingdom is seen to stand in an exclusive relationship to the church in history, the work of the Spirit as it orients the whole creation toward the kingdom cannot be separated from the Spirit's work in and through the church, and as such is intrinsically related to the work of Christ as he exercises the Father's sovereignty.

However, considering how Revelation sees the expansion of the kingdom through the prophetic ministry of the church, does this mean that there is no presence of the Spirit in the world apart from the church? No, but it does imply one has to account for the work of the Spirit in the church and the world differently from how Moltmann does it. Revelation's differentiated pneumatology may indeed point to how this may be accomplished. While τὸ πνεῦμα is used of the Spirit's work in the ecclesial communities, τὰ ἑπτὰ πνεύματα is used of how the Sprit is the power of the church's prophetic ministry to the world, is the divine presence of God and the Lamb who have not yet established their throne on earth.[184] Because of the particular geopolitical context in which the book is set, the work of God in the world apart from the church is primarily seen as judgment. However, considering the book's hope for the nations, the divine activity in the world should not necessarily be limited to judgment. Here, Moltmann's emphasis on discerning what accords with the kingdom in the world can helpfully augment the mostly one-sided emphasis in Revelation. But such a view calls for certain modifications in how Moltmann sees how the Spirit is at work

---

183. *SL*, xi; cf. *CPS*, 196; *WJC*, 91; 253–54.
184. Bauckham, *Theology of the Book of Revelation*, 112–13.

in the church in its mission to the world, and how the church in light of this discerns the Spirit in the world.

Several commentators have noted how Moltmann's account of the work of the Spirit in the world is configured so broadly that if it is not assumed to be self-evident it is nigh impossible to actually discern what is a sign of the work of the Spirit,[185] resulting perhaps in a certain privileging of one's own contemporary sensibilities.[186]

However, if the particular way the church participates in the Spirit's work in the world is the way in which the Spirit enables the church's

---

185. Farrow rightly notes that the problem with Moltmann's expansive view of the Spirit is precisely that it is too broad to provide a criteria by which to judge "which movements in human history are 'shot through by the Spirit'" ("Review," 432). Although we perhaps ought "to understand the Spirit as *the creative energy* of God and *the vital energy* of everything that lives" (*WJC*, 91; cf. 253–54), as the holistic "principle of creativity on all levels of matter and life" that keeps creation open to and aligns it toward its eschatological potentialities (*GiC*, 100–101), the perception of what is to be interpreted as this work of the Spirit must either be self-evident or can only be understood within a soteriological paradigm. Thus, for Christians, the work of the Spirit is either noetically self-evident or it must be interpret through how the work of the Spirit is revealed in the person and work of Jesus and the story of salvation in which he and his continuing ministry is embedded (Rasmusson, *Church as Polis*, 58, McIntosh, "Spirit of Life," 247). If the latter is the case, the only way to perceive the Spirit's work in the world is through the story of which Christ is the center.

186. Rasmusson argues that precisely because of Moltmann's tendency to privilege certain trajectories in modernity, his critical theology is not critical enough, it is not capable of unearthing precisely the weaknesses of the modern viewpoints Moltmann tends to adopt (*Church as Polis*, 57–62). It is true that although Moltmann is highly critical of certain aspects of modernism, he nevertheless sees the Enlightenment as a product of Judeo-Christian messianism and therefore, as "one in a series of revolutions of freedom driven by an outbreak of messianic hope for a better future," a hope that was secularised because the church had forgotten it in its defence of the status quo that favoured the privileged classes. Therefore, Christians should not reject the modern human attempt to overcome suffering. Rather, discerning how the Spirit works in the modern project, they should seek a "'fusion of horizons' between Christian hope for the coming of the Kingdom and modern hopes for emancipation," (Schweitzer, "Douglas Hall," 19, 20) or as Moltmann says, to "open its [the modern understanding of self and the world] eyes for the eschatological outlook in which revelation is seen as promise of the truth" (*TH* 44; cf. *RRF*, 21–35, *TH*, 291–303 on how Moltmann situates himself within the modern consciousness of history). However, this does not mean a capitulation to modernism, and, against Rasmusson, the confessional strand in Moltmann's theology can provide an internal critique of Moltmann's tendency to over-privilege certain aspects of modernism. Where Rasmusson's critique is relevant is in Moltmann's pneumatology, which is unduly colored by a modern emancipatory notion of universal history (Rasmusson, *Church as Polis*, 375–77; cf. 42–49, 57–60).

own ministry of the kingdom for the world, the church will always discern the work of the Spirit in the world according to its own mission to the world. What is fundamental to the church, and what therefore is fundamental to her life in the world, is the revelation of how Christ has created the kingdom to God that is the alternative to the order of the world. As such, pivotal for the church is not every way in which the Spirit may be at work in the world but the way the Spirit's work in the world is related to the church's own mission in the world.

This results in a pivotal shift from Moltmann's political theology. For Moltmann, political theology is the mediation from the *concrete* manifestation of Jesus' "Lordship" in the church to his universal "Lordship" over wider society, how the *particular* manifestation is *universally* relevant.[187] However, if it is only the church that can make any claim to the kingdom in history, the mediation is not from the concrete to the universal, but from the concrete manifestation of the eschatologically universal to the historically but provisionally universal. That is, the kingdom that now exists in exile within the ecclesial communities exists for precisely the "realm" that it one day will cover but which it as of now exercises no authority over. So it is not a matter of the mediation from a particular confession to a universal context but of the provisionally eschatological into the historically provisional. The proclamation is the proleptic manifestation of the eschatologically universal within the distortions of history. As such, the church redraws society in light of its confession rather than remoulds its confession in light of the urgencies and sensibilities of the day.[188] Although it must rightfully seek what the

---

187. See Rasmusson, *Church as Polis*, 42–48, on the mediating method of Moltmann's political theology. For Moltmann all theology is "mediating theology," a "mediation between the Christian tradition and the culture of the present is the most important task of theology" (*ThT*, 53). For him "political theology designates the field" in which this should happen, which in the modern world is the experiment to shape history toward the ideal of a human society (*EH*, 102–3). As such, as Rasmusson notes (47), this constitutes a move from the particular "history of Israel and Jesus" to the universal "interpretation of reality in general," a move made necessary "because the eschatological horizon of the Christian faith implies that this particular history anticipates the future of the whole creation."

188. Rasmusson sees this as one of the fundamental differences between Moltmann and Hauerwas. Hauerwas' adoption of the theology of the Radical Reformation "leads him to try to redescribe reality from a Christian perspective rather than to redescribe Christianity in the light of current social movements and perspectives" (Rasmusson, *Church as Polis*, 377).

appropriate form of that proclamation is within the context that is not the kingdom, that never will be the kingdom and that will be replaced by the kingdom, it nevertheless must remain its proclamation.

If this is the case, how is the church to discern the work of the Spirit in the world? First, one must make a distinction between how the kingdom cannot be present without the work of the Spirit and how the presence of the Spirit does not equate the presence of the kingdom. The kingdom is not primarily defined by God's pneumatological presence in the world but by where God resolves himself to be present as the ordering presence of the community he has made a covenant with.[189] Second, the work of the Spirit in the churches is then the way in which God is at work in shaping the churches to be communities of the kingdom that now exists in exile. Third, the work of the Spirit in the world, both as it sustains the life of all who are created through its power and as it is the power in which those who persist in opposition to God are judged, must be seen as the divine activity in which the geopolitical realm that does not exist as the kingdom of God is prepared for the day when it will be the realm of his kingdom. As the church then turns its eyes toward the world, it will discern the Spirit's work in the world not in general terms "in everything that ministers to life,"[190] but concretely as that which seems to turn the world, under the conditions it exists, toward what it believes to be true of the kingdom, as revealed in Israel's story and in the person and history of Jesus, as well as in light of its hope for the arrival of the kingdom to the earthly realm.

Considering the exclusive relationship between the future kingdom and the church in Revelation and the understanding of the work of the Spirit in both church and world, how can we respond to the basic tension we saw in Moltmann's qualitative and quantitative understanding of mission. First, it would call for a more nuanced understanding of the two aspects of the church's mission. If we use Moltmann's own terms, the quantitative mission of the church is related to its fundamental kerygmatic task, to proclaim the Gospel so men and women may be freed from their bondage to the draconic forces and may enter

---

189. Just as Israel's identity as God's people did not preclude God's involvement with the nations, so the Church's relationship to the kingdom does not preclude the presence of the Spirit in the world.

190. *SL*, xi; cf. *CPS*, 196; *WJC*, 91; 253–54.

the community that now exists as a kingdom to God.[191] This is a quantitative mission since it necessarily involves the call to become a part of the church that is the kingdom to God as it is manifested on earth in ecclesial communities. While the call to the kingdom would involve both quantitative and qualitative aspects, the church's interaction with the social, cultural and political contexts in which it lives is only the latter—it does not seek to convert present geopolitical realities into the kingdom of God (which they by definition are not) but seeks to point to how these can be informed by the light of the coming kingdom.

Second, within such an understanding these two aspects of the church's mission are in praxis inseparable from one another. The church that is not of the world but in the world cannot exist apart from calling people into the kingdom that is now not manifested geopolitically on the earth but will be. But in doing so it cannot help but let the light of the kingdom shine on the world as it is and therefore suggest ways in which the temporary geopolitical orders that now exist in the world can reflect the justice of the coming kingdom that are appropriate within them as entities that per definition are not this kingdom.[192]

Third, does this not foreclose the inter-religious dialogue fundamental to Moltmann's understanding of the church's qualitative mission since, as Moltmann claims, this dialogue cannot exist when one party seeks to convert the other?[193] However, here Moltmann seems to set up a false juxtaposition between persuasion and mutual understanding and appreciation. Although a blind and insatiable desire to prove oneself right is detrimental to dialogue, this does not preclude every attempt to convince others of what one has come to believe is true. Persuasion, as one element in the dialogue, is not closed to appreciating the other, learn from the other, and importantly, to be proven wrong by the other. A Christian who believes entrance into the kingdom is dependent on

---

191. A pivotal difference between Moltmann and Revelation then is that while both affirm that the church's "special vocation [is] to prepare the way for the coming kingdom in history" (*CPS*, 150), Moltmann sees this as finding ways in which the religions can find the path to their own future in the kingdom (*CPS*, 159), Revelation insists that it is only the church that has a future in the kingdom.

192. Although I have here questioned how Moltmann relates the church and the kingdom, one of his great strengths is how he constantly seeks ways of seeing the concrete social, economic and cultural situation in which he finds himself in the light of the coming kingdom (see e.g. *CPS*, 163–89).

193. *CPS*, 160–61.

allegiance to the Lordship of the Lamb will always try to persuade his or her dialogue partners to adopt the same viewpoint but ought also always give space to the other to do the same. What is fundamental to a Christian understanding of inter-religious dialogue is not seeking common ground but the love commandment to treat the other as one would like to be treated. In such a dialogue, whether religious or not, what is crucial is a keen ear and space for difference. If one wishes to be heard one must seek to understand the other on their own terms, and if one reserves the right to judge the other wrong one must give space for the other's "no" to oneself. Indeed, it seems difficult to see how any true dialogue could exist without this. One should seek consonances and convergences, find ways to incorporate the insight of the other in one's own and vice versa, but if this is the sole purpose of dialogue, then there is no place given for real difference, but every exclusivist claim, whether Christian or other, must by definition be excluded. But giving space for each other's categorical "no" while seeking each other's wisdom leaves the dialogue truly open, where nothing is foreclosed in advance. The church understood as a manifestation of the kingdom in exile is well equipped for such a dialogue since it must never coerce but only seek to persuade. And since the way of the kingdom is not yet self-evident it must not only give space to the other's "no" in history but it must also consider whether their "no" may show ways in which the church has misconstrued its existence as the kingdom in exile.

Fourth, although fundamental to the church's mission within this framework is to extend the invitation to enter the kingdom of God and to gather as exilic communities of this kingdom in local churches, this does not necessarily mean a homogenisation of the richness and diversity in the cultural heritages of the peoples to which the gospel of the kingdom is preached, an issue Moltmann is deeply concerned with.[194] Although it does mean that any god, idea or power that has assumed the position that is rightfully only God's must be dethroned, and although it also means that Israel's story and how the arrival of the kingdom in Jesus is embedded in it will become the new foundational story, it does not mean that the wisdom of Hinduism, Buddhism or any other ancient tradition or modern ideology must be outright rejected, just as neither

---

194. See e.g. *GSS*, 226.

Zeus or Thor were forgotten in Europe, although they have lost their divine status.[195]

[195]. The preservation of the good of the particular cultural context from which people come into the kingdom may perhaps also be explained within the asymmetric perichoresis of the two natures of Christ. Just as the divine nature did not make the human Jesus other than who he was, i.e. he did not become a universal human prototype but remained a particular Jewish man as he was the human for all, so those of other religions, when they enter the church do not lose the particularity of the tradition from which they come, while at the same time being transformed into the fulfilment of what they are meant to be. They are caught up into the messianic history of God that has its abiding origin in the history of Israel but without losing their own particular history. Is it perhaps precisely through such a paradigm we may be able to read the entrance of the nations into the eschatological city that is shaped by God's story with Israel and the apostolic community?

8

Conclusions and Anticipations

We have come to the end of our exploration of the kingdom of God in Moltmann and the book of Revelation, and it is time to both look back on what we discovered and look ahead at what further questions this study raises.

Retrospective

As the particular consonances and differences between Moltmann and Revelation on the kingdom are readily apparent in the previous two chapters, I will here only briefly summarise them before returning to an observation made both in the introduction to Moltmann and Revelation, how they respond to similar crisis situations and how their understanding of the kingdom displays a similar interplay between historical-temporal and relational-spatial concerns.

Consonances and Differences

There are some pivotal similarities between our discussion in chapters 3 and 6 on how Moltmann and Revelation see the kingdom as a symbol of hope for the future of the world. Although they develop their understanding in different (but not incompatible) ways,[1] they both emphasise the future as the arrival of the kingdom of God on earth, the time when both the social world of humans as well as the whole created order will be transformed in the arrival of God's presence. For both, this results in a complete reorientation in the present. The present should not be

---

1. Moltmann develops his understanding primarily from the dialectic between the resurrection and the cross ("which is at the heart of Moltmann's theology" [Bauckham, "Bibliography," 55]), and Revelation from the expectation of the final establishment of the victory of the Lamb, depicted in 11:15–19 as a regime change.

judged according to how things appear to be nor by the ideas and values of the powers to be. This reorientation includes for both, a Christian praxis that sets itself against everything that contradicts the light the coming kingdom sheds on our present existence. However, there is a pivotal difference between what they believe is the problem the coming kingdom resolves. Moltmann rejects the traditional understanding of sin as the basic problem in God's history with the world; although the cross responds to sin, it more fundamentally overcomes the transience that makes sin possible. Noting some significant problems in Moltmann, I suggested that Revelation's depiction of human rebellion, both as a structural and personal phenomenon, can more sufficiently account for the basic problems humanity faces in relation both to God and to the rest of creation.

As we turned to the relational aspect of the kingdom in chapters 4 and 7, we again saw that although they develop it in different ways,[2] there are some remarkable similarities between how Moltmann and Revelation see God's rule as present in the world. For both, it is a paradoxical presence in the realm otherwise characterised by the absence of God, Moltmann emphasising how in the cross God has become present to the realm characterised by his opposite, by death, and Revelation emphasising how in the ecclesial life of the earthly communities of the exalted Christ the rule of God is now present in the realm where the forces of the Dragon have usurped the position of geopolitical authority that only belongs to God. For both, the rule of God is oriented toward freedom, to the time, as the vision in Revelation concludes with, when humanity as a whole 'rules' but no one is ruled. And both see the church as standing in a fundamental relationship to the kingdom. The churches do not exist for themselves but are predicated on the lordship of Christ and are oriented toward the coming of his kingdom. Therefore, churches can only remain churches as they remain faithful to their Lord and his mission. A pivotal part of this is a critical stance to the powers to be—for John, a church cannot be a church without "coming out of Babylon" and for Moltmann a church loses its reason for existence if it functions to maintain the status quo of the state. What Moltmann says of the church is as true for the perspective we find in Revelation: "If the spirit and the

---

2. Moltmann takes his clues from the pneumatological presence of God's rule in the cross and life of Jesus while Revelation from the paradigmatic function of the martyrological witness of Jesus.

institutions of the Church correspond to the Kingdom of God, then it is the Church of Christ. If they contradict the Kingdom of God, then the Church loses its right to existence and will become a superfluous religious community."³

However, here we also noted some differences, both in how they understand the relation between God's rule and freedom, and how they relate the church to the kingdom. While Moltmann emphasises the mutual communion between God and creation in his defence of an egalitarian community, Revelation bases the egalitarian vision in the undisputed sovereignty of God. Noting problems in Moltmann's view of freedom and how he grounds it in his perichoretic kenoticism, I suggested that if we see the relationship between God and the world in the asymmetric and dynamic perichoresis between the two natures of Christ, the supposed contradiction between the absolute demand of God and human freedom dissipates and that the one cannot actually exist without the other. Noting that one of the primary reasons Moltmann rejects an exclusive relationship between the church and the kingdom is the devastating history such claims have often resulted in, I tried to show that Revelation avoids the violence of triumphalism although it makes such a claim. While churches, as communities of conversion, are the only earthly communities that can make a claim to be the present manifestation of God's kingdom, they do not exist in the form of a kingdom in history. The advantage of this view is that it gives a theological rationale against both ecclesial and political triumphalism. Just as churches deny their own identity when they assume geopolitical powers, so political entities lose their reason to exist when they deny their own provisionality.

Moltmann, Revelation in the Context of Crises of the Kingdom

In order to bring out more clearly one particular contribution of Moltmann's and Revelation's view of the kingdom, let us return to the crises they respond to in their respective portraitures of the kingdom. Although the dialogue between Moltmann and Revelation I have sought to construct here does not depend on it, one of the main reasons why the two are such fitting dialogue partners, is the similarity between the

---

3. "Jesus and the Kingdom of God," 16.

contexts they respond to. Questions of the kingdom, both where it is to be located and how God's rule is to be understood, are key to their thought precisely because the origin of their work is in contexts where the kingdom had in some way been rendered questionable. While Moltmann, during and in the aftermath of the Second World War, intimately and painfully experienced the collapse of the evolutionist notion of the kingdom in Cultural Protestantism, John wrote Revelation in the aftermath of the demise of the religio-political nature of Second Temple Judaism.[4] Despite their differences, both these contexts naturally raise the question of what the true nature of the kingdom is. We also noted that the flipside of this crisis is the question of the absence of God in contexts where nothing but evil and suffering seem to rule. While Moltmann approaches these questions from his own experience of suffering during the war, from the inexplicability of the suffering of Jews in the holocaust and the atheistic protest against a God who allows such unspeakable suffering, Revelation sees this concern in the concrete question of the incongruence between the confession of God as sovereign over his creation and the apparent universal geopolitical reign of his primordial enemy on earth. For both, however, the answer to this question is found in how Easter shows God and his rule as present in the earthly realm in hidden and paradoxical ways.

Both Moltmann and Revelation respond to this double crisis by developing an understanding of the kingdom in which historical-temporal and relational-spatial aspects of the kingdom are intrinsically bound together. For heuristic purposes we discussed these two aspects separately but sought also, in places, to show how they are interrelated. For Moltmann the hope for the coming of the kingdom is merely an escapist dream if divorced from the "liberating rule of God"[5] within history. However, the experience of the latter becomes a blind force when separated from the former since it loses its orientation toward its eschatological homeland. The church of Christ exist within the dialectic between how the paradoxical presence of God's liberating rule is revealed in the cross of Christ, and how the future of the kingdom has been opened up to the world in his resurrection. Therefore, Christian

---

4. Even if Revelation was written during the reign of Nero, it is written within a context when the religio-political aspects of Second Temple Judaism is severely limited and is rapidly approaching its cataclysmic end.

5. *CPS*, 190.

praxis, while bound by the possibilities the present offers, seeks the transformation of the present in the light of the future of the crucified one who was raised. As such, the church is bound by the horizon of the kingdom, and "if the spirit and the institutions of the Church . . . contradict the Kingdom of God, then the Church loses its right to existence and will become a superfluous religious community."[6] We see a very similar dynamic at work in Revelation. Its expectation of the eschatological regime change cannot be seen apart from how God is already confessed as the sovereign over heaven and earth and how he now, in Christ and by the Spirit, is already orienting the world toward its coming transformation. And it is precisely this hope and how it has been made certain in the paradoxical victory of the slain Lamb that is now the motivating and shaping power of the martyrological praxis of the followers of the Lamb in the world. As in Moltmann, it is within this larger canvas of the kingdom, that the church is to be understood in Revelation. As is made abundantly clear in Revelation 2–3, the ecclesial communities ought and can only exist as the earthly communities of the kingdom when they orient themselves toward the coming city according to how Christ has paved the way for them.

The Concrete Identity of the Displaced Kingdom

In the way they correlate the temporal and relational aspects of the kingdom, both Moltmann and Revelation point us away from seeing the kingdom in purely abstract terms. This is one of their great contributions to our understanding of the kingdom. It is common in both theological and exegetical discussions to first note how βασιλεία τοῦ θεοῦ does not refer to the realm of God's kingdom but rather to his rule, and then proceed to interpret this in purely abstract terms.[7] Moltmann's

---

6. Moltmann, "Jesus and the Kingdom of God," 16. Elsewhere (*CPS*, 75) he accounts for this interrelationship christologically, the church's "remembrance of Jesus, his mission, his self-giving and his resurrection is past made present and can be termed 'remembrance in the mode of hope'. Its hope of his parousia is future made present and can be termed 'hope in the mode of remembrance.'"

7. In a recent article, Mary Ann Beavis notes ("Kingdom of God," 92) that most scholars do not see ἡ βασιλεία τοῦ θεοῦ in "primarily spatial, territorial, political, or national" terms. Similarly France claims ("Church and the Kingdom," 32) that as a reference to God's rule, the kingdom of God "is the abstract idea of God being king, his sovereignty, his control of his world and its affairs," and as such, functions "to evoke a whole complex of ideas, even emotions, relating to the deeply rooted belief that God is

early theology was a sustained attack on how such notions were individualized and existentialized in especially the theology of Bultmann; and more recently he has critiqued the trend in Protestant theology "to interpret βασιλεία τοῦ θεοῦ solely as the present rule of God," which usually results in moralistic reduction of the symbol.[8] The thrust of his political theology is to reclaim the public relevance of the kingdom of God, to show how the confession of Christ the center cannot exist apart from the worldly horizon of his kingdom. Our discussion of Revelation suggests this is not simply a matter of mid-twentieth-century theological urgencies but has deep roots in the biblical tradition itself, or at least in Revelation.

Considering kingdom language in Revelation, we concluded that it eschews any neat "reign-realm" distinctions that are often assumed in biblical studies. As we discovered in our discussion on 11:15–19, βασιλεία refers to the position of geopolitical authority that orders the social world around it. And since this is not an abstract notion but a concrete actuality, how this βασιλεία shapes the social realm ordered around it cannot be separated from it. 11:15–19 anticipates when the powers in the world that now occupy this central position of geopolitical authority will be replaced by the political rule of God and his Christ in the earthly realm.

It is precisely when we consider ἡ βασιλεία τοῦ θεοῦ in this richly textured and eschatological sense that we see how it retains its full political meaning although it is not geopolitically manifested now. The

---

king" (38). Although this may be the case, it is hard to see how it can have any effective power if it is not more concretely, although eschatologically, located in the hope for the actual geopolitical rule of God. Barbour notes ("Kingdom," 370) that G. Dalman's study, *Words of Jesus*, has been particularly important for the emphasis on "rule" separated from any notion of "realm" in the interpretation of the kingdom of God in the New Testament. Although this distinction has persisted, a greater variety of perspectives on what the phrase actually means has emerged (Duling, "Kingdom of God," 65). Interestingly, at least half of the scholars Beavis mentions as seeing a political reference in ἡ βασιλεία τοῦ θεοῦ, Beasley-Murray, Caird, and N. T. Wright, have a particular interest in apocalyptic and/or have written extensively on Revelation. Whether Beavis is correct or not that the expansion of the referent of the kingdom to include non-Jewish people had already occurred in Jesus or not, this expansion has occurred in Revelation. However, against Beavis ("Kingdom of God," 102–6), this does not suggest that the utopianism of the kingdom "emphasized the 'no-place' (οὐ–τόπος) character of the βασιλεία" (105).

8. *WJC*, 98.

"a-topic" character of the kingdom of God in history is not grounded in some "u-topic" existential or ethical concept of the rule of God in the world. Rather, as we explored in our discussion of the woman in Rev 12, the kingdom of God does not have an actual *place* in the world now because it has been *displaced*. It is not that the reign of God does not have a claim to an actual earthly realm but that the position of geopolitical authority that rightfully belongs to God is now occupied by his enemies. Since God's purpose is to reclaim this position, the *placelessness* of the kingdom of God is a temporal anomaly. Seen within the spatially and temporally expanded vision of Revelation, the concrete location of the political rule of God is now in heaven but its eschatological destiny is in the descent of the heavenly city to the earth. As such, "the church can demonstrate the reality neither of her kingship nor of her priesthood during the time of her pilgrimage," but "the great moment of Christ's revelation will bring what she really is to light."[9]

Although the present manifestation of the kingdom per definition does not appear in a political form, Revelation 12 makes clear that it has lost none of its political significance. During the time of the Dragon, the earthly city of God has migrated to the wilderness, where it is being protected by God and prepared for its exodus from its geopolitical desert into the eternal city of God. This is crucially important because although the emphasis of the placelessness of the kingdom of God in history is crucial in debunking any kind of Christian ecclesial or political triumphalism, if left on its own, it can also lead to a Christian apathy in relation to the political situations Christians find themselves in. The kingdom is not simply an existential re-orientation of the individual who experiences the reign of God but the end toward which all social worlds ought to be reoriented. The church, since it does not exist in the form of a kingdom, must not take on political power, but because it is the heir of the kingdom it must form a contrast society, an expatriate community of the coming kingdom in the middle of the kingdom of the world.

While Revelation unflinchingly reminds us that fundamental to the church's political praxis is resistance to any participation in the world that compromises the way of the Lamb, Moltmann can help us translate this vision into situations where we not only can but have a

---

9. Rissi, *Future of the World*, 34.

responsibility to take an active part in the social processes of the world without denying the lordship of Christ. So, for example, when Western Christians read how Rome was the Babylon of its day partially because of the unjust flow of material goods (18:3, 9–19), Moltmann reminds us that we must read such text in light of the way the Western world is getting drunk on the intoxicating wine of the luxuries it drains from the rest of the world. Christians who participate in these processes without a concern of justice for the poor are shifting their allegiance from Christ to the Dragon and its contemporary beasts. Faithfulness to the Gospel does not only mean rejecting every form of idolatry but also an orientation toward the rule of God in which those who suffer injustice now are exalted to the throne-room of God. For privileged Christians, the call "to *come out* of her" means also to *enter more consciously into* these processes in order to change the flow of goods. Likewise, although not a major focus in the book, we noted how Richard Bauckham has shown that the book holds out the hope that the nations themselves will repent of their allegiance to the Beast.[10] In this way, Revelation leaves the door open for the actual transformation of present social structures. Moltmann can in many ways point us in the direction of how we can enter through this door as we seek to

> enquire about still closer political correspondences to the lordship of Christ, to the messianic mission and to the church's existence in a world-wide context. . . . The politically responsible concept of the church . . . leads to the church that suffers and fights within the people and with peoples, and to an interpretation of this people's church in the framework of the divine history of liberation, whose goal is the new creation in peace and righteousness.[11]

Prospective

Having looked at some pivotal aspects of what this thesis sought to accomplish, it is now time to make a few forward looking notes on questions it poses.

---

10. Bauckham, *Climax of Prophecy*, 238–37.
11. *CPS*, 18.

The Situatedness of the Authorial "I" and the Limitations of the Present Study

I have attempted to construct a dialogue between Moltmann and Revelation. Since these are the two dialogue partners that actually appear in the text, it can be easy to forget that there is a third partner in the dialogue, who, although hidden on the page is embedded in the text, constructs the dialogue. In contrast to an in the flesh, live dialogue, a literary dialogue always involves the author as the interested convener of the dialogue. In this thesis, I have chosen who will speak to whom, what they will speak about and whose voice will be privileged. Although hopefully I have given sufficient reasons for why I have constructed the dialogue as I have and although I have sought to let each voice speak in its own notes, it still remains the dialogue *I* have constructed. As such the dialogue is colored by my own 'situatedness.' This situatedness comes perhaps closest to the surface in my critiques of Moltmann and in the way I have consistently privileged what I perceive to be the voice of Revelation over Moltmann's. This, as discussed in chapter 2, is due to my view of Scriptural authority and my posture of trust toward basic trajectories of traditional Christian dogma.

Having confessed elements of the subjectivity that has guided my own judgments, the questions remains, can this study still be seen as a real dialogue, both as I have constructed it between Moltmann and Revelation, and my own interaction with them? I think it can and am convinced it cannot be done otherwise. Being aware of and making known where we come from enables us to give a better account of where we situate ourselves. In such a dialogue, if it is truly to remain a dialogue, we must always be open to hear the other, whether that be in voicing the perspective of the other or evaluating how it challenges our own. As such, if we are truly going to hear the challenge of the other, we must be willing to give reason for our own perspective and not impose it on the other as what is self-evident. For example, although I have privileged the voice of Revelation in this dialogue, I have sought to do so, whether successfully or not, by trying to reason why my particular interpretation of Revelation points in a better direction than Moltmann. So, in my critique of Moltmann's understanding of sin I tried to show how Revelation's depiction of the fundamental problem as rebellion both can account for Moltmann's critique of traditional understandings of sin and can better account for some of Moltmann's core concerns.

Precisely because one must both hear the voice of the other and give account of one's own, a fundamental aspect of such a dialogue is giving space for one another. If a dialogue is to happen between two that may hold potentially irreconcilable positions, it is simply not enough to try to understand one another and seek consensus, one must also give space for the other's rejection when stating one's own "no."

This reflection on the *partial* nature of the dialogue I have constructed in this thesis also reminds us that it can only be seen as a *part* of a larger whole, if it is not to lose significance as merely another arbitrary academic exercise.

The limitations of this study are first seen in light of my self-confessed situatedness. If I claim to have a high view of Scriptural authority, that the Scriptures provide us with a foundational and authoritative perspective of the world in which Christians are to construct their view of reality, then this particular study can only be seen as a part of a much larger canonical task. It needs to be placed within a context where other Scriptural voices augment the particular view of the kingdom I have developed here. And if I truly believe that it is in ecclesial communities that the kingdom is present by the Spirit, the present study cannot rest with my analysis of how John understood the kingdom in the first century and how Moltmann understands it in our own era, but must be seen within the long history of how the church, in its multiple institutional and social manifestations, has struggle with making sense of what it means to live for and be shaped by the coming kingdom of God.

What I have briefly claimed about the basic posture necessary for such a dialogue to be possible turns us to a second set of concerns that the present study can only be seen as one small part of. If I am not only concerned with making sense of the kingdom within my own particular ecclesial location but want to see it within the larger context of the church, the present dialogue can only be seen as a contribution toward a larger ecumenical dialogue which includes other voices different from my own. Although the present study does this partially as it highlights the difference between myself and Moltmann, it will benefit further from being set in dialogue with other traditions, both perspectives it would situate itself critically against (e.g. the Catholic claim that the See of Rome is the visible manifestation of the unity of the church or the national-territorial claims made by many Orthodox churches) and perspectives it would share many affinities with (such as the Mennonite shaped perspectives of Yoder and Hauerwas). A particularly important ecumenical context that this study should be placed in is with how the kingdom of God is understood by those who occupy the margins of the church and who find themselves on the socio-economic margins of society. Revelation is written from a context of those socially and economically ostracised because of their faithfulness to the Lamb and Moltmann has consistently emphasised how the kingdom comes first to the poor. This naturally leads to the conclusion that an examination into the reality of the kingdom of God cannot find rest before it is seen in the context of those who now suffer most acutely for it. Also, even if this exploration into the kingdom is seen primarily within a larger Christian ecumenical task, it must not close its ears to the questions and critiques that those outside this context raise. Therefore, as one seeks to place the present study within a larger ecumenical theological context, one must also listen to the voices that protest against it, and always be ready to give an account of the hope for it with these critics in mind.

Millenarianism and Jewish-Christian Dialogue

In addition to these broad concerns within which this thesis should be seen, there are two particular issues that space has not allowed us to explore here that would be of interest in further research on the role of the kingdom in Moltmann's thought and in Revelation, namely millenarianism and the relationship between Jews and Christians.

Although millenarianism has only existed on the fringes of the Christian tradition after Constantine and was usually eyed with suspicion, Moltmann stand within a new stream of interest in the this-worldly hope of early Christian millenarianism.[12] For him the expectation of the messianic *interregnum* not only provides a robust refutation of the triumphalist assumption of the millenarian vision in historical institutions or structures, but it also provides the motivation for a historical

---

12. "In this type of outlook," says Rowland, "there is the conviction that the present moment is one of critical significance within the whole gamut of salvation history, in which action is necessary, as it is no ordinary moment but one pregnant with opportunity for fulfilling the destiny of humankind" (Rowland, *Radical Christianity*, 3; cf. 3–4, 10–12).

praxis that anticipates the coming of the *interregnum* in history.[13] For this reason, Moltmann reads Rev 20:1–10 as an anticipation of the fulfilment of the kingdom of Christ within the conditions of history. How Revelation 20 is to be read is of course a contested issue.[14] If the dialogue between Moltmann and Revelation I have constructed here would be extended into this issue, some of the questions one may level against Moltmann's reading are as follows: 1) Does Rev 20:1–10 function to provide such this-worldly hope or is it simply an anticipation of the vindication of the martyrs? 2) If the passage anticipates an actual messianic *interregnum* that encourages a this-worldly historical praxis, how are we to interpret the seemingly pessimistic view of its end?[15] 3) Since Rev 21:1—22:5 expects not only the transformation of the earth but also the fulfilment of God's covenantal life with his people in history, and since this vision seems to have an unambiguously positive place for the nations (Rev 21:24–26), might this final vision not provide a better motivation for historical praxis than a possible *interregnum* in Revelation 20?

In addition to the reasons stated above, Moltmann sees millenarian hope as crucial to Jewish-Christian dialogue; he says, "there is no affirmative community between the church and Israel without the messianic hope for the kingdom ... [and therefore] no adequate Christian eschatology without millenarianism."[16] This is an important concern in our present appropriation of Revelation for a very simply reason— although the vision John receives is steeped in Jewish tradition, for

---

13. As Moltmann rightfully points out, the problem of the early church, and especially in the post-Constantinian grasping of political power, was not the delay of the parousia but an over-realized eschatology, an assumption that the reign of Christ had arrived before either he or the throne of God had arrived on earth (*CoG*, 153–54, 161–62). For Moltmann, it is then not only the promise millenarianism holds for a this-worldly praxis that is important, but precisely also its critique of any triumphalist historical assumption of the 1,000 years reign.

14. For an overview of various interpretations of Revelation 20, see Mealy, *Thousand Years*, 15–58 (cf. Grenz, *Millenial Maze*). For a debate between Moltmann and Bauckham on Millenarianism, see Bauckham, "The Millenium"; and Moltmann, "Hope of Israel."

15. Although there is global peace for a 1,000 years, as soon as Satan is released he is able to deceive "the nations in the four corners of the world" to make battle against "the camp of God's people, the city he loves;" there these nations come to a blazing end in an inferno sent on them from heaven (20:8–9).

16. *CoG*, 197; cf. 196–99; *CPS*, 138–39, 149–50.

most of its history it has been received in non-Jewish and often anti-Jewish contexts.[17] This is a particular acute question for the argument I have developed, since I have consistently assumed that John transforms and expands "Israel" to identify the people of the kingdom as the international crowd gathered around the Lamb. However, this raises the question whether there is any place for Jews as Jews within the people of God? Although this "expansionist" view of the imagery does suggest that there is only one people of God, this does not necessarily mean an obliteration of national and ethnic distinctives within this one people. Further research in this area would pay particular attention to the pluriform way in which John describes the one people, that they come from every tribe, language, people, and nation (Rev 5:9; 7:9; cf. 10:11; 14:6). That Israel, as the first covenant people of God, plays a distinct role within this community of nations, is perhaps suggested by the names of the twelve tribes on the gates of the New Jerusalem (Rev 21:12).[18] Perhaps it is only when Israel's particular role in the economy of God (which, in the perspective I have developed, cannot be separated from faith in Jesus as the Messiah for Jews) is fulfilled that the other nations can enter the one eternal city.[19]

If one were to consider Revelation in light of the urgencies Moltmann sees in Jewish-Christian relations, an important dialogue partner would be precisely a group that is usually excluded from such conversations, messianic Jews. They are often seen as an anathema in

17. Wengst notes ("Babylon," 202) that "it is a bitter irony of history that, as I have indicated, the church in the course of its further development abandoned Israel and let itself be defined in terms of Rome."

18. Although Mathewson, "Foundation Stones," 487–98, rightly points out that the multi-ethnic population of the New Jerusalem is now based on the testimony of the apostles (21:14), he does not sufficiently consider what the significance of that the names of the twelve tribes are associated with the city's gates (21:12).

19. David Rudolph, "Commonwealth," suggest that something like this is at work in Paul's thought: "In Paul's thought, the church was a prolepsis of the royal commonwealth of Israel ... [He] appears to have viewed the prophetic depiction of Israel and the nations in the Messianic era as a Scriptural ideal and the body of Jews and Gentiles in the church as the 'already but not yet' manifestation of this ideal.... The implications of this nuanced reading are significant. Whereas supersessionism leads to erasure of the Jew/Gentile distinction and the formation of a 'third race,' and dispensationalism leads to dualism, the commonwealth model uniquely emphasizes unity between Messianic Jews and Gentile Christians without loss of their respective identities, a vision consistent with Paul's 'rule in all the churches' and the apostolic decree (1 Cor 7:17; Acts 15)."

such dialogue—they are impure because they have broken precisely the boundary that has defined the difference between Christian and Jews over centuries, they insist that one can remain and has an obligation to remain a Torah observant Jew while professing faith in Yeshua as the Messiah for both Jews and Gentiles.[20] Although Moltmann emphasises that the Jewish "no" to Christ is an important and lasting reminder that Israel's messianic hope is still awaiting its final fulfilment,[21] there are some particularly good 'Moltmannian' arguments for including messianic Jews in the dialogue. In *The Church in the Power of the Spirit*, Moltmann argues that in interreligious dialogue Christians should not seek to convert bur seek reasons for faith in Jesus within the other religious traditions themselves,[22] and he argues that the relationship of Christianity with other religions must be patterned after the church's first partner for the Kingdom, Israel.[23] Messianic Jews, standing at the end of a long history where Jews have been persecuted or assimilated into 'Christian' cultures, have actually found a way to do precisely what Moltmann calls for, find a way to believe in Jesus as the Messiah for the whole world without loosing their own particular tradition.[24] From within a Moltmannian perspective may this not suggest that it is precisely from this group of the first people of the kingdom that we might find a pivotal key for how Gentiles and Jews can together live toward the kingdom. And is it from them that we may learn new models

---

20. This is clearly seen in the recent decision of the Presbytarian Church USA to withdraw funding and ties with Avodat Yisrael, a messianic congregation in Philadelphia. As one of the primary reason for the decision, Rev. William Borror noted the congregation's use of distinct Jewish liturgical practices within a PCUSA context, seeing, e.g., its use of Torah scrolls in worship as "a nonnegotiable." Reflecting a the same sentiment, Burt Siegel of the Jewish Community Relations Council of Greater Philadelphia believes the decision "is a clear indication of an increased understanding on the part of the Presbyterian leadership that churches that claim to incorporate aspects of both Judaism and Christianity are inherently inauthentic" (Remsen, "Church"). A more sympathetic portrait of Avodat Yisrael is found in a recent cover story in *The Christian Century* (toward the end of April 2005—unfortunately it was taken off the web when I was looking for bibliographical references for it).

21. *WJC*, 32–37; cf. *CPS*, 136–37, 148–49.

22. *CPS*, 162.

23. Ibid., 135.

24. For a defense of the position of messianic Jews in Jewish-Christian dialogue, see Rudolph, "Messianic Jews."

of spreading the Gospel in cultures and traditions foreign to our own without moulding emerging ecclesial communities in our own image?

Bibliography

Major Works by Jürgen Moltmann

The Church in the Power of the Spirit: A Contribution to Messianic Ecclesiology. London: SCM, 1992 [1977].
The Coming of God: Christian Eschatology. Minneapolis: Fortress, 1996.
The Crucified God: The Cross of Christ as the Foundation and Criticism of Christian Theology. Minneapolis: Fortress, 1993 [1974, 1991].
Experiences in Theology: Ways and Forms of Christian Theology. London: SCM, 2000.
God in Creation: A New Theology of Creation and the Spirit of God. Minneapolis: Fortress, 1993 [1985].
Jesus Christ for Today's World. London: SCM, 1994.
The Spirit of Life: A Universal Affirmation. London: SCM, 1992.
Theology of Hope: On the Grounds and the Implications of A Christian Eschatology. Minneapolis: Fortress, 1993 [1967, 1991].
Trinity and the Kingdom of God: The Doctrine of God. London: SCM, 1981.
The Way of Jesus Christ: Christology in Messianic Dimensions. London: SCM, 1990.

Other Works by Jürgen Moltmann

"Antwort auf die Kritik der Theologie der Hoffnung." In *Diskussion über die "Theologie der Hoffnung" von Jürgen Moltmann,* edited by Wolf-Dieter Marsch. Munich: Kaiser, 1967.
"Christian Theology and Political Religion." In *Civil Religion and Political Theology,* edited by Leroy S. Rouner, 41–58. Notre Dame: University of Notre Dame Press, 1986.
The Experiment Hope. Philadelphia: Fortress, 1975.
The Future of Creation. London: SCM, 1979.
Die Gemeinde im Horizont der Herrschaft Christi: Neue Perspektiven in der Protestantische Theologie. Neukirchen: Neukirchener Verlag, 1959.
God for a Secular Society: The Public Relevance of Theology. London: SCM, 1999.
"God's Kenosis in the Creation and Consummation of the World." In *The Work of Love: Creation as Kenosis,* edited by John Polkinghorne, 137–51. London: SPCK, 2001.
"God's Kingdom as the Meaning of Life." In *Why Did God Make Me?*, edited by H. Küng and J. Moltmann. New York: Seabury, 1978.

History and the Triune God: Contributions to Trinitarian Theology. New York: Crossroad, 1992.
"Homecoming for Abraham's and Sarah's Children and Augustine's Lonely Soul." *Dialog* 37 (1998) 277–81.
"Hope and Confidence: A Conversation with Ernst Bloch." *Dialog* 7 (1968) 42–55.
Hope and Planning. New York: Harper & Row, 1971.
"The Hope of Israel and the Anabaptist Alternative: Response to Richard Bauckham." In *God Will Be All in All: The Eschatology of Jürgen Moltmann*, edited by Richard J. Bauckham, 149–54. Edinburgh: T. & T. Clark, 1999.
"How I have Changed." In *How I Have Changed*, edited by Jürgen Moltmann. Harrisburg, PA: Trinity Press International, 1997.
Im Gespräch mit Ernst Bloch: Eine theologische Wegbegleitung. Munich: Kaiser, 1976.
In the End—the Beginning: The Life of Hope. Minneapolis: Fortress, 2004.
"The Inviting Unity of the Triune God." *Concillium* 177:1 (1985) 50–58.
"Jesus and the Kingdom of God." *Asbury Theological Journal* 48 (1993) 5–17.
"The Liberation of the Future and Its Anticipation in History." In *God Will Be All in All: The Eschatology of Jürgen Moltmann*, edited by Richard J. Bauckham, 265–89. Edinburgh: T. & T. Clark, 1999.
Man: Christian Anthropology in the Conflicts of the Present. London: SPCK, 1974.
"Messianic Atheism." In *Knowing Religiously*, edited by Leroy S. Rouner, 192–206. Notre Dame: Notre Dame University Press, 1985.
On Human Dignity: Political Theology and Ethics. London: SCM, 1984.
"Progress and Abyss: Remembering the Future of the Modern World." *Review and Expositor* 97 (2000) 301–14.
Religion, Revolution and the Future. New York: Scribner, 1969.
Science and Wisdom. Minneapolis: Fortress, 2003.
The Source of Life: The Holy Spirit and the Theology of Life. London: SCM Press 1997.
Theology Today: Two Contributions towards Making Theology Present. London: SCM, 1988.
"The World in God or God in the World? Response to Richard Bauckham." In *God Will Be All in All: The Eschatology of Jürgen Moltmann*, edited by Richard J. Bauckham, 35–41. Edinburgh: T. & T. Clark, 1999.
"Die Zunkunft des Christentums." *Evangelische Theologie* 63 (2003) 148–57.
"Zwölf Bemerkungen zur Symbolik des Bösen." *Evangelische Theologie* 52 (1992) 1–6.

Other Works

Aulen, Gustav. *Christus Victor: An Historical Study of the Three Main Types of the Idea of the Atonement.* London: SPCK, 1970 [1931].
Aune, David E. "The Apocalypse of John and Graeco-Roman Revelatory Magic." *New Testament Studies* 33:4 (1987) 481–501.
———. *Revelation 1–5.* Word Biblical Commentary 52A. Dallas: Word, 1997.
———. *Revelation 6–16.* Word Biblical Commentary 52B. Nashville: Nelson, 1998.
———. *Revelation 17–22.* Word Biblical Commentary 52C. Nashville: Nelson, 1998.
Aus, Roger D. "The Relevance of Isaiah 66:7 to Revelation 12 and 2 Thessalonians 1." *Zeitschrift für neutestamentliche Wissenschaft* 67 (1976) 252–68.

Barbour, R. S "Kingdom of God." In *The Oxford Companion to Christian Thought*, edited by Adrian Hastings, 370–71. Oxford: Oxford University Press, 2000.
Barr, David. "The Apocalypse as a Symbolic Transformation of the World: A Literary Analysis." *Interpretation* 38 (1984) 39–50.
Barr, James. *The Concept of Biblical Theology: An Old Testament Perspective*. London: SCM, 1999.
Bauckham, Richard J. "Bibliography: Jürgen Moltmann." *Modern Churchman* 28:2 (1986) 55–60.
———. *The Climax of Prophecy: Studies on the Book of Revelation*. Edinburgh: T. & T. Clark, 1993.
———. "Jesus and the Wild Animals (Mark 1:13): A Christological Image for an Ecological Age." In *Jesus of Nazareth: Lord and Christ: Essays on the Historical Jesus and New Testament Christology*, edited by Joel B. Green and Max Turner, 3–21. Grand Rapids: Eerdmans, 1994.
———. "Jürgen Moltmann." In *The Modern Theologians: An Introduction to Christian Theology in the Twentieth Century*, edited by David Ford, 209–24. Oxford: Blackwell, 1997.
———. "The Millennium." In *God Will Be All in All: The Eschatology of Jürgen Moltmann*, edited by Richard J. Bauckham, 123–47. Edinburgh: T. & T. Clark, 1999.
———. *Moltmann: Messianic Theology in the Making*. Basingstoke: Pickering, 1987.
———. *The Theology of the Book of Revelation*. New Testament Theology. Cambridge: Cambridge University Press, 1993.
———. *The Theology of Jürgen Moltmann*. Edinburgh: T. & T. Clark, 1995.
———. "The Throne of God and the Worship of Jesus." In *The Jewish Roots of Christological Monotheism: Papers from the St. Andrews Conference on the Historical Origins of the Worship of Jesus*, edited by C. G. Newman, et al., 43–69. Journal for the Study of Judaism Supplement Series 63. Leiden: Brill, 1999.
Bauckham, Richard J., and Trevor Hart. *Hope Against Hope: Christian Eschatology in Contemporary Context*. London: Darton, Longman & Todd, 1999.
Beale, G. K. *The Book of Revelation: A Commentary on the Greek Text*. The New International Greek Testament Commentary. Grand Rapids: Eerdmans, 1999.
———. "The Origins of the Title 'King of Kings and Lord of Lords.'" *New Testament Studies* 31 (1985) 618–20.
Beasley-Murray, G. R. *The Book of Revelation*. New Century Bible Commentary. Grand Rapids: Eerdmans; London: Marshall, Morgan & Scott, 1981 [1978].
———. "Revelation, Book of." In *The Dictionary of the Later New Testament and Its Development*, edited by R. P. Martin and P. H. Davids, 1025–38. Downers Grove, IL: InterVarsity, 1997.
Beavis, Mary Ann. "The Kingdom of God, 'Utopia' and Theocracy." *Journal for the Study of the Historical Jesus* 2:1 (2004) 91–106.
Beckwith, Isbon T. *The Apocalypse of John: Studies in Introduction with a Critical and Exegetical Commentary*. New York: Macmillan, 1919.
Berger, Peter L. *The Sacred Canopy: Elements of a Sociological Theory of Religion*. Toronto: Doubleday, 1967.
Bloesch, Donald G. *Holy Scripture: Revelation, Inspiration & Interpretation*. Christian Foundations. Downers Grove, IL: InterVarsity, 1994.

Bouma-Prediger, Steven. "Creation as the Home of God: The Doctrine of Creation in the Theology of Jürgen Moltmann." *Calvin Theological Journal* 32 (1997) 72–90.

———. *For the Beauty of the Earth: A Christian Vision for Creation Care*. Grand Rapids: Baker, 2001.

———. *The Greening of Theology: The Ecological Models of Rosemary Radford Ruether, Joseph Sittler, and Jürgen Moltmann*. American Academy of Religion Academy Series 91. Atlanta: Scholars, 1995.

Bovon, Francois. "John's Self-Presentation in Revelation 1:9–10." *Catholic Biblical Quarterly* 62 (2000) 693–700.

Boxall, Ian. *The Revelation of Saint John*. BNTC. London: Continuum, 2006.

Braaten, Carl E. "Toward a Theology of Hope." *Theology Today* 24 (1967) 208–26.

Bredin, Mark. *Jesus, Revolutionary of Peace: A Nonviolent Christology in the Book of Revelation*. Carlisle, UK: Paternoster, 2003.

Bromiley, Geoffrey W. *Karl Barth: Letters 1961–1968*. Edinburgh: T. & T. Clark, 1981.

Brown, R. E., K., et al., eds. *Mary in the New Testament: A Collaborative Assessment by Protestant and Roman Catholic Scholars*. Philadelphia: Fortress, 1978.

Bruns, J. Edgar. "The Contrasted Women of Apocalypse 12 and 17." *Catholic Biblical Quarterly* 26 (1964) 459–63.

Bryan, David J. "Exile and Return from Jerusalem," In *Apocalyptic in History and Tradition*., edited by C. Rowland and J. Barton, 60–80. Journal for the Study of the Pseudepigrapha Supplement Series 43. London: Sheffield Academic, 2002.

Buri, Fritz. "Zur gegenwärtigen Diskussion über das Problem Hoffnung." *Theologische Zeitschrift* 22 (1966) 196–211.

Bush, George W. "Second Inaugural Address." No pages. Online: http://www.whitehouse.gov/inaugural/.

Caird, George B. *The Revelation of St. John the Divine*. New York: Harper & Row, 1966.

———. *The Revelation of St. John the Divine*. 2nd ed. London: A. & C. Black, 1984.

Campbell, Gordon. "Findings, Seals, Trumpets, and Bowls: Variations upon the Theme of Covenant Rupture and Restoration in the Book of Revelation." *Westminster Theological Journal* 66 (2004) 71–96.

Carrell, Peter R. *Jesus and the Angels: Angelology and the Christology of the Apocalypse of John*. Society for New Testament Supplement Series 95. Cambridge: Cambridge University Press, 1997.

Carroll, John T. "Creation and Apocalypse." In *God Who Creates: Essays in Honor of W. Sibley Towner*, edited by William P. Brown, and S. Dean McBride, 251–60. Grand Rapids: Eerdmans, 2000.

Chapman, G. Clarke. "Hope and the Ethics of Formation: Moltmann as an Interpreter of Bonhoeffer." *Studies in Religion* 12 (1983) 449–60.

———. "Jürgen Moltmann and the Christian Dialogue with Marxism." *Journal of Ecumenical Studies* 18 (1981) 435–50.

Charles, R. H. *A Critical and Exegetical Commentary on the Revelation of St. John*. Volume I. International Critical Commentary. Edinburgh: T. & T. Clark, 1920.

———. *A Critical and Exegetical Commentary on the Revelation of St. John*. Volume II. International Critical Commentary. Edinburgh: T. & T. Clark, 1920.

Childs, Brevrand S. *Biblical Theology of the Old and New Testaments: Theological Reflections on the Christian Bible*. London: SCM, 1992.

Clutterbuck, Richard. "Jürgen Moltmann as a Doctrinal Theologian: The Nature of Doctrine and the Possibilities for its Development." *Scottish Journal of Theology* 48 (1995) 489–505.

Collins, Adela Yarbro. *The Combat Myth in the Book of Revelation*. Harvard Dissertations in Religion 9. 1976. Reprinted, Eugene, OR: Wipf & Stock, 2001.

———. *Crisis and Catharsis: The Power of the Apocalypse*. Philadelphia: Westminster, 1984.

———. "Eschatology in the Book of Revelation." *Ex Auditu* 6 (1990) 63–72.

———. "The Political Perspective of the Revelation to John." *Journal of Biblical Literature* 96 (1977) 241–56.

———. "Revelation, Book of." In *Anchor Bible Dictionary*, edited by D. N. Freedman, 5:694–708. New York: Doubleday, 1992.

———. "Vilification and Self-Definition in the Book of Revelation." *Harvard Theological Review* 79 (1986) 308–20.

Collins, John J. *The Apocalyptic Imagination; An Introduction to Jewish Apocalyptic Literature*. 2nd ed. Grand Rapids: Eerdmans, 1998.

Conyers, A. J. "The Revival of Joachite Apocalyptic Speculation in Contemporary Theology." *Perspectives in Religious Studies* 12 (1985) 197–211.

Cornelison, Robert T. "The Reality of Hope: Moltmann's Vision for Theology." *Asbury Theological Journal* 48 (1993) 109–20.

Cottingham, David C. "Rosen, Moltmann, and the Anticipatory Paradigm." *Perspectives on Science and Christian Faith* 42 (1990) 239–45.

Dalman, Gustaf. *The Words of Jesus: Considered in the Light of Post-Biblical Jewish Writings and the Aramaic Language*. Edinburgh: T. & T. Clark, 1902.

Davies, John A. *A Royal Priesthood: Literary and Intertextual Perspectives on an Image of Israel in Exodus 19.6*. Journal for the Study of the Old Testament Supplement Series 395. London: T. & T. Clark, 2004.

Davies, W. D., and Dale C. Allison. *A Critical and Exegetical Commentary on the Gospel According to Saint Matthew*. International Critical Commentary Edinburgh: T. & T. Clark, 1997.

Deane-Drummond, Celia E. *Ecology in Jürgen Moltmann's Theology*. Texts and Studies in Religion 75. Lewiston, NY: Mellen, 1997.

de Moor, J. C., and E. van Staalduine-Sulman. "The Aramaic Song of the Lamb." *Journal for the Study of Judaism* 24 (1993) 266–79.

Duling, Dennis C. "Kingdom of God, Kingdom of Heaven." In *Anchor Bible Dictionary*, edited by D. N. Freedman, 5:49–68. New York: Doubleday, 1992.

du Rand, J. A., and Y. M. Song. "A Partial Preterist Understanding of Revelation 12–13 within an Intertextual Framework." *Acta Theologica* 24:1 (2004) 26–44.

Ellul. Jacques. *Apocalypse: The Book of Revelation*. New York: Seabury, 1977.

Eckert, Michael. "Zukunft als Tranzendenz." In *Ernts Blochs Vermittlungen zur Theologie*, edited by H. Deuser and P. Steinacker, 128–43. Munich: Kaiser, 1983.

Escobar, S. "The Return of Christ." In *The New Face of Evangelicalism: An International Symposium*, edited by R. Padilla. Downers Grove, IL: InterVarsity, 1976.

Farrer, Austin. *The Revelation of St. John the Divine: Commentary on the English Text*. Oxford: Clarendon, 1964.

Farrow, Douglas B. "Review Essay: In the End is the Beginning: A review of Jürgen Moltmann's Systematic Contributions." *Modern Theology* 14 (1998) 425–43.

Fee, Gordon D. *God's Empowering Presence: The Holy Spirit in the Letters of Paul.* Peabody, MA: Hendrickson, 1994.

———. Lectures on Revelation. Vancouver: Regent College, 1999.

Fekkes, Jan III. *Isaiah and Prophetic Traditions in the Book of Revelation: Visionary Antecedents and Their Development.* Journal for the Study of the New Testament Supplement Series 93. Sheffield: Sheffield Academic, 1994.

Fernandez, Dagoberto Ramirez. "The Judgment of God on the Multinationals: Revelation 18." In *Subversive Scriptures: Revolutionary Readings of the Christian Bible in Latin America*, edited by Leif Vaage, 75–100. Valley Forge, PA: Trinity, 1997.

———. *Priester für Gott: Studien zum Herrschaft und Priestermotiv in der Apokalypse.* Münster: Aschendorff, 1972.

Ford, Josephine Massyngberde. *Revelation: Introduction, Translation and Commentary.* Anchor Bible 38. Garden City, NY: Doubleday, 1975.

———. "*Shalom* in the Johannine Corpus." *Horizons in Biblical Theology* 6:2 (1984) 67–89.

Fowl, Stephen E., editor. *Engaging Scripture: A Model for Theological Interpretation.* Oxford: Blackwell, 1998.

———. *The Theological Interpretation of Scripture: Classic and Contemporary Readings.* Oxford: Blackwell, 1997.

France, R. T. "The Church and the Kingdom of God: Some Hermeneutical Issues." In *Biblical Interpretation and the Church*, edited by D. A. Carson, 30–44. Exeter, UK: Paternoster, 1984.

Fries, Heinrich. "Spero ut intelligam: Bemerkungen zu einer Theologie der Hoffnung." In *Wahrheit und Verkündigung: Michael Schmaus zum 70. Geburtstag*, vol. 1, edited by L. Scheffczyk et al, 353–75. Munich: Schöningh, 1967.

Friesen, Steven J. *Imperial Cults and the Apocalypse of John: Reading Revelation in the Ruins.* Oxford: Oxford University Press, 2001.

———. "Satan's Throne, Imperial Cults and the Social Settings of Revelation." *Journal for the Study of the New Testament* 27 (2005) 351–73.

Garrow, A. J. P. *Revelation.* New Testament Readings. London: Routledge, 1997.

Gaventa, Beverly Roberts. "The Cosmic Power of Sin in Paul's Letter to the Romans: Toward a Widescreen Edition." *Interpretation* 58 (2004) 229–40.

Gelston, A. "The Royal Priesthood." *Evangelical Quarterly* 31 (1959) 152–63.

Geoghegan, Vincent. "Bloch, Ernst Simon (1885–1977)." In *Routledge Encyclopedia of Philosophy*, edited by E. Craig, 787–90. London: Routledge, 1998.

Giblin, C. H. *The Book of Revelation: The Open Book of Prophecy.* Collegeville, MN: Liturgical, 1991.

Giesen, Heinz. *Studien zur Johannesapokalypse.* Stuttgarter Biblische Aufsatzbände 29. Stuttgart: Katolisches Bibelwerk, 2000.

Gilbert, Kevin James. "Jürgen Moltmann's Theological Method: Evangelical Options?" *Restoration Quarterly* 41:3 (1999) 163–78.

Gilbertson, Michael. *God and History in the Book of Revelation: New Testament Studies in Dialogue with Pannenberg and Moltmann.* Society for New Testament Supplement Series 124. Cambridge: Cambridge University Press, 2003.

Gilkey, Langdon. *Reaping the Whirlwind: A Christian Interpretation of History*. New York: Seabury, 1976.

Gowan, Donald E. "The Fall and Redemption of the Material World in Apocalyptic Literature." *Horizons of Biblical Theology* 7:2 (1985) 83–103.

Graham, Gordon. "Biblical Hope and Moral Endeavour." *Evangelical Quarterly* 72 (2000) 347–57.

Grenz, Stanley J. *The Millennial Maze: Sorting Out Evangelical Options*. Downers Grove, IL: InterVarsity, 1992.

Grenz, Stanley J. *Theology for the Community of God*. Grand Rapids: Eerdmans, 1994.

Gundry, Robert H. *Matthew: A Commentary on His Literary and Theological Art*. Grand Rapids: Eerdmans, 1982.

———. "The New Jerusalem: People as Place, not Place as People." *Novum Testamentum* 29 (1987) 255–64.

Gunton, Colin E. "'Until He Comes': Towards an Eschatology of Church Membership." The Drew Lecture on Immortality. London: Spurgeon's College, 1999.

Hannah, Darrell. "The Throne of His Glory: The Divine Throne and Heavenly Mediators in Revelation and the Similitudes of Enoch." *Zeitschrift für die neutestamentliche Wissenschaft* 94 (2003) 68–96.

Harrington, Wilfrid J. *Revelation*. Sacra Pagina 16. Collegeville, MN: Liturgical, 1993.

Hart, Trevor. "Imagination for the Kingdom of God? Hope, Promise, and the Transformative Power of an Imagined Future." In *God Will Be All in All: The Eschatology of Jürgen Moltmann*, edited by Richard Bauckham, 49–76. Edinburgh: T. & T. Clark, 1999.

Heil, John Paul. "The Fifth Seal (Rev 6,9–11) as a Key to the Book of Revelation." *Biblica* 74 (1993) 220–43.

Hellholm, David, ed. *Apocalypticism in the Mediterranean World and the Near East: Proceedings of the International Colloquium on Apocalypticism, Uppsala, August 12–17, 1979*. Second Edition. Tübingen: Mohr/Siebeck, 1989.

Herzog, Frederick, ed. *The Future of Hope: Theology as Eschatology*. New York: Herder & Herder, 1970.

Hirzel, R. "Die Talion." In *Philologus Zeitschrift für Das Classische Alterthum Supplementband XI*, edited by Otto Crusius, 405–480. Leipzig: Dieterisch, 1910.

Höhne, David. "What Can We Say about Perichoresis? An Historical, Exegetical and Theological Examination of Colin Gunton's Use of the Concept." M.Th. thesis, Moore College, 2003.

Howard-Brook, Wes, and Anthony Gwyther. *Unveiling Empire: Reading Revelation Then and Now*. Maryknoll, NY: Orbis, 1999.

Humphrey, Edith McEwan. *The Ladies and the Cities: Transformation and Apocalyptic Identity in Joseph and Asenath, 4 Ezra, the Apocalypse and the Shepherd of Hermas*. Journal for the Study of the Pseudepigrapha Supplement Series 17. Sheffield: Sheffield Academic, 1995.

Hunsinger, George. "The Crucified God and the Political Theology of Violence: A Critical Survey of Jürgen Moltmann's Recent Thought: I." *Heythrop Journal* 14 (1973) 266–79.

———. "The Crucified God and the Political Theology of Violence: A Critical Survey of Jürgen Moltmann's Recent Thought: II." *Heythrop Journal* 14 (1973) 379–95.

———. "The Daybreak of the New Creation: Christ's Resurrection in Recent Theology." *Scottish Journal of Theology* 57 (2004) 163-81.

Jaeger, John. "Abraham Heschel and the Theology of Jürgen Moltmann." *Perspectives in Religious Studies* 24 (1997) 167-79.

Jeanrond, W. G. "After Hermeneutics: The Relationship between Theology and Biblical Studies." In *The Open Text: New Directions for Biblical Studies?* Edited by F. Watson, 85-102. London: SCM, 1993.

Jansen, Henry. "Moltmann's View of God's (Im)mutability: The God of the Philosophers and the God of the Bible." *Neue Zeitschrift für Systematische Theologie* 36 (1994) 284-301.

Jenson, Robert W. "Jesus, Father, Spirit: The Logic of the Doctrine of the Trinity." *Dialog* 26 (1987) 245-49.

Jeske, Richard L. "Spirit and Community in the Johannine Apocalypse." *New Testament Studies* 31 (1985) 452-66.

Johns, L. L. *The Lamb Christology of the Apocalypse of John: An Investigation into Its Origins and Rhetorical Force.* Wissenschaftliche Untersuchungen zum Neuen Testament 2/167. Tübingen: Mohr/Siebeck, 2003.

Karrer, Martin. *Die Johannesoffenbarung als Brief: Studien zu ihrem literarischen, historischen un theologischen Ort.* Göttingen: Vandenhoeck & Ruprecht, 1986.

Kelsey, David H. "Whatever Happened to the Doctrine of Sin?" *Theology Today* 50 (1993) 169-78.

Kim, Jean K. "'Uncovering Her Wickedness': An Inter(con)textual Reading of Revelation 17 from a Postcolonial Feminist Perspective." *Journal for the Study of the New Testament* 73 (1999) 61-81.

Kingsbury, Jack Dean. *Matthew: A Commentary for Preachers and Others.* London: SPCK, 1977.

Koch, Michael. *Drachenkampf und Sonnenfrau: Zur Funktion des Mythischen in der Johannesapokalypse am Beispiel von Apk 12.* Wissenschaftliche Untersuchungen zum Neun Testament 2/184. Tübingen: Mohr/Siebeck, 2004.

Kovacs, Judith, and Christopher R. Rowland. *Revelation: The Apocalypse of Jesus Christ.* Blackwell Bible Commentaries. Oxford: Blackwell, 2004.

Kraybill, J. Nelson. *Imperial Cult and Commerce in John's Apocalypse.* Journal for the Study of the New Testament Supplement Series 132. Sheffield: Sheffield Academic, 1996.

LaCocque, André, and Paul Ricoeur. *Thinking Biblically: Exegetical and Hermeneutical Studies.* Chicago: University of Chicago Press, 1998.

Lash, Nicholas. *Theology on the Way to Emmaus.* London: SCM, 1986.

Lossky, Vladimir. *The Mystical Theology of the Eastern Church.* Cambridge: James Clarke, 1991.

Lønning, Per. "Die Schöpfungstheologie Jürgen Moltmanns—eine nordische Perspektive." *Kerygma und Dogma* 33 (1987) 207-23.

Lull, Timothy F. "The Trinity in Recent Theological Literature." *Word and World* 2 (1982) 61-68.

Luz, Ulrich. *The Theology of the Gospel of Matthew.* New Testament Theology. Cambridge: Cambridge University Press, 1995.

Malina, Bruce J. *On the Genre and Message of Revelation: Star Visions and Sky Journeys.* Peabody, MA: Hendrickson, 1995.

Marion, Jean-Luc. *God without Being: Horse-Texte*. Chicago: University of Chicago Press, 1991.

Marsch, Wolf-Dieter, ed. *Diskussion über die "Theologie der Hoffnung" von Jürgen Moltmann*. Munich: Kaiser, 1967.

Mathewson, David. "The Destiny of the Nations in Revelation 21:1—22:5: A Reconsideration." *Tyndale Bulletin* 53 (2002) 121–42.

———. "A Note on the Foundation Stones in Revelation 21.14, 19–20." *Journal for the Study of the New Testament* 25 (2003) 487–98.

McGowan, A. T. B. *The Divine Spiration of Scripture: Challenging Evangelical Perspectives*. Nottingham, UK: Apollos, 2007

McGrath, Alister, E. *The Genesis of Doctrine*. Oxford: Blackwell, 1990.

McDonough, Sean M. *YHWH at Patmos: Rev 1:4 in its Hellenistic and Early Jewish Setting*. Wissenschaftliche Untersuchungen zum Neuen Testament 2/107. Tübingen: Mohr/Siebeck, 1999.

McIntosh, Ian. "The Spirit and Life: An Assessment of Jürgen Moltmann's Pneumatology, with Particular Reference to the Theology of Gregory Palamas." Ph.d thesis, King's College, London, 2000.

McWilliams, Warren. "Trinitarian Doxology: Jürgen Moltmann on the Relation of the Economic and Immanent Trinity." *Perspectives in Religion* 23 (1996) 25–38.

Mealy, J. Webb. *After the Thousand Years: Resurrection and Judgment in Revelation 20*. Journal for the Study of the New Testament Supplement Series 70. Sheffield: Sheffield Academic, 1992.

Meeks, Douglas M. *Origins of the Theology of Hope*. Philadelphia: Fortress, 1974.

Moo, Douglas J. "Nature in the New Creation: New Testament Eschatology and the Environment." Unpublished Essay. Wheaton, IL: Wheaton College, 2003.

Morse, Christopher. "God's Promise as Presence." In *Love: The Foundation of Hope: The Theology of Jürgen Moltmann and Elisabeth Moltmann-Wendell*, edited by F. B. Burnham, et al, 143–57. New York: Harper & Row, 1988.

———. *The Logic of Promise in Moltmann's Theology*. Philadelphia: Fortress, 1979.

Moyise, Steve. "Does the Lion Lie down with the Lamb." In *Studies in the Book of Revelation*, 181–94. Edinburgh: T. & T. Clark, 2001.

Müller-Fahrenholz, Geiko. *The Kingdom and the Power: The Theology of Jürgen Moltmann*. London: SCM, 2000.

Musfeldt, Klaus. "Wird der Löwe Stroh fressen." *Zeitschrift für Systematische Theologie und Religionsphilosophie* 33:3 (1991) 300–315.

Musvosvi, J. N. *Vengeance in the Apocalypse*. Andrews University Seminary Doctoral Dissertation Series 17. Berrien Springs, MI: Andrews University Press, 1993.

Neuhaus, Richard John. "Moltmann vs. Monotheism." *Dialog* 20:3 (1981) 239–43.

Nogueira, Paulo Augusto de Souza. "Introduction." *Journal for the Study of the New Testament* 25 (2000) 123–26.

O'Donnell, John. *Trinity and Temporality: The Christian Doctrine of God in the Light of Process Theology and the Theology of Hope*. Oxford: Oxford University Press, 1983.

———. John. "Saved by Hope." *Gregorianum* 79 (1998) 55–83.

———. "The Trinity as Divine Community: A Critical Reflection Upon Recent Theological Developments." *Gregorianum* 69 (1988) 5–34.

O'Donovan, Oliver. "The Political Thought of the Book of Revelation." *Tyndale Bulletin* 37 (1985) 61–94.

Ollenburger, Ben C. "What Krister Stendahl 'Meant'—A Normative Critique of 'Descriptive Biblical Theology.'" *Horizons in Biblical Theology* 8:1 (1986) 61–98.

Osborne, Grant R. *Revelation*. ECNT. Grand Rapids: Baker, 2002.

Otto, Randall. "Moltmann and the Anti-Monotheism Movement." *International Journal of Systematic Theology* 3 (2001) 293–308.

———. "The Resurrection in Jürgen Moltmann." *Journal of the Evangelical Theological Society* 35 (1992) 81–90.

Perrin, Norman. *Jesus and the Language of the Kingdom: Symbol and Metaphor in New Testament Interpretation*. Philadelphia: Fortress, 1976.

Peters, Ted. "Moltmann and the Way of the Trinity." *Dialog* 31 (1992) 272–79.

Peterson, Erik. *Theologische Traktate*. Munich: Wild, 1951.

Petri, Heinrich. "Theologie der Hoffnung: Fundamentaltheologische Aspekte." *Catholica* 24:4 (1970) 257–69.

Pieper, Josef. *Abuse of Language—Abuse of Power*. San Francisco: Ignatius, 1992.

———. *Hope and History: Five Salzburg Lectures*. San Francisco: Ignatius, 1994.

Pippin, Tina. *Death and Desire: The Rhetoric of Gender in the Apocalypse of John*. Louisville: Westminster John Knox, 1992.

———. "Eros and the End: Reading for Gender in the Apocalypse of John." *Semeia* 59 (1992) 193–210.

Porteous, Norman W. "Jerusalem-Zion: the Growth of a Symbol." In *Living the Mystery: Collected Essays*, 93–111. Oxford: Blackwell, 1967.

Prigent, Pierre. *Commentary on the Apocalypse of St. John*. Tübingen: Mohr/Siebeck, 2001.

Rad, Gerhard von. *Old Testament Theology*. Vol. 1: *The Theology of Israel's Historical Traditions*. Translated by D. M. G. Stalker. London: SCM, 1975.

Radlbeck-Ossmann, Regina. "...in drei Personen. Der trinitarische Schlüsselbegriff 'Person' in den Entwürfen Jürgen Moltmanns und Walter Kaspers." *Catholica* 47 (1993) 38–51.

Räisänen, Heiko. *Beyond New Testament Theology: A Story and a Programme*. London: SCM, 1990.

Rasmusson, Arne. *The Church as Polis: From Political Theology to Theological Politics as Exemplified by Jürgen Moltmann and Stanley Hauerwas*. Notre Dame: University of Notre Dame Press, 1995.

Remsen, Jim. 2005. "Church Aimed at Jews Loses Presbyterian Funding." *Philadelphia Enquirer* (March 30). No pages. Cited Spring 2005. Online: http://www.philly.com/mld/inquirer/living/religion/11261983.htm

Reventlow, Henning Graf. "Theology (Biblical), History of." In *Anchor Bible Dictionary*, edited by D. N. Freedman, 6:483–505. New York: Doubleday, 1992.

Richard, Pablo. *Apocalypse: A People's Commentary on the Book of Revelation*. Maryknoll, NY: Orbis, 1995.

Rissi, Mathias. *The Future of the World: An Exegetical Study of Revelation 19.11—22.15*. Studies in Biblical Theology 1/23. London: SCM, 1972.

Roloff, Jürgen. *The Revelation of John: A Continental Commentary*. Minneapolis: Fortress, 1993.

Roose, Hanna. *Eschatologische Mitherrschaft: Entwicklungslinien einer urchristlichen Erwartung*. Novum Testamentum et Orbis Antiquus 54. Göttingen: Vandenhoeck & Ruprecht, 2004.

———. "Sharing in Christ's Rule: Tracing a Debate in Earliest Christianity." *Journal for the Study of the New Testament* 27 (2004) 123–48.

Rossing, Barbara. *The Choice Between Two Cities: Whore, Bride, and Empire in the Apocalypse*. Harrisburg, PA: Trinity, 1999.

Rowland, Christopher R. "The Apocalypse in History: The Place of the Book of Revelation in Christian Theology and Life." In *Apocalyptic in History and Tradition*. Journal for the Study of the Pseudepigrapha Supplement Series 43, edited by C. R. Rowland and J. Barton, 151–71. London: Sheffield Academic, 2002.

———. "The Apocalypse: Hope, Resistance and the Revelation of Reality." *Ex Auditu* 6 (1990) 129–44.

———. *The Book of Revelation*. In *The New Interpreter's Bible*, edited by Leander E. Keck, et al, 12:501–736. Nashville: Abingdon, 1998.

———. *Christian Origins: An Account of the Setting and Character of the most Important Messianic Sect of Judaism*. 2nd ed. London: SPCK, 2002.

———. "Ἰωάννης συγκοινωνός...." In *Understanding, Studying and Reading: New Testament Essays in Honour of John Ashton*, edited by Crispin H. T. Fletcher-Louis and Christopher R. Rowland, 236–46. Journal for the Study of the New Testament Supplement Series 153. Sheffield: Sheffield Academic, 1998.

———. "The Lamb and the Beast, the Sheep and the Goats: 'The Mystery of Salvation' in Revelation." In *A Vision for the Church: Studies in Early Christian Ecclesiology in Honour of J. P. M. Sweet*, edited by Marcus Bockmuehl and Michal B. Thompson, 181–91. Edinburgh: T. & T. Clark, 1997.

———. *The Open Heaven: A Study of Apocalyptic in Judaism and Early Christianity*. London: SPCK, 1982.

———. *Radical Christianity: A Reading of Recovery*. Cambridge: Polity, 1988.

———. *Revelation*. Epworth Commentaries. London: Epworth, 1993.

Rowland, Christopher. R., and Mark Corner. *Liberating Exegesis: The Challenge of Liberation Theology to Biblical Studies*. London: SPCK, 1990.

Rudolph, David J. "The Commonwealth Model Universalism and Particularism in the Pauline Church-Israel Configuration." Unpublished Essay. Cambridge, 2005.

———. "Messianic Jews and Christian Theology: Restoring an Historical Voice to the Contemporary Discussion." *Pro Ecclesia* 14 (2005) 58–84.

Ruggieri, Giuseppe. "God and Power: A Political Function of Monotheism?" *Concillium* 177:1 (1985) 16–27.

Ruiz, Jean-Pierre. "The Politics of Praise: A Reading of Revelation 19:1–10." In *SBL Seminar Papers 1997*, 374–93. Atlanta: Scholars, 1997.

Runia, Klaas. "Eschatology in the Second Half of the Twentieth Century." *Calvin Theological Journal* 32 (1997) 105–35.

———. "The Kingdom of God in the Bible, in History and Today." *European Journal of Theology* 1:1 (1992) 37–47.

Sals, Ulrike. *Die Biographie der "Hure Babylon."* Forschungen zum Alten Testament 2/6. Tübingen: Mohr/Siebeck, 2004.

Sauter, Gerhard. *Einführung in die Eschatologie*. Darmstadt: Wissenschaftliche Buchgesellschaft, 1995.
Schindler, Alfred, ed. *Monotheismus als politisches Problem? Erik Peterson und die Kritik der politischen Theologie*. Studien zur evangelischen Ethik 14. Gütersloh: Gütersloher, 1978.
Schnabel, Eckhard J. "John and the Future of the Nations." *Bulletin for Biblical Research* 12:2 (2002) 243–71.
Schüssler Fiorenza, Elisabeth. *The Book of Revelation: Justice and Judgment*. Philadelphia: Fortress, 1985.
Schuurman, Douglas J. "Creation, Eschaton, and Ethics: An Analysis of Theology and Ethics in Jürgen Moltmann." *Calvin Theological Journal* 22 (1987) 42–67.
Schweitzer, Don. "The Consistency of Jürgen Moltmann's Theology." *Studies in Religion* 22 (1993) 197–208
———. "Douglas Hall's Critique of Jürgen Moltmann's Eschatology of the Cross." *Studies in Religion* 27 (1998) 7–25.
Seitz, Christopher R., and Kathryn Greene-McCreight, editors. *Theological Exegesis: Essays in Honor of Brevrand S. Childs*. Grand Rapids: Eerdmans, 1999.
Selvidge, M. J. "Powerful and Powerless Women in the Apocalypse." *Neotestamentica* 26 (1992) 157–67.
Skorupski, John. "The Future of Ideals." In *Philosophy at the New Millennium*. Royal Institute of Philosophy Supplement 48, edited by Anthony O'Hear, 193–208. Cambridge: Cambridge University Press, 2001.
Slater, Thomas B. *Christ and Community: A Socio-Historical Study of the Christology of Revelation*. Journal for the Study of the New Testament Supplement Series 178. Sheffield: Sheffield Academic, 1999.
———. "'King of Kings and Lord of Lords' Revisited." *New Testament Studies* 39 (1993) 159–60.
———. "On the Social Setting of the Revelation." *New Testament Studies* 44 (1998) 232–56.
Smalley, Stephen S. *The Revelation to John: A Commentary on the Greek Text of the Apocalypse*. Downers Grove, IL: InterVarsity, 2005
Smith, Christopher R. "The Portrayal of the Church as the New Israel in the Names and Order of the Tribes in Revelation 7.5–8." *Journal for the Study of the New Testament* 39 (1990) 111–118.
Smith, Morton. *Tannaitic Parallels to the Gospels*. Journal of Biblical Literature Monograph Series 6. Philadelphia: Society of Biblical Literature, 1951.
Staedke, Joachim. "Die Hoffnung des Glaubens und die Veränderung der Welt." *Kerygma und Dogma* 18 (1972) 71–81.
Stendahl, Krister. "Biblical Theology, Contemporary." In *Interpreter's Dictionary of the Bible*, vol. 1, edited by G. A. Buttrick, 418–32. Nashville: Abingdon, 1962.
Stichele, Caroline Vander. "Apocalypse, Art and Abjection: Images of the Great Whore." In *Culture, Entertainment and the Bible*, edited by G. Aichele, 124–38. Journal for the Study of the Old Testament Supplement Series 309. Sheffield: Sheffield Academic, 2000.
Stott, Wilfrid. "A Note on the Word ΚΥΡΙΑΚΗ in Rev I.10." *New Testament Studies* 12 (1965) 70–75.
Sweet, John P. M. *Revelation*. London: SCM, 1979.

Swete, Henry Barclay. *The Apocalypse of John: The Greek Text with Introduction, Notes and Indices*. London: Macmillan, 1911.

Thiselton, Anthony C. *New Horizons in Hermeneutics*. Glasgow: HarperCollins, 1992.

———. *The Two Horizons: New Testament Hermeneutics and Philosophical Description with Special Reference to Heidegger, Bultmann, Gadamer, and Wittgenstein*. Exeter, UK: Paternoster, 1980.

Thompson, Leonard L. *The Book of Revelation: Apocalypse and Empire*. Oxford: Oxford University Press, 1990.

Torrance, Alan J. "*Creatio ex Nihilo* and the Spatio-Temporal Dimensions, with Special Reference to Jürgen Moltmann and D. C. Williams." In *The Doctrine of Creation: Essays in Dogmatics, History and Philosophy*, edited by Colin E. Gunton, 83–103. Edinburgh: T. & T. Clark, 1997.

Vanhoozer, Kevin J. *Is There a Meaning in This Text? The Bible, the Reader and the Morality of Literary Knowledge*. Grand Rapids: Zondervan, 1998.

Volf, Miroslav. "Not Optimistic." *Christian Century* 121:26 (2004) 31.

Wainwright, Arthur W. *Mysterious Apocalypse: Interpreting the Book of Revelation*. Nashville: Abingdon, 1993. Reprinted, Eugene, OR: Wipf & Stock Publishers, 2001.

Wakefield, James L. *Jürgen Moltmann: A Research Bibliography*. Lanham, MD: Scarecrow, 2002.

Walsh, Brian J. "Theology of Hope and the Doctrine of Creation: An Appraisal of Jürgen Moltmann." *Evangelical Quarterly* 59 (1987) 53–76.

Watson, Francis. "Liberating the Reader: A Theological-Exegetical Study of the Parable of the Sheep and the Goats (Matt. 25.31–46)." In *The Open Text: New Directions for Biblical Studies?*, edited by F. Watson, 57–84. London: SCM, 1993.

———. *The Open Text: New Directions for Biblical Studies?* London: SCM, 1993.

———. *Text, Church and World: Biblical Interpretation in Theological Perspective*. Edinburgh: T. & T. Clark, 1994.

Wengst, Klaus. "Babylon the Great and the New Jerusalem: the Visionary View of Political Reality in the Revelation of John." In *Politics and Theopolitics in the Bible and Postbiblical Literature*, edited by Henning Graf Reventlow, et al, 189–202. Journal for the Study of the Old Testament Supplement Series 171. Sheffield: JSOT Press, 1994.

Wenham, Gordon J. *Genesis 1–15*. Word Biblical Commentary 1A. Waco, TX: Word, 1987.

Wheelwright, Philip. *Metaphor and Reality*. Bloomington: Indiana University Press, 1962.

Witherington, Ben. *Revelation*. New Century Bible Commentary. Cambridge: Cambridge University Press, 2003.

Williams, George H. *Wilderness and Paradise in Christian Thought: The Biblical Experience of the Desert & the Paradise Theme in the Theological Idea of the University*. New York: Harper, 1962.

Williams, Stephen N. "On Giving Hope in a Suffering World: Response to Moltmann." In *Issues in Faith and History*, edited by Nigel M. de S. Cameron. Edinburgh: Rutherford, 1989.

Wright, N. T. *Jesus and the Victory of God*. Christian Origins and the Question of God 2. Minneapolis: Fortress, 1996.

———. *The New Testament and the People of God*. Christian Origins and the Question of God 1. Minneapolis: Fortress, 1992.

Yeago, David S. "The New Testament and the Nicene Dogma: A Contribution to the Recovery of Theological Exegesis." *Pro Ecclesia* 3 (1994) 152–64.

Yoder, John Howard. *The Politics of Jesus: Vicit Agnus Noster*. Grand Rapids: Eerdmans, 1972.

www.ingramcontent.com/pod-product-compliance
Lightning Source LLC
Chambersburg PA
CBHW071245230426
43668CB00011B/1598